# OM

*An Indian Pilgrimage*

Also by Geoffrey Moorhouse

*The Other England*
*Against All Reason*
*Calcutta*
*The Missionaries*
*The Fearful Void*
*The Diplomats*
*The Boat and the Town*
*The Best Loved Game*
*India Britannica*
*Lord's*
*To the Frontier*
*Imperial City*
*At the George*
*Apples in the Snow*
*Hell's Foundations*

# Geoffrey Moorhouse

# OM
## An Indian Pilgrimage

Hodder & Stoughton
LONDON SYDNEY AUCKLAND

**British Library Cataloguing in Publication Data**

Moorhouse, Geoffrey
OM: An Indian Pilgrimage
I. Title
915.404

ISBN 0-340-57059-8

Published by Hodder and Stoughton,
a division of Hodder and Stoughton Ltd,
Mill Road, Dunton Green, Sevenoaks, Kent TN13 2YA.
Editorial Office: 47 Bedford Square, London WC1B 3DP.

Designed by Gerald Cinamon

Photoset by Rowland Phototypesetting Ltd,
Bury St Edmunds, Suffolk

Printed in Great Britain by St Edmundsbury Press Ltd,
Bury St Edmunds, Suffolk

# Contents

*OM This eternal word is all; what was, what is and what shall be, and what is beyond eternity. All is OM . . . It is beyond the senses and it is the end of evolution. It is non-duality and love. He goes with self to the supreme Self who knows this, who knows this.*

MANDUKYA UPANISHAD

*And do thy duty, even if it be humble, rather than another's, even if it be great. To die in one's duty is life: to live in another's is death.*

BHAGAVAD GITA 3-35

*Religion is indeed man's self-consciousness and self-awareness so long as he has not found himself or has lost himself again . . . Religious suffering is at the same time an expression of real suffering and a protest against real suffering. Religion is the sigh of the oppressed creature, the sentiment of a heartless world, the soul of soulless conditions. It is the opium of the people.*

KARL MARX Introduction to the Critique
of Hegel's Philosophy of Right

Puttaparthi

KARNATAKA

Brindavan
Bangalore•

*Western Ghats*

Mysore•

*ARABIAN
SEA*

*Cauvery River*

Ootacamund•
*Nilgiri Hills*

Calicut•

**KERALA**

•Coimbatore

•Palghat

*Anaimalai
Hills*

*Palni Hills*

Kodaikanal

*M
a
l
a
b
a
r*

Cranganore•
Vypeen I.  Ernakulam
Cochin•

*C
o
a
s
t*

Shertally•   •Kottayam
Alleppey•

*Cardamom
Hills*

Sengottai•
•Tenkasi

Quilon•

0        miles        100

0      kilometres      150

Trivandrum•

Padmanabhapuram
Kanya Kumari•

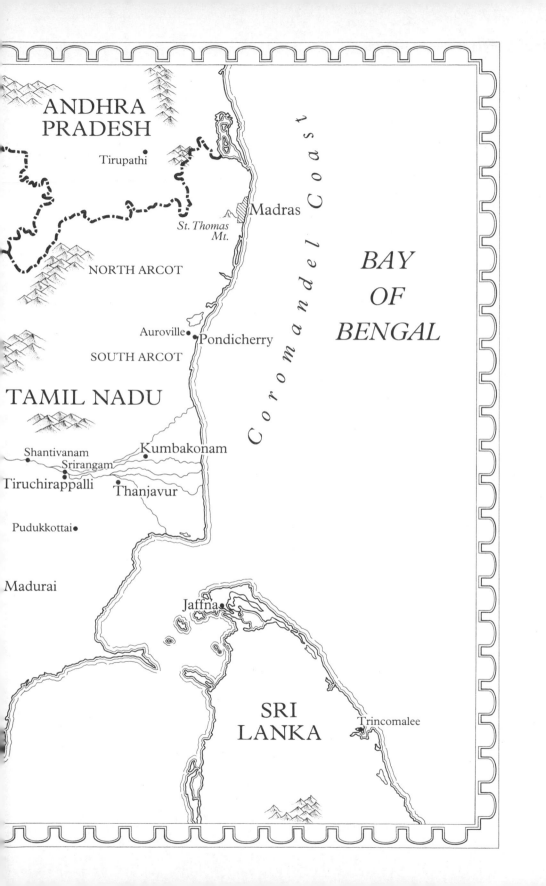

# Kanya Kumari

This is where India begins. On this curve of land, whose stained shore is washed by the jade green sea, an entire subcontinent is poised as if upon a sharpened point. Navigators rounded it in ancient times when extending the boundaries of the known world, among them the Greeks, whose geographer Ptolemy identified this extremity as Κομαρια αϰρον – ultimate Komari. Behind those early voyagers was an emptiness of ocean, separating the subcontinent from Africa; ahead, the tear-drop shape of Taprobane, which we now call Sri Lanka. Yet this was no barren headland, valuable only because it gave mariners their bearings. Just offshore, beating their way home against high winds and curling white water, are fishermen whose ancestors have worked this coast for centuries. Their craft are the same today as they always have been: a few tree trunks lashed together, with a bamboo pole bending to the pull of a swollen brown lateen. A line of them cant at such an angle to the waves that their shapes are transformed, so that from the shore they have the appearance of beetles crawling across the stormy sea. Men balance on these vessels like acrobats, gripping the slippery logs with fiercely splayed toes. And slowly they make their way into the lee of the land, to the beach lying beside the subcontinent's most southerly point, and the huddle of white-walled houses rising in terraces above. The sand is well studded with rocks which, at low tide, become increasingly coated in yellow slime, as the fisherfolk squat on them and empty their bowels. As the sea flows into and over the shore, all is miraculously cleansed, so that with the ebbing of the tide the illusion of purity is established again.

Purity matters here. This is a holy place, and the most ardent of the pilgrims who travel the length and breadth of the subcontinent to reach it are obsessed, above all, with what is pure and what is impure. Such considerations can shape their whole lives, everything they do, all that happens to them from conception to the pyre. And yet they live by paradox, as do no other people on earth; so that anyone utterly and shamefully defiled will only be made acceptable again by consuming a potion made from five substances emitted by the cow, including its dung and its piss. Urine is seen as the best purifier of any uncleanliness by the very people who speak of the left hand – in the Tamil tongue native to this holy place – as "the hand of filth".

The pilgrims come by train and by bus, entering the sacred pre-cincts down a narrow road lined by hoardings which clamour to sell accommodation, handicrafts, gimcrack souvenirs, food. Another exhortation more soberly advises them to Beware of Thieves. People pause beside stalls offering bananas, ugly plastic toys, and seashells which have been gaudied with paint and glued together to resemble rabbits, elephants, butterflies and boss-eyed fish. Persistent young men waylay each newcomer and attempt to press postcards, transpar-encies, sunglasses, beads upon all who do not wave them aside con-temptuously. Beggars position themselves artfully where they are almost impossible to avoid. The air swirls with dust blown up by gusts of wind off the sea, and it tantalises the hungry with promising smells of woodsmoke and spicy things ready to eat. It is deafening with sounds that are neither Indian nor musical, merely amplified noise which mutilates the ears.

At the bottom of that road rises a wedge-shaped gopuram above the principal shrine. This is dedicated to Parvati, who was betrothed to Lord Shiva but lost his hand in marriage through some trickery of the gods, who required her to slay the demon king, a feat that could only be managed by one destined to remain for ever kumari – virginally pure; in another version of the myth, Parvati came here to do penance in order to be worthy of her god but, being neverthe-less rejected, she vowed to embrace celibacy to the end of her days.

Endlessly the crowds do homage to this immaculate deity, where she sits on her temple throne, her diamond nose-rings glittering in the lamplight, her visible features embalmed in sandalpaste.

Then most of them board a hazardous old bucket with its wheelhouse aft, which lurches across the short space of tumultuous water separating the land from an enormous rock. This is surmounted by a domed building of much more recent origin than the temple of Kumari. It marks the place where the Swami Vivekenanda meditated for several months in 1892 upon the syncretistic teachings of his guru Ramakrishna, lately dead, until he reached the conclusion that he must take enlightenment to the West; which he did the following year at the Parliament of Religions in Chicago. The West, holding narrower views than his, had much earlier staked its own claim by building a Portuguese church above the pink pantiled roofs of the fishing village, which faced the Bengali sage as he sat and pondered possibilities before making eagerly for the impressionable warmth of America. Hundreds every day cross the water to be with the spirit of Vivekananda, and to make their obeisance to the sacred Sanskrit characters graven in stone; while in the all but empty dolly-blue interior of Our Lady of Ransom, a woman does the Stations laboriously on her knees, after prostrating herself before the Disney-coloured altar with her arms outstretched to their fingertips.

Few come here without cleansing themselves ritually from the ghats below the seafront. A squad of noisy youths stripped to their Y-fronts splash water at three shrill girls dressed in the shalwar kameez of North India. A young South Indian with his head shaven, apart from a small pigtail at the back, picks his way carefully across some rocks beyond the ghats until he comes to a lonely pool, where he bathes in solitude, before rearranging his lunghi round his hips. A trio of well-fleshed men descend the bathing steps and jump in boisterously, one of them a Brahmin with the confirming thread of the twice-born slung over his right shoulder and under his left arm. A fourth man stands on the edge of the water nervously, while the others dare him to take the plunge. Eventually and tentatively he does, with a weakly inane grin: whereupon the Brahmin, most pot-bellied and loudest of the others, wades heavily towards him, seizes his hand and leads him to the deeper part, as gently as if the fellow were his infant son.

When the pilgrims have completed their rituals of hygiene and prayer, they saunter along the promenade running above the ghats and below the most substantial hotels. They do not investigate the adjacent fishing village because that would involve an intrusion into caste, which would certainly occasion astonishment and might even result in catastrophe. The ones who have planned their visit after consulting the lunar calendar can savour a unique spectacle, moments before twilight begins: the pale disc of a full moon rising from the waters as the molten sphere of the sun lowers itself into the self-same sea. These reverent people regard this as another form of holiness. So did Mahatma Gandhi, who also came here to meditate, and whose memorial on the seafront strangely echoes pre-war British cinema buildings, a 1936-ish Odeon, perhaps. With the exception of its fishing village, there is something about Kanya Kumari as a whole, especially along its promenade, that conveys a whiff of Herne Bay, or some other English watering place that has known distinctly better days.

But this is where India begins; and she is inimitable. The land rises very shallowly from the sea, its sandy scrub soon giving way to palms and other trees, and plots of irrigated land which villagers till. Presently the first high ground rears above the coastal plain, a ridge of barren rock running northwards in a series of swerving pinnacles, all flaring with heat so intense that they are effectively unclimbable. The scenery is being assembled for topographical drama. Barren rock is soon clad with vegetation and the Western Ghats barricade the occidental seaboard against the rest of the country, shielding lush Kerala from the harsh and bony landscape further inland. Eventually the Ghats subside into the deserts of Rajasthan, which themselves give way to the mighty rivers of the North, that in one season will confer life on millions, and in another cause disaster and death on a frightful scale. When the rains come and the rivers swell there is nothing on earth like the sight of them, running torrentially, a mile or more wide, sweeping everything out of their path. Yet the greatest drama the eye can see is saved for the last and lies well above the Gangetic plain. Foothills rise from the rasping dust of early summer, and shimmer in a palpitating haze, which suddenly lifts when these tops, forested with rhododendron and deodar, have climbed to the point at which snow is a real possibility rather than a lowland fantasy; to reveal the most sensational range of mountains in the world, white and gleaming and utterly impregnable, as improbable as any theatrical backcloth in their operatic grandeur. They fill the horizon and half the heavens when first seen from any of those foothills in upper Garhwal. If there is such a thing as a terrestrial abode of the gods, then it will surely be there.

Stand with your back to the sea at Kanya Kumari, which is 2,000 miles from that stupendous barrier, and sense the weight, the full immensity, the huge variety of this subcontinent bearing down upon you. Beyond this scrubby littoral a tale unfolds such as no other land can tell in such measure as this. No other nation has ever known such a natural diversity of tongues, the result, for the most part, of slow evolution since the beginning of mankind. No other country has lived with so complicated a past so equably, assimilating everything that has happened to it, obliterating naught, so that not even the intricate histories of European states have produced such a rich pattern as that bequeathed by the Mauryas, the Ashokas, the Pahlavas, the Guptas, the Chalukyas, the Hoysalas, the Pandyas, the Cholas, the Mughals and the British – to identify only a few of the peoples who have shaped India's inheritance. Nor is there another land that constantly provokes in the stranger such elation and despair, so much affection and anger, by powerful contrasts and irreducible opposites of behaviour: wickedness and virtue, caring and indifference, things bewitching and disgusting and terrifying and disarming, often in quick succession. India has nuclear power and other advanced technology close by some of the most obscene slums in creation; she has never failed to hold democratic elections at the appointed time, yet these too frequently elevate men whose own votes can be bought with rupees and other emoluments; she has a high and mighty self-esteem and a taste for moral posturing which equals anything suffered by her people when the British were here; she has been capable of unparalleled generosity to her last imperial rulers, but she bickers endlessly and meanly with her closest neighbour and twin; she gave birth to the creed of massive non-violent protest and once practised this effectively, yet in the first generation of independence she has assassinated three of her own leaders, starting with the begetter of satyagraha ... Such contradictions and anomalies as these run through India from end to end, and help to make her incomparable.

As does another characteristic. Religion, too, flourishes here as it does nowhere else. Other lands may surrender themselves totally to a particular faith, but in India most creeds are deeply rooted and acknowledged fervently. Virtually the whole population practises some form of devotion: the Indian without the slightest feeling for the divine, without a spiritual dimension to his life, is exceedingly rare. By this means the wretched can entertain the possibility of improvement, and are sustained in their wretchedness until something better comes their way in another form, or until they are even more blessedly released from the cycle of life and death. The comfortable find in it a justification of their prosperity and an assurance that their submission will continue to bring them rewards. The most truly spiritual merely hope that with perseverance they will one day achieve enlightenment.

Incomparable and inimitable she is; but in this as in much else, India is also our great paradigm.

For a quarter of a century, the great subcontinent had captivated me. I first came to it out of simple curiosity and was almost overwhelmed by that introduction, in which everything was so much more powerful and intense than I had been led to expect. For a moment I was tempted to retreat from it to some bland place where all the senses were not so relentlessly assailed, to some less harrowing society where one's spirits were not so regularly lowered by human misery, to a more restful haven in which it was not so necessary to be for ever on guard against persistent and unwanted attention. Plenty of Westerners do not survive their initial experience of the subcontinent, fleeing in anxiety, in disgust and with indignation from its darknesses, condemned never to know it properly. But many more are vouchsafed in that first encounter a glimpse of something so enchanting, so inspiring, so utterly and attractively outside all previous experience, that they know they will return as often as possible, to be thrilled by it afresh.

I was one of these fortunates, and I had many times revisited the subcontinent in order to increase my understanding of it, once in a journey across Pakistan, otherwise repeatedly in India. In the beginning I had chiefly been interested in the local history which, through the coincidence of my English birth, was part of my history, too; to that extent I was trying to find something of myself in this strangely compelling land, even though I was the first member of my family ever to set foot in Asia. But gradually I became more fascinated by the texture of society here, by its very complexity, and especially by the way it had been formed from and was still dominated by religious attitudes, notwithstanding its secular democracy. My earliest visits to India had been confined to the North, which is where most of the great historical events associated with the British took place. When eventually I went south, I discovered a region that was never less than subtly different, and was sometimes obdurately so. It had not been shaped as much as the North had once been by a mighty zeal for Islam, but continental Europeans had left a greater impression here than elsewhere, especially the Portuguese and the French. It was possible to envisage the South as Hinduism's centre of gravity, and I had concluded that this was the reason why a high proportion of the foreigners wandering the southern states were not merely sampling an alien culture, but were more intently looking for spiritual nourishment. This, it seemed to me, distinguished them from almost all the outsiders criss-crossing other parts of India, except those who took themselves to Ladakh and similar anchorholds in the more mountainous recesses of the far North.

In a way, I had become one of them. And here I was again, on a further stage of my own Indian pilgrimage, hoping to understand something more of the great subcontinent. Also, trying to find another part of myself.

# Trivandrum

The old man caught my eye because he was not actually begging. Most indigents in Kerala, like those everywhere else in India, let no potential benefactor pass them by without, at least, an intimidating expression of hope and grievance. Unless they are utterly immobilised they generally do much more than that. At Kanya Kumari there had been a youth who, in spite of a paralysis from the waist down, wriggled into my path when I tried to avoid him, causing me to quicken my stride to get out of his way. Ashamed, I later sought him out and gave him notes instead of coin, which he took uncomprehendingly without acknowledgment; but when I looked back he raised a hand and smiled at me as dazzlingly as if I had made him whole. And here in Trivandrum there were cripples like him, who squirmed across the pavements of the city in order to intercept prosperity.

But the old man was different. He was squatting beside a pile of stone chippings where the buses came to a stop outside the university. He paid no attention to the crowds waiting to get on, though occasionally someone watched him curiously and would doubtless have been good for a few paise if he had responded; nor did he seem to be aware of the black fumes the buses gusted over him as they laboured up the hill towards the stadium. He was completely pre-occupied, sorting out his possessions, indifferent to anything else. He didn't have many belongings, but he couldn't have been more careful with them if they had been heirlooms: a bundle of rags that seemed to contain torn-up newspaper more than anything else, also a tin, possibly a large soup can with its top cut away. He spent minutes shredding some of the paper and packing it tightly into a matchbox. Then he took rubbish from one part of his swag and methodically stowed it away in another. Everything he had was filthy, including the sacking that did as his skirt, the clout wound round his head to protect it from the sun, the rags that bound two broken flip-flops to his feet. There were patches of dirt on the deeper darkness of his back, his drooping moustache was naturally white but had become grey; and this was a measure of his plight much more than his obvious poverty. He was a grimy, half-naked old man no longer in thrall to the most basic fixation of this society. If he wasn't outcast, then he had cast himself outside its norms.

But he had retained a dignity. He had just about finished his preparations for moving off when two men who had been watching him intently – one a well-dressed manager or superior clerk, the other a peon or some other dogsbody – stepped forward and gave him something as their bus arrived. He took the coins with the curtest of nods. He had not solicited these gifts and he was not going to abase himself in gratitude. He was merely receiving his dues. As his benefactors vanished in a thick cloud of diesel smoke, the old man got to his feet, hitched his swag on to his shoulder and shambled away, a small and bent figure moving slowly and unsteadily.

He turned a corner and went down another road, where there was less traffic, not so many people about. He was no more than a quarter of a mile from his starting place when he squatted again, began to smoke a kind of bidi made from shredded newspaper, and rummaged once more in his bundle of rags. This time, a passer-by donated two rupees, again without any supplication from the crumpled figure in the gutter, and very little by way of thanks: the old man simply wasn't paying attention to anyone unless they pressed money on him. Nor did this resolve, or this eccentricity, or whatever it was, lessen at any time during the remainder of that day. Regularly, he would rest for half an hour or so, ruminating and rummaging, occasionally smoking one of his acrid gaspers, and then move on, whether or not he had acquired more funds. In mid-morning he lingered in a lane where palm trees rose above pink-tiled roofs and where a broken water pipe had made a pool in the road, deep enough for him to dip his tin into and to wash his hands and face; but no more. About midday he came to a collection of thatched shanties beside a noisome drain, where a woman picked nits from her daughter's hair and a pi-dog snatched a chicken leg from a putrid refuse heap, and there was a little market for the capital's poorest folk. Here the old man spent some of his money on a small tuber of tapioca and on three morsels of fish, which a woman hacked from the carcass where it lay upon the dusty ground. Then he went on his way even more slowly than before, because the day was very hot and his energy was running low. But he did not eat until the sun was beginning to go down and he found a patch of wasteland against a tumbled mud wall. By then he had crossed the centre of the city many times in his meandering, indifferent to the auto-rickshaws and the scooters and the other traffic that often came within inches of flattening him. And there the old man settled down for the night, in solitude, as he had spent his day. He had collected enough rubbish to make a fire with, spent a precious match in setting this alight, heated some water to render the fish and tapioca more edible, restored somewhat his vigour, which had been dribbling away since the dawn.

I spoke to him just once in all those hours. I gave him some money and because I had a camera he stood dutifully before me, his shoulders slumped, his sharp sunken face expressionless of anything but total exhaustion. This wasn't a photograph I cared to take; I simply wanted to talk to him. I wanted to know why he was spending so much of his feebleness on moving restlessly around the city, when he might have sat beside the other beggars lined up to tap the charity of the faithful emerging from the Sri Padmanabhaswamy Temple; or he could have taken post outside one of the bigger hotels, to prick the consciences of rich people from other parts of India and overseas. The student I had recruited for this purpose asked him in Malayalam where had he come from and where was he going? But he waved the questions away without a word, turned, and shambled off down the street, past the Thara Engineering Works, which was a cubby-hole containing several half-empty shelves and its proprietor bent over a small lathe. I left him alone after that, and followed him at a distance as unobtrusively as I could.

He was a strange sort of loner and a proud one, his own man still, in spite of his penury. But he had slipped a little from where his karma had originally placed him, or else he had been born at the very bottom of India's intricate hierarchy of caste, where Aryan notions of purity are of less account. Whichever it was, the old man was resigned, at odds with the prevailing attitude locally. Not far from where he settled down that night was a black plinth and bust in honour of Bhimrao Ramji Ambedkar, an Untouchable who rose high in government and became the principal author of the Indian Constitution; he then dedicated the rest of his life to teaching the lowliest Hindus that a more felicitous existence might be theirs if they adopted the beliefs and habits of Buddhism.

Dr Ambedkar was not Malayali (he was born near Indore in central India) but it was appropriate that his centenary should be honoured by a monument in the state capital of Kerala. For this had once been the most caste-ridden society in all India, notoriously rigid in its observances: Vivekananda had called it "a madhouse of caste" at the end of the nineteenth century. Much later than that, someone calculated that the Hindus here were divided into hundreds of distinctly different groups, all graded irrevocably according to their breeding, their occupation and their domicile. This was the basis of caste throughout the land, as was the concept of one group polluting another by physical contact, or the sharing of common resources; the family into which Dr Ambedkar was born had been forbidden to take water from the public well in their native village. But in the princely states of Cochin and Travancore, which were amalgamated into Kerala upon surrendering their sovereignty after independence, a superior caste could be polluted if an inferior one merely came closer than certain severely regulated distances. It was ordained that every Pulaya – the word means "polluted man" – must advance no nearer than ninety-six feet towards a Nambudiri Brahmin, who alone had religious authority here even when, as sometimes happened, he was an illiterate with only a hearsay know-ledge of scripture. The Pulaya must also keep no less than sixty-four feet between him and every Nair, who represented the warrior caste in these parts, and thirty feet was the minimum distance to be maintained between him and anyone from the Ezhava community, who were cultivators and skilled labourers. A Pulaya was obliged to call out "Po! Po! Get away! Get away!" wherever he went, so that his superiors might take evasive action in good time. Failure to give warning meant a beating by the servants of those who would have to go through tiresome and expensive rituals to cleanse themselves; and sometimes the penalty had been death.

Since November 1949, the Indian Constitution had prohibited caste discrimination in general and the practice of Untouchability in particular* – Dr Ambedkar saw to that – yet both concepts remained living issues throughout the country and were at the bottom of many gruesome stories still to be heard almost everywhere, but especially in the northern state of Bihar which continued to function, in this and in other lawless ways, on medieval lines at the end of the twentieth century. Kerala may well have come closer to a casteless Indian society than anywhere else, not excluding the great metropolitan cities, and one reason for this would be that the state had been run intermittently by Marxists for the past thirty-odd years: it was the first place in the world to elect a communist Prime Minister by impeccably democratic vote, subsequently imitated in this country only by West Bengal and Tripura. Yet so powerful were the historic prerogatives and inhibitions of caste, so infectious its fundamental premise of hierarchy, that not only did vestiges still cling to the Hindus of South India – marked, for example, by the reluctance of pilgrims to enter the fishing village at Kanya Kumari – but, it was said, the infection had long ago spread to the principal non-Hindu communities of this area, to the Christians and the Muslims who between them accounted for two-fifths of the population.

It even impinged upon the lives of the Das family, who were as far from blind submission to the traditional orthodoxies of India as anyone I had ever known on the subcontinent. This is not to say that they defied all the conventions in order to demonstrate their independence. They were as unswervingly vegetarian as the most scrupulous Brahmin might be. I never saw Kamala in anything but a sari, nor did Das ever wear anything but a lunghi below his shirt. His letterheads announced him as K. Madhava Das, but neither his

---

*  "Article 17 – 'Untouchability' is abolished and its practice in any form is forbidden. The enforcement of any disability arising out of 'Untouchability' shall be an offence punishable in accordance with law."

wife nor anyone else ever called him anything but Das. He was a retired banker and a sophisticated one, who had wooed and won his cousin partly with his knowledgeable talk of Aldous Huxley and Bertrand Russell. In those younger days he had written verse and prose pieces that found their way into print, but it was Kamala Das who would make the much greater mark in literature. I had first come across her poetry in an anthology, where its passion stood out from everything else in the collection. She composed in both English and Malayalam, and not only in verse: she had become celebrated outside India's bookish circle for her autobiography, which recounted the facts of her life with a candour that well-bred Indian ladies are not supposed to exhibit publicly.

A mutual friend in England had given me the Das's phone number, which I rang on reaching Trivandrum. It was Kamala who answered and asked me to meet her at somebody else's book launch that evening. This was held in an hotel round the corner from the white and classically pedimented building that could easily have been mistaken for one of the more extravagant imperial clubs erected during the British time on the subcontinent. It was, in fact, the State Secretariat, an appropriate proximity when we had been summoned to celebrate the exposure of corruption in every area of Kerala's public life, from politics to the judiciary, by a former civil servant who had once been the state government's Director of Publicity. He was a shock-headed man who greeted me warmly on my arrival and led me to an empty seat at the front of the room. Kamala did not arrive until the rows were full of people, almost entirely male, some wearing slacks and shirt, as many wearing local dress. She was in the platform party and moved to her place there without a glance at me. On one side of her was a film director, who looked as if he was weighing up the chances of a big deal. On the other was a tall spare man who kept using a ventilator to soothe wrecked lungs. "That's Bannu," the man next to me whispered as the platform party sat. "He was one of our most famous freedom fighters." My informant grinned at me mischievously, as though he was half-hoping I might need that interpreted.

The author rose and began to explain himself. He spoke vehemently without a pause for half an hour, his flow of Malayalam punctuated with English phrases – "social leper", "corruptions exposed" and the like – which enabled me to get the drift of his argument without understanding another word. His hands were as voluble, as articulate as his speech, splaying, pointing, beseeching, dismissing eloquently. There was clapping to applaud the more forceful passages, but by the time he had finished Kamala Das was not the only person in the room who seemed to have heard enough. I assumed she was there because she was the South's most famous living writer after Narayan, that this was a chore inseparable from celebrity. She sat perfectly still, a middle-aged woman in a purple sari with very black hair in two plaits, a jewel in her left nostril, a red bindi dotting her forehead. Behind horn-rimmed spectacles, her eyes looked down at her hands, folded on the table in front of her, and never once appeared to be deflected by either the speaker or anyone to whom he spoke. I couldn't make up my mind whether she was playing the demurely proper female in a congregation of men, or whether she was simply concentrating hard. Before the author ran out of steam I had come to the conclusion that she was a little bored.

Another figure from the platform arose, a corpulent man with a dreamy face, who stood like a politican on the hustings, belly thrust forward, hand on hip, expression of challenging probity on his face. "He's a famous story-teller," my neighbour hissed, "a village troubador!" And he was unquestionably beginning a performance, teeth flashing, lips palpitating with Dravidian polysyllables that bubbled forth in an unbroken spate and fell indistinctly upon my ear; unlike speech in the various languages of North India, whose words are distinguishable to most Westerners even when they are quite incomprehensible, because they developed from the same linguistic roots as our own. I should have liked to have heard the presumably model diction of this orator a little longer, to see if I could pick any of it up, but almost as soon as he got into his stride, Kamala stood, said something to the chairman and headed for the way out, beckoning to me as she went. "I told them that my husband was not well," she said when we were out of earshot, "but that man will go on for an hour now and I shall be asleep if I stay." She looked faintly, defiantly amused as she peered along the street and gestured towards a line of parked cars; and presently a Das servant drove up in the battered old family Ambassador to take us home.

She had been speaking no less than the truth about Das, who was holding his own against Parkinson's disease. He got up from his chair as we entered their living room, but it was obviously an effort to raise himself on those thin and halting legs. He had been a tall man in his prime but now he was bent and he seemed to be all cranium and twinkling eyes. Kamala plucked the bindi from her brow as soon as she got home, rather as a European matron might have peeled off her gloves on coming through the door, and launched into a sharp description of the book event which made her husband giggle, as it was meant to do. Her autobiography had portrayed their relationship as a difficult one, especially in its early years, with Das dominating his younger wife more than was good for any partner-ship. This did not seem to have damaged her much. She was utterly self-possessed, confident of her ability to amuse, strong in the know-ledge that the power now resided in her. But she did not exult in that shift of emphasis and, had I not read her revelations of the marriage, I would have assumed that they had always been uncom-monly and tenderly devoted to each other. At supper that evening she surreptitiously helped him with his food when necessary, and when the meal was finished she went to a sideboard, where her cook had left a freshly washed betel leaf. Kamala smeared it with lime paste, added some crushed nut, twirled her fingers as though she were rolling a cigarette, pushed the pale green wad into her mouth and began to chew.

"They maintain," she said beforehand, "that women who take paan will not let their husbands die."

She let her hand rest lightly on his shoulder for an instant as she went behind his chair again. Before I left, some turn in the conver-sation caused them to break into a duet that originated a long time ago in a culture that was not their own. "Que sera, sera, whatever will be, will be . . ." Her voice held its line better than his, which trembled a little as he sang. But what occurred to me first was Darby and Joan.

I became incorporated into the generosities of the Das household throughout my time in Trivandrum because I brought tidings of that knowing and alien world which both of them relished as much as anything in their own inheritance. Das in his turn supplied anec-dotes of people he had met on banking expeditions all over the globe, while Kamala described the Adelaide and other international arts festivals she had attended in terms which suggested that the libido was much more important than literature to most participants. But I was never quite sure how much to believe when she toyed with a prurient speculation or strayed towards a carnal diversion from some earnestly proper dialogue. There was about her still, in her fifties and a grandmother, the desire to shock and thrill an audience that most women leave behind in their early twenties, if they haven't already done so before finishing adolescence.

One lunchtime, with half a dozen people enjoying the Das hospitality, the talk had turned to Hinduism's cyclical view of existence, which Kamala interrupted, glowing at the company with an expression of sheer enjoyment. "I want to come back as a *child*," she announced, uttering the last word with great relish; and then, leaning forward with eyes wide and sparkling, she added, "God is a *beast*, full of sexual energy!" She reached for a piece of jackfruit, popped it into her mouth and sucked it with appetite.

The old freedom fighter Bannu, at the other end of the table, brought the ventilator from the folds of his garment, gave his lungs a shot of vapour, and looked as if he was lost in the non sequitur. The Sinologist next to him smiled fondly, as she must have done a hundred times at some unexpected sally from her friend Kamala Das. That great rambling bungalow in Sasthamangalam, with its yantras and other pieces of Indian art on the walls, and with its heavy Victorian furniture, was above all an old-fashioned intellectual salon, in which the very wide and varied circle of Das acquaintances enjoyed almost certainly the most catholic and occasionally the most startling views to be heard in Trivandrum, possibly in the whole of Kerala.

There was a price to be paid for free-thinking in this society, however, and part of the cost to the Das household was anonymous and abusive telephone calls. Some of these were connected with the corruptions the former Director of Publicity had exposed. The eldest Das son, Monoo, had publicised these in the newspaper he edited up in Bangalore; his mother had attended the book launch in his stead because he had been unable to get away from his office that day, to travel south. But she was also vilified in her own right, one of the accusations levelled at her being that she'd been instrumental in having a member of the state legislative assembly killed. "Luckily for me, he disappeared for only a few weeks. If he hadn't surfaced again, I'd have been in trouble." Not all the hostility was political, though. Some was directed at Kamala because of things she revealed in her autobiography. A great deal of venom had come the entire family's way because of Monoo's own separate domestic life.

He had courted and eventually married Lakshmi, a princess of the royal House of Travancore, and this was a much more serious breach of convention than a union between royalty and commoner would be in Europe. For one thing it involved Kerala's adherence to the concept of Marumakkathayam, by which descent and inheritance proceed through the female line, very rare in India. But beyond that there was the matter of caste. The Das family were Nairs, who have been likened to the Japanese Samurai in the evolution of the South: a warrior aristocracy. The royal House of Travancore were a sub-caste of the Koil Tampurans, Kshatriyas with very strict rules about marriage. The custom was that their males married into the families of other Rajahs or took Nair wives; their females were allowed husbands only from among the Nambudiri Brahmins. The offence of Monoo and his princess therefore was not just that they had defied these strictures, but that they had dared to turn the convention upside down. Lakshmi had, in fact, run away from her home in the Kaudiar Palace in order to be married and, although the rupture with her family had started to heal, some sticklers for the old ways in Trivandrum were less forgiving.

The Maharajahs of Travancore were never the most powerful of India's native rulers; but in the order of precedence which the British painstakingly worked out to mollify the princes they rated a nineteen-gun salute on ceremonial occasions, which was only a couple of volleys fewer than the noise made for the really big men of Hyderabad, Kashmir, Mysore, Gwalior and Baroda. Originally of no more account than scores of other rulers in South India, their fortunes were transformed early in the eighteenth century with the accession of Martanda Varma. The historian K. M. Panikkar has summarised his importance as follows:

When he came to the throne his state was one of the smallest in Kerala. Royal power was practically non-existent. There was no money in the treasury. The army obeyed the commands of rebellious nobles and his own life was in constant danger. In Kerala politics the Dutch [East India] Company put forward pretensions of suzerainty and claimed the right to intervene in all affairs. In a few years' time he changed the whole map of Kerala. The Dutch Company was forced to abandon its proud position and had to be content with that of mere traders dependent on the goodwill of the Travancore Ruler. The minor principalities from Cochin to Quilon were all conquered and annexed and the rule of Travancore established firmly over them. An efficient and trained army was raised which gave to Travancore a predominance in Kerala affairs which no State had enjoyed before. Great irrigation works, roads and canals of communication were undertaken and carried out. Charitable institutions were founded. These results could not have been achieved except by a man who possessed rare foresight, strength of will, energy and decision. He was, thus, with all his faults, the greatest Ruler of the Travancore line.*

The faults Dr Panikkar refers to were embodied in a savage ambition from the moment Martanda Varma came to the throne at the age of twenty-three. A potential rival was assassinated while making a friendly visit and forty-two of his attendant noblemen were hanged, their women and children disposed of as slaves. He was never known to offer clemency to anyone who offended him and he was prepared to invoke alien assistance – from Hyder Ali one minute, from the English and then from the French at another – in order to subdue his own people if necessary. And yet, rather like the Mughal Emperors who began to encroach on India from Central Asia in the sixteenth century, and who were brutal aesthetes almost to a man, this ruler of Travancore's barbarity was offset by a sensitivity to civilised things. Long before Christian mission schools were opened here and added their own impressive weight to the same end, he was responsible for the beginnings of popular education in Kerala, which has resulted in a level of literacy far higher than the Indian average: something above 90 per cent among both males and females, with the state government confident of reaching 100 per cent before the end of this century.

None of Martanda Varma's successors had quite matched his

* *A History of Kerala 1498–1801* by K. M. Panikkar (Annamalai UP, 1960) p 258.

viciousness; none needed to after he had made Travancore stronger than any state below Mysore, a highly independent fiefdom which had its own currency, eventually its own stamps, and which kept time according to the sun, twenty-two and a half minutes slower than the rest of India. Another side of the royal reputation had been carefully maintained, it seemed, from one generation to the next. The very last Maharajah of Travancore as a young man passed a law in 1936 which allowed Untouchables, for the first time, to enter any temple in his realm. Eight years later he enacted the legislation which made Kerala the first state in all Asia to abolish capital punishment. He eventually authorised 40 per cent of the state budget to be spent on education when no other princely state spent more than 5 per cent. When he died, a devout old bachelor, six months before my return to India, Kerala mourned him with genuine sorrow and her communist ministers added their own expressions of sadness that he was gone. His younger brother, the Elaya Rajah, sat in the Kaudiar Palace now with other members of the royal family, and pursued his interest in the Indian company which makes the Royal Enfield motorbike.

"Would you like to see it?" said Kamala Das one afternoon. I had, in fact, glimpsed its roofline from the nearest road, an intriguing arrangement of pinnacled cupolas among trees, well behind the high boundary wall that ensured palatial privacy: there was something distinctly Far Eastern, Thai perhaps, about the delicacy of those little spires and the way they rose from the warmth of russet tiles. The Kaudiar looked as if it might be a more lavish version of Martanda Varma's old palace at Padmanabhapuram, which I had inspected on the way up from Kanya Kumari. There, white walls supported galleries of marvellous carpentry and, above these, gently pitched roofs with deeply overhanging eaves, all clad in the ubiquitous local tile. It was unlike any other major domestic Indian architecture I had ever come across, comfortable and homely, very quiet and understated compared with the extravaganzas of Mysore or Baroda or Ramnagar. It felt like the life's work of village craftsmen and not as though hundreds of specialists had been imported to create a showpiece at vast expense.

The thought of visiting the Kaudiar hadn't even crossed my mind, given the recent strain between the two families; but I had already discovered that Kamala's charm could fix almost anything once she'd applied her considerable sense of purpose to it. So, yes, I said; I'd like that very much. Apart from anything else, the Padmanabhapuram Palace had long been uninhabited and was now a museum run by the state authorities: it would be interesting to see how the royal House of Travancore lived a full generation after losing its sovereignty.

Meanwhile I investigated the rest of Trivandrum, which was much more like a busy provincial town than a fairly important state capital. MG Road, its principal thoroughfare, was lined with small shops for most of its length and did not widen enough to accommodate three lines of traffic until it passed the Secretariat, when it didn't have much further to go. Off it ran even narrower streets, almost rural in their unpretentiousness, plunging uphill or down along the rolling contours of the city, which everywhere were smothered in a luscious growth of shrubbery and trees. The suburbs in particular were curiously familiar in a way that had nothing to do with India, and it took me a while to remember where I'd seen something similar before. Those countrified roads with their multitude of small buildings separated from each other by flowering bushes, with little black pigs and poultry and other domestic animals scuttering about, and everywhere shaded by tall canopies of palm, were remarkably like the outskirts of St George's, on the island of Grenada, which I'd visited once. As in the West Indies, these surroundings concealed and prettified a great deal of poverty.

Some time earlier, just after the Iraqi invasion of Kuwait, I had chanced to arrive in Bombay the night refugees flew in from the Gulf, all Indians who had worked out there as dhobeywallahs, drivers, cooks, houseboys or other forms of servant to wealthy Arabs. A majority of them were Malayalis, and half the Kerala State Transport System's buses seemed to have been mobilised outside the airport, waiting to take them home down the long road south. With a kind of peace now restored to the Gulf, the Malayalis had gone back to whatever they could pick up from the sweepings of the sheikhdoms: there were twenty-one direct flights a week in each direction between Trivandrum and Jeddah, Dubai, Abu Dhabi, Muscat and other places in the region. The money orders the migrant workers sent home month by month helped, when the statistics of hardship in Kerala were not much better than those of Calcutta. Only the setting was a lot more agreeable.

MG Road began not far from another of Martanda Varma's buildings, the Sri Padmanabhaswamy Temple which was topped uncharacteristically by a richly carved gopuram, which is a gateway style of Tamil Hinduism, unknown anywhere else in Kerala.* It was possible to admire this slowly while walking towards the temple along an extensive avenue that served as an approach and as a market place, whose stallholders constantly called out to worshippers to come and inspect their wares. It was not, alas, possible to go further than the gate, and a huge hairy-chested man, a temple guard, naked from the waist up, with a friendly smile and a club dangling from his wrist, was there to prevent passage beyond him by any who were not Hindu. This was an inviolable rule throughout Kerala, something I had never encountered in any other part of India. I could think of odd shrines where the unbeliever was unwelcome, and many whose inner sanctum was accessible to the faithful alone; but in no other state had I found the inside of every temple totally out of bounds. And this was paradoxical as well as perverse. For the Hindus of the Malabar coast, of this whole area now known as Kerala, had been unusually warm in welcoming the stranger to their land throughout their history. They had early looked to the outside world with more anticipation than other Indians because they were effectively cut off from the rest of the subcontinent, hemmed in against the sea, by the great barrier of the Western Ghats. Their lack of insularity made them less fevered about their Dravidian blood, which had in any case been blended with other strains in the course of time. This explained a number of characteristics that set them apart from their nearest neighbours, the Tamils, including their attitude to the rest of the modern republic, which was wholly benign. They had in particular always shown the most gratifying tolerance of other religions; and while this would to some extent be because they had not at the outset been threatened by other faiths – all of which arrived here on trade winds, not in conquest – the benevolence

* Padmanabha, as in the name of the temple and of the palace further south, refers to a local form of Vishnu, who is the household god of the Travancore family.

said something about a fundamental openness in Hinduism, even though it could be cruelly shut against many of its own votaries; which was another paradox.

The Christians especially flourished in this climate, from the moment St Thomas Didymus arrived on the Malabar coast in AD 52 (as all Indians with any interest in the subject unshakeably believe; whereas Western Biblical scholars, who will unhesitatingly accept even more remarkable claims about the early Church, profess to be less than completely convinced). The apostle is supposed to have made his landfall at Malankara, near the Roman port of Muziris, some little distance north of Cochin, and there to have founded the Malankara Orthodox Syrian Church, which claims historic precedence over all other Christian sects in India today. It is not to be confused with the Malankara Jacobite Syrian Church, or the Malankara Syrian Catholic Church, nor yet with the Mar Thoma Syrian Church, the Chaldean (or Nestorian) Church, the Thozhiyoor (or Anjoor) Church, certainly not with the St Thomas Evangelical Church of India, the Pentecost Church, the Russell Church, the Seventh Day Adventists, the Jesus for India Society or any other of the permutations into which the Christians of Kerala have arranged themselves in the past nineteen centuries: more than a score of different denominations all told. And so completely had the Christians become assimilated by the fifteenth century, so indistinguishable were they from their Hindu neighbours in many respects, that when the good Roman Catholic Vasco da Gama reached Calicut in 1498, he mistook a temple for a church, a statue of Kali for one of the Virgin Mary, and solemnly knelt to say his prayers in front of it. He was perhaps pardonably confused, having only just got over the shock of discovering that the Gospel had been preached here for hundreds of years. The Portuguese had arrived in the belief that they were about to introduce Christianity to the subcontinent.

At the other end of MG Road from Trivandrum's principal Hindu temple was an impressive testimony to Kerala's traditional religious tolerance, with no fewer than three cathedrals, two other churches and a mosque all situated within half a mile. Each of these buildings filled with worshippers during the major rituals of their week, but only in Warsaw at the height of the Cold War, when Cardinal Wyszinski was preaching fire and brimstone against the communists, had I ever known a Christian church to be as suffocatingly crammed with devout people as was the Syrian Orthodox Cathedral of St George at the nine o'clock mass one Sunday morning in Trivandrum. The congregation was packed inside and out like a football crowd, overflowing into the churchyard and everywhere standing so close together that when people crossed themselves, as they did repeatedly, it was with little dabs of the fingers and articulated wrists, so as to avoid putting their elbows into their neighbours' ribs. The building was not at all what I had expected, with what looked suspiciously like Victorian Early English lancet windows, and a minimum of decoration on its pillars and walls: three ikons placed at intervals and nothing more. Instead of the great dividing screen which regulates so much of the liturgy in the Orthodox churches of Russia and Greece, there was here a red curtain embroidered with doves in gold; but generally the altar and all activity round it was revealed for everyone to see. The bearded priest in his red robe and black biretta circumnavigated the altar periodically, accompanied by acolytes swinging incense, and others carrying wands which were each tipped with several metal discs: the wand-bearers shook these from time to time so that they produced a subdued clashing sound to represent the fluttering of angel wings. At the same time a handbell was rung discordantly, while a deeper sound came from the bellcote on the cathedral's roof.

There was a great deal of unaccompanied singing, whose measure and tread were unmistakably Orthodox, the tone and the range of sound being unfamiliar, less weighty than anything you might hear on Athos or in Zagorsk, and less controlled. A single loud drum beat announced the sermon, which the priest gave standing on a podium brought onstage for the purpose; and he continued for half an hour while no one below him moved. When he had finished, the people immediately in front of him turned round to those behind, who did the same thing, as did everyone else one after the other, so that something like a miniature Mexican wave rolled right down the church. But it was the Peace, conveyed with such natural grace and ease by everyone present that it made the embarrassed version practised by most English Anglicans seem clumsy and contrived. I had thought at first that people must be passing some object to those at the back; but it was simply their fingertips, lightly touching their neighbour's open palms, a fastidious gesture made gravely and swiftly to one other; and to me with a kindly twinkle in the eye. It was almost the final act of worship. After it the whole congregation, first the men and then the women, surged forward to put their alms in a box after being tapped on the head with a little wand held by the priest. That done, each person in turn walked straight outside to pick up chappals and other footwear that had been discarded before the service began.

As revealing as anything in the city was the building that had once belonged to the Anglicans but now housed the ecumenically minded souls who created the Church of South India a generation ago. As I walked through the crumbling graveyard of Christ Church a half-wild dog snarled at me with menace, but fled with its tail tucked in when I flung a stone its way. There were table-tombs, drunken memorial slabs and upright stone crosses rising out of an undergrowth of weed and bramble, with neem trees affording some shade from the scorching heat. Every name I discerned on those decaying stones was that of an Indian, but I was more interested to see what mark, if any, my own people had left behind. Had this been a church in North India, I should have known what to expect: an interior whose walls were encrusted with tablets in metal and stone memorialising a variety of people who had represented British rule in some form: as businessmen and their wives who had profited hugely from our imperialism, as civil servants who had kept it in good repair, as soldiers who were on the subcontinent to enforce the will of this white minority upon the native population where necessary. Almost always, a disproportionately high number of memorials in such churches recollected military glory, military tragedy, military might. But it was not so in Trivandrum, where the British had no more than an advisory role to play in the affairs of the autonomous little state. In Christ Church there was the name of but one soldier, a 2nd Lieut. Chalmers, a Reservist called up at the outbreak of the Great War, killed in Persia in 1916; the rest were all civilians, in Travancore to make neither war nor an indecent fortune. Here was Stanley Neville Ure MA (Oxon), Tutor to His Highness the Elaya Rajah of Travancore 1932–39. Here was Robert Harvey MA LLD (Glasgow), Professor of English and Moral Philosophy at HH the Maharajah's College, Trivandrum, for twenty-two years and Principal 1884–90. Here was Charles Schofield Boyle, Scholar of Pembroke College, Oxford, and Professor of English Literature at the Maharajah's College 1892–1903. Here was James Macdonald Houston MD (Edinburgh), Physician to HH the Maharajah 1875–88. Here was Augusta Mary Blandford "who for 43 years laboured as a Christian missionary among the women of this land". Here was the Rev Maitland Dalrymple Wardrop, Chaplain of Trivandrum and Quilon 1906–11. And here was Henry Bidewell Grigg CIE MA, formerly Resident in Travancore and Cochin, died 1895. He, and only he, was part of the ruling process during the British imperium; also well educated by the look of it. These memorials were consistent with the reputation of a state which had long set a high store on education and which had always opened itself to outside influence.

It was impossible to be in Trivandrum for long without being conscious of its vaunted literacy. There was a huge population of university students, judging by the vast numbers perpetually moving about the campus and adjacent streets at the top of MG Road, the young men conspicuously not wearing the customary lunghi of South India but casual shirts and slacks. In the centre of the city you could not walk 500 yards in any direction without coming across yet another bookstore, though none of them was very large. The bulk of the stock in most cases was textbooks and other material that might help someone obtain qualifications; but there was some surprising extra-curricular reading available to the discerning bookworm in this part of Kerala. I was searching one day for anything that might guide me through the maze of local Christianity when I found myself confronted with half a dozen paperbacks (Penguin Classics edition) of the *Orkneyinga Saga*, which is marvellously rousing stuff, especially if it is read after a stormy morning at Skara Brae, or after walking across the sea cliffs to check out the Old Man of Hoy, but which isn't exactly a bestseller south of Kirkwall and Stromness. I pulled a copy from the shelf and held it up for the bookseller to see.

"What on earth," I asked, "is this doing in Trivandrum? Surely it isn't on somebody's syllabus?"

He wiggled his head, a little testily I thought. "No, sir. We take literature from many lands. This is coming to us from wholesalers."

"But do you really expect to sell many copies? Most people in

England have never even heard of it. I'm the only Englishman I know who's actually read it. *Have* you sold any copies yet?"

The head wiggled again, thoughtfully this time. "Only few copies are going so far, sir. Rather a slow mover, you might say."

Only a few copies! It was, I supposed, conceivable that somewhere out there, amid the palm trees, the bougainvillaea, the foraging hens and the sopping humidity of this equatorial coast, some insatiably questing Malayali was at that moment glued to the epic of good King Magnus, Earl Rognvald, Svein Breast-Rope and those other medieval Northmen, and was trying to picture the bleak and tempestuous, the so utterly other land in which it was set. Anything inherently improbable in other parts of India, it seemed to me, was quite possible here. I had already discovered that. Trivandrum was the only place I had known where the auto-rickshaw drivers, without being urged, and the moment you stepped aboard, turned on their meters and didn't press for more than the fare clocked up at the end of the ride. It was the only place where I had not seen a single sacred cow wandering the public thoroughfares unchecked, thereby holding up the traffic and committing other nuisances, without anyone daring to complain (and it was whispered that Hindus had been known to eat beef in Kerala!). This was the only place where I had not been continually pestered by small boys asking, "Where are you coming from? What is your name?" as a preamble to soliciting ballpoint pens and other gifts. Trivandrum, I decided some time before I left, was my sort of place.

My last weekend there coincided with Republic Day, which in New Delhi produces one of India's great and unique spectacles, with a parade down Rajpath that goes on magnificently for hours, and a moving ceremony at sunset, when the gorgeous massed bands of the military Beat Retreat, and the Indian tricolour is slowly hauled down to the strains of "Abide With Me". In Trivandrum the celebration started the night before when fireworks suddenly exploded across the sky with such a din that I rushed to the verandah of my hotel, as did the man in the next room, both of us expecting some emergency, quite unprepared for the sight of star shells, rockets and flares making the darkness light.

"Had this been the Punjab," he said, "I should have assumed it meant trouble." The entire country was braced for trouble up north that weekend though not, for once, involving the Sikhs. The bully boys of the Bharatya Janata Party were heading for Srinagar, where they were as clearly bent on provoking a confrontation with Pakistan as the Union government in New Delhi was anxious to avoid it. Weeks earlier, these Hindu fundamentalists had left Kanya Kumari on a highly publicised march up the length of the land to Kashmir where, on Republic Day, they intended to raise their standard on the state assembly building, a gesture guaranteed to inflame the local community. They had already done much harm during their passage through northern Kerala, where the majority of the state's Muslims lived. On reaching Palghat just before Christmas, the BJP convoy had traded insults and worse with some local Islamic fundamentalists, their sworn adversaries, and a Muslim child had been killed by accident. Nothing like this had happened in Kerala since the Moplah Rising of 1921: the state had managed to avoid the communal disturbances that have wracked almost every other part of the nation periodically in the last fifty years. People now wondered whether the long and proud history of religious tolerance in Kerala was about to end.

Trivandrum's Republic Day ceremonies began shortly after sunrise, so that they would be over before it was too hot for comfort on the parade ground behind the State Secretariat. As it was, the most uncomfortable place to be was in the rows of special seating for the Governor of Kerala and his numerous guests, scores of whom were sitting with the sun dazzling them, low and straight between the eyes, when five trumpeters blew the opening tantivy with the sun at their backs on the stroke of 7.30 a.m. Hundreds of lesser folk had a much better view, ranged on the terraces of the shallow amphitheatre which encircled the rest of the ground, also opposite the enclosure for the celebrities. There were several parties of schoolgirls, vivid in colourful draperies, with teachers distributing fruit and drink among them the moment they sat down; but no one seemed to have organised the local schoolboys, who were not to be seen except in ones and twos. It was a well-behaved crowd, which had strolled along MG Road and entered the compound gates decorously, under the eyes of police who had arrived by the truckload long before anyone else. They easily outnumbered the spectators, a paramilitary cohort in khaki drills and steel helmets, each figure nonchalantly swinging his lathi so that no one would miss the point of their presence. A police charge in India, every man armed with three feet of stout bamboo tipped with iron, which he usually employs without much mercy, is as frightening as anything on the subcontinent.

The military were not dressed for business but for carnival. Foot-soldiers marched in first behind bandsmen and pipers, dramatic in their uniforms of scarlet and viridian, ultramarine and saffron, with their white spats and their multicoloured pugris, with their epaul-ettes, their tassels and their braid, with high cockades laundered stiffly into pleats, pert hackles pluming from their heads and wide sashes worn boldly across their chests. Each new rank was cheered as it emerged under an archway into the open, and was identified by the man operating the public address system which boomed across the parade. The biggest cheer came when the 17th Mahratta Light Infan-try appeared and it was explained that they had recently covered them-selves in glory against the Tamil Tigers in Sri Lanka. I must have looked a bit surprised at the obviously partisan edge to that applause, because the man sitting next to me on the terrace decided to put me straight.

"Those are the wicked miscreants who murdered our Prime Minis-ter," he said. He screwed up his face in great distaste as he thought of something else. "Besides," he added, "the Tamils are very dirty people. We are very poor but we are very clean also."

After the infantry came cavalry, men in blue and gold uniforms, with golden pith helmets, the horsemen bearing lances with little burgees below their points. The animals were superb and so were the riders, holding themselves stiffly as they entered the arena at the trot, hooves stubbing flurries of red dust from the ground, burgees streaming in the breeze, every forearm at a regulation right angle to a vertical lance. They wheeled and came to a fidgeting standstill in the middle of the ground, the horses nodding deeply under the restraints of the bridles, pawing the ground delicately, not yet exer-cised enough. Surrounding them by now were not only the infantry units, but a squadron of women from the Air Force in white and blue uniforms. A silence until the Governor appeared, a small spare figure in a white achkan and a dun Congress cap, whose approach to the saluting base was preceded by the thump and crackle of more fireworks being loosed off somewhere out of sight. The bands struck up the National Anthem, the tricolour was raised and everyone in the stadium stood; and for once an Indian crowd was absolutely motionless. Then a turquoise jeep rolled up and the Governor stepped aboard with an aide-de-camp, who clutched a handrail with one hand and held a gleaming sword at the present with his other. The vehicle cruised round the parade, and each rank came to the salute as the Governor passed, making the vague gestures of a civilian who isn't at all sure of military etiquette.

The jeep restored him to the saluting base before it rolled offstage; whereupon His Excellency began to address this Republic Day assembly in the language of the old imperialism. He didn't have much choice if he wished to be generally understood, for his invited audience was Malayali, he himself came from Kannada-speaking Karnataka, the native tongue of some troops was Marathi, and English was the only speech intelligible to everyone. And in this manner the freedom fighters who had shamed the imperialists off their land were saluted first of all, which drew politely token applause. A gesture was made to Mahatma Gandhi as "architect of modern India", another to Dr Ambedkar for his authorship of the Constitution, both without acknowledgment from the spectators, and a halting causerie came to an end. The Governor put his spectacles away, the officer in charge of the military stamped up to him, saluted, and asked for permission to dismiss the parade.

It was soon done, with splendid bravura, perfect drill from the Mahrattas, and a swirl of tartan capes from the pipers, who played everybody else out of the amphitheatre to "Cock of the North", in the quick time of light infantry. As the last platoons of men marched under the archway and out to the side streets, where Army trucks were waiting to bear them off, the spectators rose from their terraces and filed out under the eyes of the police; who, I now saw, had not only outnumbered the watching crowd, but were more numerous than the military as well. Just as in imperial times, the biggest show of force had been mustered to intimidate the civilian populace. I walked back to my hotel through streets full of people obediently making their ways home or to church under the mounting sun.

I reached my room in time to watch the televised spectacular from New Delhi, which still had much of that Sunday morning to run. It had not long been finished when the telephone rang.

"Mr Moorhouse, I believe you've expressed a wish to see the Kaudiar Palace?"

The voice was cultured, self-possessed, not given to speaking except on its own terms; it could easily have been developed in an English public school. I did not doubt that it belonged to the Elaya Rajah. He did not need to announce himself. I said I'd be grateful.

"Then would you be good enough to call on us this coming Thursday, some time after lunch?"

"Oh dear. I'm afraid I'm leaving for Quilon on Tuesday, and I can't get out of it now."

"I understood you were going to be here for three weeks."

"No. I've been here for three weeks already, but I have to go now. I'm expected in Quilon on Tuesday." Silence at the other end of the line.

"I could quite easily come tomorrow – or even in what's left of today if that were convenient."

"Ah, well," said the voice, "I think we'd better leave it at that."

The phone was put down. I thought I had detected a note of relief.

# *Quilon*

As the train pulled out of the capital, houses with tiled roofs quickly fell away and all dwellings were covered instead with a thatch of dried palm. There were palm trees everywhere, on either side of the track, with small clearings here and there for buildings or for paddy fields of tapioca and rice. Cactus was flourishing in sand, but the food grew out of bright russet earth, and the gleam of liquid was almost perpetually visible. This was the lushest country in all India, apart from her borderlands in the far north-east. Egrets were poised watchfully beside swamps and saturated paddies, dark country boats were drawn up on the edge of a backwater, and as we neared Quilon the sea hove into view not far to our left, on the other side of a sandbar, where a red bus was bouncing north along a tarmacked road, going much faster than the train. A cool antiseptic breeze reached the stifling carriage from the waves. Passing the edge of the backwater I had almost retched at the sulphurous stench coming off the muddy banks.

Not only was it one of the lushest, but also one of the most densely populated areas on the subcontinent, though the palm forest was so thick and so interminable that it concealed all but a handful of its people. Some women strode along a bank with woks full of charcoal on their heads. A boat drifted down a backwater, poled by two men, with a third sitting between two piles of earth. We went through a station which was deserted apart from a man in a white uniform, who held out a green flag, giving us permission to continue along the next stretch of single line. A girl walked beside the track a bit further on, reading what was almost certainly a textbook, without once looking up at us. The appetite for advancement, for self-expression, was as keen here in the countryside as ever it was in the big town. In the middle of nowhere a pukka blue-rinsed building stood in a shaft of sunlight which broke through the canopy of palms. Painting School, said the notice above its door. In a tiny trackside village the most prominent structure was Premier College English and Maths. Very few walls, unless they were made of palm, had not been daubed with some motif, some announcement or exhortation, the hammer and sickle of communism competing with the open hand of Congress for dominance, Seven Days Without Safety Make One Weak giving way to Save Change India and other opaque sentiments. Kerala's people were as politically conscious as they were literate.

Quilon had once marked the northern limit of the old kingdom of Travancore, when this extended all the way down to Kanya Kumari. It had also been a principal port along the Malabar coast, long before Cochin reached its present primacy. In the thirteenth century Marco Polo knew it as Koulam, remarking on its population of Christians and Jews, its sandalwood, its pepper and its indigo, and on its intense heat ("so violent as to be scarcely supportable"). That other great medieval traveller Ibn Battuta spent three months here several decades later, recovering from a fever which had threatened his life. Nowadays, Quilon's importance was as a market for the surrounding countryside and as a terminus for all the considerable traffic of the backwaters. This mostly consisted of heavy longboats, carvel-built with dark planks set edge to edge and caulked with coir, their ribs lashed into place with the same fibre, devoid of any metal except along the gunwales, which were bolted on to the rest of the hull. Where other parts of the nation shifted bulk cargoes by road or railway, the tradition here had been to do so by country boat along the vast network of canals and lagoons that connected every community between Quilon and Cochin. But there were also ferries which plied the backwaters with the regularity of bus services ashore, low-lying launches capable of holding a hundred or more passengers, each with its wheelhouse perched for'ard on the cabin roof so that its captain would have an uninterrupted view ahead, and with a corrugated iron thunderbox hanging over the stern for the relief of people travelling long distances. It could take up to nine hours to travel one of the main routes, from Quilon to Alleppey. Every evening, with kites wheeling overhead in the fading light and crows flapping cumbersomely from tree to tree, the faint throb of diesels would be heard round a distant bend in the wide water, and presently the last ferry of the day from the northern terminus would come into sight through the trees, its navigation lights twinkling, its shape becoming indistinct as darkness fell. The muezzin's call would by then be drifting across that edge of town, competing with the sound coming out of the most prominent building in Quilon: the Shrine of Our Lady of Velamkani, which was a gigantic gimcrack pyramid with a glass base exposing its altar and its worshippers, gaudy with fairy lights inside, rising to a point on which balanced a lotus blossom enclosing a crown, not far above a golden Virgin who gazed towards the ferry building from her niche high above the street. The music coming out of the loudspeakers sounded as if it was made by an Indian James Last.

I had promised Joy Thomas that I would make my way upcountry that Tuesday, and he had applied for leave of absence as a result. He was a civil servant in the Secretariat at Trivandrum, who commuted between there and Quilon throughout the working week, which took an hour and a half each way. He was also a writer of short stories, who had been at the book launch on my first night in the capital. It was he who provided the running commentary on the platform personalities for my benefit, and a few days later we had lunched together at one of the coffee houses along MG Road. He was a stocky, immensely cheerful man, with a frizz of curly hair, which was uncommon in Kerala and the result of European or Levantine blood somewhere up the line. When I asked him about his first name he grinned and held up a hand, to count fingers one by one. "Eldest of six," he said. "Joy, Angel, James, John, Mercy and Mary – good Catholic family with hard-working parents, full of joy and thanksgiving to start with but crying out for mercy before the end." And doubled up at the jest.

The family saga that he then explained in all its bewildering detail was far from a laughing matter, however. Its crux was the Indian tradition of providing dowry at a daughter's marriage and the crippling burden this placed on poor families, and those who were no more than moderately well off, when they had several daughters to settle in matrimony. In Kerala the tradition was especially burdensome because the custom there was that the eldest daughter must always be married before any other child, even if several boys had been born before her; in other words, the parents would have to find a dowry before they could begin to recoup their outlay at the marriage of their sons. In the Thomas family, Angel was therefore the first to be married, in 1977; and her father, in addition to carrying all the expenses of the considerable celebrations that were expected of him, had to hand over to the bridegroom's father one-third of all his land, which was productive rice paddy, together with 10,000 rupees in cash and ten gold sovereigns, valued at another 1,000 rupees apiece. He was a minor official in local government, of modest means, and he was heavily stretched by this demand, even though it was the basic minimum for somebody at his end of the pay scale. For anyone better off, the dowry requirement could have been almost anything. It would have taken him, and any other average Indian wage-earner, seventy-five days of his labour to obtain just one of those sovereigns.

Joy's turn came a couple of years later. He had already turned down several offers of marriage, including one that would have brought him half an acre, a lakh of rupees (100,000) and twenty-five sovereigns. He didn't make it clear to me why he waved this wealth away, though it's possible that he was then more interested in making a career for himself. His professional life reached its first high point when he was working for the only Malayalam newspaper that carried the news of President Nasser's death, which broke in the middle of the night. Joy persuaded the printers to stay on to rejig the front page long after their normal shift was done. I could see him managing that: he was an essentially good-natured man and they'd do it because they liked him.

He beamed at the memory of that trifling success. "The editor acclaimed me like anything."

The following year he became a civil servant, at the age of twenty-two, but not until he was thirty did he receive the proposal from Annamma's parents, which needed some thought. They were poor people and marriage into the Thomas family was something of a step up for them, even though her father was a proud man who claimed descent from the Syrians who arrived with the apostle in the first century. Joy, an Information Officer in Cochin by now, had expected a dowry of 50,000 rupees but the family could offer no more than 10,000 and five sovereigns; at the same time there was the additional inducement that Annamma had a small job in a hospital, which meant extra wealth until she began childbearing. The proposal of marriage came accompanied by a photograph of the prospective bride, and Joy had liked the look of her.

"First criterion is liking girl but there are other criteria when you have responsibilities. However, my father was principled and I am an obeying boy. Father said, 'Marriages are made in heaven; engagements, too.'" So Joy and Annamma married on the terms offered by her parents. Twelve months later, Joy's father died and the newly wed civil servant became head of the Thomas family, with the sole responsibility for steering his four unmarried siblings through matrimony and for taking care of their widowed mother. At the very moment he took this on, Annamma had their first child: a daughter.

Joy's mother was soon pressing him to get Mercy married off, but for a year or two there wasn't a single offer, and Joy was in no hurry to find the dowry with his personal expenses beginning to mount. Then Mercy got a job as a clerk, the marriage offers suddenly began to come in, and matters could be delayed no longer. Joy looked at one man who was interested, "but he was black and a bit baldy also", and so his suit was dismissed. Eventually, a deal was struck with someone else, for a dowry of half the remaining Thomas land, 13,000 rupees and ten sovereigns.

After two more years, 1986 was eventful. First of all James, a clerk, married a girl who obtained a job within the month to augment her dowry of 10,000 rupees and ten sovereigns, together with one-fifth of an acre; which, however, was such poor land that even by 1992 it hadn't yet yielded a crop. John, meanwhile, had got a job as a bus conductor, and helped his remaining unmarried sister to do a teaching course. The moment Mary qualified, the marriage proposals began to come in. Her mother began to put pressure once again on the head of the family and I could well imagine it ("Our Mary's not getting any younger, y'know. Think of the shame, Joy, if she ends up on the shelf! Think of the shame!"). Joy had wanted time to recover financially from the outlay on Mercy and rejected Mary's first suitors; but his youngest sister *was* indisputably twenty-six by now, and his mother wasn't going to stop nagging until she was safely wed.

So Joy submitted, and began to make provision for Mary's marriage to another teacher. He collected all the money that was in his Provident Fund as a civil servant, so that he could muster 15,000 rupees and twelve gold sovereigns. The rest of the dowry consisted of all that was left of the Thomas land apart from a tiny plot: Joy, James and John now had only one-sixth of an acre between them. The week before the wedding there was crisis and panic when they found that some of their expectations had not materialised and they were still short of money for the dowry and the necessary wedding feast. They tried to persuade their sister Angel to lend some of the gold – jewellery and sovereigns – that she had taken into her own marriage nine years earlier; but both her husband and her mother pressed her to keep out of it. The day was saved only when Annamma chipped in with some of her family money and when James and John, without telling Joy what they were up to, went to the moneylender to raise 10,000 rupees for the shortfall in Mary's sovereigns. Six months later the moneylender called in his loan at interest of 50 per cent, on Joy's personal guarantee, which had been given entirely without his knowledge.

He was telling me all this at the age of forty-two, with a wife and three children by now, whom he supported on a salary of 3,000 rupees a month, which wouldn't go more than halfway to buying a small refrigerator for his family. He was up to his neck in debt, which he might never be able to pay off and which would be increased in a few years' time when he had to start the whole wretched dowry business all over again, as his own daughters came of marriageable age, two more females who would be reduced to mere bargaining chips. Even that wasn't the sum of Joy Thomas's problems. James's marriage had run into difficulties because his wife had become a high school teacher, worth 2,000 rupees a month, a sum which her parents had demanded for their own coffers or, instead, the return of their dowry. She had taken the children of the marriage and gone to live with the avaricious parents. James had abandoned the home he had been sharing with his wife, and had gone to live with his mother; I assumed he did so because he was incapable of looking after himself. Unfortunately, the senior Mrs Thomas happened to be living, according to the custom of Indian widowhood, in her eldest son's house. Fed up with this latest visitation of the fates, Joy, Annamma and their children had therefore moved out of their own home and shifted to quarters some distance away, rented by the government to Annamma's sister, who was a nurse.

It could have been worse. No bride had been burned to death mysteriously in her mother-in-law's kitchen because of greed for yet more dowry: this had been an appalling fact of life in North India, certainly during the past twenty years, and probably for a lot longer than that. The moneylender who was after Joy Thomas for 50 per cent interest was by no means the most rapacious creature plying that trade on this subcontinent: moneylenders always had been at the bottom of most Indian misery and even today some habitually extorted as much as 120 per cent.

When I asked this buoyant, uncomplaining little man whether he saw any possibility of improvement in his circumstances, he shrugged, but without a hint of hopelessness. "I can't say," he replied, as though my enquiry had been about the weather or about the chances of the communists returning to power in Trivandrum soon. "But God will help me in some way or other." We were sitting in my hotel lobby as he spoke, directly across the road from Our Lady of Velamkani. At that moment a bus pulled up at the stop outside the shrine. A man leapt off, put something into an offertory box set into the wall, crossed himself, turned and jumped back aboard as the bus lumbered off down the road. "If you have faith," said Joy, "everything comes goodly in the end. I think so, anyway."

We were in Quilon together because we both wanted to visit Amritananda Mayi, one of the most celebrated gurus in India, a woman whose fame had also spread abroad, especially to the United States, where she was said to be the subject of a flourishing cult. She was supposed to have great healing powers, which both Das and Kamala had briefly thought of invoking against his illness: in the end they had rejected the idea on the grounds that neither of them had any orthodox faith, which seemed to me to be taking

scruple a bit too far. It was they who had told me what little I knew
about Amritananda Mayi, and Joy was no better informed than I.
Now thirty-eight years old, she had been born in a village beside
the sea, a few miles north of Quilon, and was betrothed at the age
of thirteen, though for some reason the marriage fell through. She
then took to isolating herself from everyone, going off to the shore
or into the palm forest, to sit alone and meditate, and people began
to take note of this. One day she had a vision in which she was told
by Lord Krishna that she was His reincarnation; in this guise therefore no longer she, but She. And people believed the girl as soon as
she told them this apparently, being even more credulous than the
French peasants who accepted the word of Bernadette Soubirous
that she had encountered the Virgin Mary in a grotto at Lourdes.
In one other respect, the adolescent in Kerala conformed to an
ancient pattern that runs through every faith: the self-proclaimed,
utterly simple holy person with little or no schooling, in her case
scarcely literate. There are ten grades of basic education in India,
and she had passed only four when she became divine. Amritananda
Mayi stood in a line that began with the Delphic Oracle, whose
priests retained the services of untaught peasant girls much given
to strange utterances which seemed to come from their bellies, and
were taken to signify that they were *en theos*, "with the god".

We struggled to board a bus that was already crammed full when
it came through from Trivandrum, listing heavily to port when it
rattled to a standstill near the ferry terminus. As we braced ourselves
much more tenaciously than any strap-hangers on the London
Underground, while the bus canted this way and that with the driver
careering at speed around all other traffic, I reflected on the part
played by India's public transport in eroding the caste system. The
ancient rigidities simply could not have survived on the old scale
once the railway and especially the omnibus came along. So cooped
up were we on this ride that I could feel sweat from the man standing
next to me mingling with my own through both our shirts. He
looked very uneasy at this, but there was nothing either of us could
do about it.

After half an hour, Joy and I got off in the middle of a township,
where we had to wait for another bus heading due west towards the
coast. Beside the main road stood the huge and ornate frontage of

a temple; but that's all the building there was. The land behind, open ground apart from a number of trees, was the temple and the trees were the objects of veneration. We had time to kill and we wandered through this holy grove, where people sat cross-legged in attitudes of devotion before their chosen trees; which now, I could see, in every case had ribbons tied to branches, even pieces of grubby rag, in one case a half-deflated balloon. The only other time I'd seen tree worship had been years before in the hills above Islamabad, where the devotees had been Muslims, rather out of favour with the local religious authorities, who regarded the practice as disturbing evidence of a pagan past. In Pakistan the trees had been decorated with flags, and fires had sometimes been lit in front of them. There was no evidence of that here; only the decorations, the quiet wor-shippers, a handful of beggars slumped in the heat of noon, a number of people prone and snoozing in the shade.

The second bus ride was more comfortably seated, winding along country lanes with dry paddies on either side and palm trees growing well back, until we came to a village, which was the end of the road. It contained a handful of shops, each no bigger than a garden shed at home, and all were selling vegetables, fruit, spices, bottles of soft drinks. Where the bus route ended a canal began and along this longboats were tethered at intervals, all low in the water because they were loaded with stinking mud. It looked as if the canal was being dredged, but there was other activity here, too. A man was husking a pile of coconuts and I could see a great raft of these floating in a pond beside the canal. The man paused as Joy and I walked past and, to give himself more time to inspect us before resuming his task, he rearranged his lunghi, taking its hems almost primly in his fingertips and hitching them up to his waist so that the skirt would fall no lower than his knees. It was an angular, elbowy movement made without haste, like a seabird composing its wings when it has just touched down. There was a pestilential smell of rot coming off the nearby raft, which made us gulp and quicken our stride to leave it behind. A few hundred yards further on, with the palm forest now thick and enclosing on every side, the air improved as we came to a wide and clear waterway.

A country boat was coming down the middle, very low in the water with two mounds of white sand amidships, the hump of a mat shelter further aft, a man standing at the stern by his steering oar, an occasional puff of wind in the lateen up for'ard just enough to keep the boat moving gently along. Another boat, empty and without sail, came in the opposite direction, its crewman steering and propelling it at the same time, using a long pole as if he had charge of an oversize punt. Both men had cloths wound round their foreheads, to stop sweat trickling into their eyes, but it was the punter who needed his most. They did not speak to each other as their boats passed; both were more interested in people ashore. On our side of the water there was only Joy and me, and the man preparing to take us across on a miniature version of the cargo boats; but it was sharper at the prow than the bigger craft, which were upturned at each end into a crude scroll. On the far side of the water a dozen or more people, both brown and white, were standing on the landing stage, waiting for our ferry to arrive. Beside them was a large notice in white capitals on a red ground: MATA AMRITANANDAMAYI MATH.

These people paid us no attention as we stepped ashore; coming and going was evidently so usual that it occasioned no curiosity here. A narrow path fenced in by hurdles of palm branch led directly to some buildings a few hundred yards away, all but invisible before we reached them through a thickness of trees. Most of them were of conventional pukka construction without upper floors, but one was extravagantly more ambitious than that.* It loomed high above a compound in which many people stood about gossiping as we arrived, as though they had just emerged from a lecture or some other collective event. There were four storeys of pre-stressed concrete, starting with a steep flight of steps up to an entrance beneath a jutting canopy, which might have been built anywhere in the world, and above that was a medley of chhatris and other shapes that belonged to this subcontinent alone, pillared vantage points and cupolas, domes and canopies shaped like open umbrellas, all of which might have had ritualistic significance or have simply been built to provide a view across the surrounding palm forest, sheltered from

---

* A pukka building is one made of cemented bricks or masonry, with or without a plastered exterior: the traditional alternative is a kutcha building of mud, matting or timber. The essential difference is one between affluence and poverty.

the sun. Work on the building was obviously not yet finished. The
flight of steps was still mostly in rough concrete, though a start had
been made on cladding these with marble slabs. A young blond man
started down them, with carpenter's tackle arranged round his waist
on a belt. Coming up towards him was another Westerner with an
infant in the crook of one arm and a plastic potty held in his other
hand. They paused and exchanged greetings, Americans both.

Joy and I walked round this structure, which had windows, evidently for a series of rooms, running on each level down both sides.
Behind it was a thatched hut in which a Western woman was sweeping the floor. She was dressed in a long white cotton wraparound
which also covered her head, and made her look like a nun; every
female we'd seen in the compound was similarly garbed. She greeted
us and sounded very French when she said that of course we could
come in and look around. At the far end of the hut was an
upholstered bench on which was spread a leopard skin. The walls
were hung with many portraits of Indian sages, among whom I
recognised Vivekananda and Ramakrishna; and there was also a copy
of a famous fourteenth-century Russian ikon, the Virgin of the Don.
The only other woman pictured there was an Indian, dressed like
the sweeper. She had a chubby face, plump hands, and the sort of
smile that cannot be produced for effect. She looked a very warm
person with brilliantly white teeth and a jewel, possibly diamonds,
in her nose.

"This is Amritananda Mayi?" I asked the Frenchwoman.

"Yes, that is Mother."

"Would it be all right if I took a photograph of this room?"

An odd expression crossed her face, faintly nervous, almost furtive.
"Mother wouldn't like that," she said, "and it's quite possible she'd
tell one of the brahmacharyn to remove your film." She didn't say
no, but I let it go. The hut was gloomy and the auto-flash would
have given the game away.

We went outside and Joy wandered off while I sat on a wall
to watch the activity of the ashram. People were moving about
purposefully in all directions, mostly Westerners and a majority of
them young women, more often than not extremely attractive. There
were a lot of mixed couples and most of these seemed to have
children with them, not one of whom showed temper or other

unhappiness while we were there. A number of people went into a small building, one at a time, each staying for a little while before emerging. It had a notice over the door

OM Sweet OM
One in All      All in One

and during a small interval in the traffic I looked inside: it was a tiny conventional shrine, with room for no more than a handful of people to kneel or sit cross-legged at the same time.

Joy returned to tell me that close to the shrine was the house in which Amritananda Mayi had been born. "And over there," he said, pointing to a modern villa whose upper floor could be seen behind a fence with a No Entry sign on its gate, "that is where Mother lives now." He sounded impressed. Someone had taken him into the refectory for food and tea, feeding him with information, too. The ashram had a permanent population of 200 or so, no more than thirty of them from the West, the others Indian; but there was a huge floating population from America and Europe, especially at this time of the year, before the great heat of early summer and the subsequent monsoon.

"Come and see inside the temple, which is very fine and interesting." He led the way across the dusty compound, where a couple of dogs lay panting in the shade of a wall. I assumed they had somehow got inside the ashram from the village, but no one seemed to be bothered by that. Every Westerner, I noticed, very carefully steered clear of them.

The temple had several functions to fulfil in addition to the liturgical. Its ground floor consisted of offices and other working rooms. At the top of the outside steps was the entrance to a large auditorium, with a wide balcony running right round it at normal ceiling height; and people reached their private rooms by going up to the balcony first. The rooms all seemed to have two occupants and, when people emerged, they did not fail to padlock the doors. There were more stairs leading higher still to the chhatris and the roof and, when I went up, half a dozen people were sitting there as though mesmerised, each wrapped in some private world, soothed by a pleasant breeze, when not a breath of air stirred on the ground. The view was one of treetops on every side; but half a mile or less to the west, I could see the waters of the Arabian Sea, shimmering in the glare of the late afternoon sun.

There were notices on the wall of the balcony, one of which gave details of another world tour Mother was undertaking during the high summer, exceptional because, although she would be reworking ground in America and Europe that she had already found to be fertile, she would now be going to Moscow for the first time. One other thing was being pushed in 1992, and that was the circulation of the magazine put out by the Mata Amritanandamayi Mission Trust, whose publishers addressed themselves to the faithful on a balcony wall as follows:

Blessed Self,
Surely you are all aware by now that the Math and the devotees of the Divine Mother have decided to observe 1992 as Matruvani year with the aim of vastly enhancing our circulation, thus bringing the nectar of Mother's Divine Love to all souls who suffer in the heat of samsara. The central methods we will employ in this venture is to form groups of volunteers (Pracharaks) which will make house contacts and visit institutions, introducing people to Matruvani and Amma's teachings . . .
                              Yours in the service of the Divine Mother

There was a shop beside the entrance to the auditorium, and I picked up a copy of the magazine, together with some pictures of this divine but very guarded lady, as I obviously wasn't going to get any of my own. The journal was of about the same pocketable size and inexpensive appearance as the average parish magazine in the Church of England, and in it I discovered that Amritananda Mayi's activities were wider than I had supposed. She was associated with a Free Eye Camp at Ernakulam, a Medical Centre in Trivandrum, and clearly got herself involved in good works all over the place. There was also an Amrita Institute of Computer Technology, which offered courses as short as three months, as long as one year, and was well into Wordperfect, Wordstar, Foxpro, Clipper and Lotus 1-2-3. Its advertisement said nothing at all about fees, the only guidance to cost being that twenty-eight rupees were required simply to acquire a prospectus and an application form. That would represent nearly two and a half days' work to the average Indian wage-earner.

But it was the tone of the editorial texts that interested me most of all. The first few pages were occupied by Divine Mother's Message, addressed to "Darling children". What followed was unexceptional and unexceptionable, fairly simple observations about human frailty and the possibility of solution by belief in God. The ending, though, was intriguing. "Therefore, my darling children, take refuge in the Supreme Atman. Surrender totally to God. Then you will enjoy a strong and sound mind, and be able to rise above all sorrows. What-ever you require will be brought to you. If that does not happen, tell Amma. Amma gives you Her word that such an occasion will never occur, for Amma is speaking directly from Her own experience over all these years." Wherever any reference anywhere in the maga-zine was made to Amritananda Mayi in the third person, She or Her was always capitalised. The assumption of divinity was made more explicitly a few pages further on, where a disciple described what had happened some years earlier, when Amma went to a festival in the Tamil temple town of Tiruvannamalai.

The memory of Amma's first visit . . . still lives in my heart with unfading glow. The train journey with Amma, who often behaved like a frolicsome and naughty teenaged girl, was very lively and joyful. Full of enthusiasm, Amma would run along the length of the compartment, making enquiries like "Son, did you get peanut? Who wants bananas?" etc. She would come and sit beside each of us in turn, singing devotional songs. The other passengers looked at each other with surprise, wondering who was this crazy girl in shirt and skirt, making such a commotion! Little did they know that their rambunctious compartment-mate was actually the incar-nate Goddess of the Universe, sole Author, Director and Actor of the cosmic play.

Eventually, of course, word got out; it was bound to, and passen-gers began to prostrate themselves before Amma, while at every station in Tamil Nadu there were devotees waiting to garland her. The reason for going to Tiruvannamalai was to see the big chariot festival, when enormous decorated raths would be manhandled through the streets by acolytes, watched by hundreds of thousands. So that Amma would not be exposed to the dangers of humanity in the mass going berserk with religious fervour – a commonplace in India, which too often results in people being fatally crushed – she was taken to the terrace of a two-storey house, where she could watch in safety and comfort. After a while, obviously not enjoying herself, she demanded to be taken to the local ashram of her followers, and her bodyguard had a thoroughly frightening time escorting her through the heaving streets. They thought at one point that they probably weren't going to make it.

The danger of being trampled loomed in the air ... Then, as if by the Grace of God, the owner of a roadside house came out and, seeing our predicament, he invited Amma and the whole group of us inside; thus we narrowly escaped being trampled to death. Soon, a horsecart was arranged and Amma and the rest of us returned to our Ashram. Upon reaching the Ashram, Amma began to laugh continuously. Nealu and the others soon arrived. With a tinge of sorrow and anger Nealu complained "What did you do that for, Amma?" Amma's reply was, "My children, you wanted me to enjoy the festival from the safety of the terrace, when thousands were suffering all the brutal kicks and pushes below. You can never expect to get Amma to enjoy Herself when others are suffering."

Those words reverberated in my ears again and again.

The auditorium began to fill with people as the heat went out of the day and the sun came down the sky. Men to the left and women to the right was the rule, as each found a space on the bare marbled floor, put down a mat or a cushion and sat cross-legged among the stumpy Doric pillars holding up the balcony. They faced a stage with wooden doors screening something at the back but at each end of the stage, in front of the doors, was a large photograph of Mother, one in colour, the other in black and white. The stage and its contents were framed in a surrounding tableau of pale pinks and blues and yellows and greens, thin and dulcet colours which had also been used to decorate the pillars of the hall. Upstairs, other members of the community emerged from their rooms, from showers, from the coolness of the roof, and brought their cushions to vantage points by the balcony rail, from where they could look down on whatever happened below. Many had a book with them, containing verses printed in transliterated Sanskrit and English. Just before five o'clock the wooden doors on the stage slid open to reveal a small shrine, with the effigy of a goddess in the middle. In front of this was the upholstered bench and the leopard skin I had seen earlier in the thatched hut, and in front of that was a small battery of microphones. Down in the hall, packed by now, a man fiddled with the knobs of a stereo control centre. A young woman came bustling on to the balcony, stepped over two or three people to get to a friend with a good view, put down a drugget and whispered, "Mother's coming at any moment." She was close to trembling with excitement.

Mother entered swiftly, backstage right, accompanied by four men: she and two of them were clad in white garments, the other two in saffron robes. She was shorter than I expected, a little barrel of a woman whose robes concealed most of her plumpness. She was smiling broadly as she walked forward until she prostrated herself to the congregation across the leopard skin. The people bowed low to her in turn. The men arranged themselves on either side and just in front of Mother, two of them with brass percussion instruments, one paddling the skin of a tabla with the flat of his hands, the fourth squeezing a harmonium. We were obviously in for an evening of hymn singing, whatever else developed. And it was artfully stage-managed. The musicians were so positioned that they would look up to Mother, throughout her performance; the cue for absolute attention by everybody else.

She went straight into the first bhajan without preamble, chanting a line in a high reedy voice, which her audience then repeated fortissimo, with a verve that suggested pent-up emotion more than ready for release. Then another line from Mother, who swayed from side to side as she sang, sitting amid her musicians in the traditional Hindu manner, but with all the fluent body language of a happy West Indian praising the Lord in a Pentecostal mission. There was nothing of the stylised grace, the flowing arms, the eloquent hands of the Hindu temple artist here; instead, Mother and her devotees were adapting Indian music and sentiment to the clapalong fervour of Western revivalists. For ten minutes the first set continued, statement and answer, soloist leading chorus, until it ended not with a sharp cut-off, but with a dwindling of sound to something like a choral sigh, as though everyone was reluctant to let it go. In the brief silence that followed, an Indian girl crawled across the stage on hands and knees and placed before Mother an open book, before retreating in the same manner to the wings. She would do this repeatedly until all the singing was done. Mother evidently didn't have the songs off by heart, or else she wasn't confident enough to do without a prompt. The second set began to a different tune and different words, but the form was exactly as before; as it would be for every bhajan that rocked the building for the next couple of hours.

Excitement mounted progressively with each new number. In the third set, Mother began to gesture more extravagantly than before, placing her hands together in prayer, then throwing her arms to heaven, then outstretching them towards the audience, changing the direction, the object of her supplicating cry. This produced a response well on the way to frenzy from some people. A bearded Indian near the sound system was soon beside himself with ecstasy, flinging his body this way and that in an exaggerated parody of Mother's first swaying motion, clapping his hands resoundingly in time with the brass manjira and the drum. He was not the only one to behave with such abandon, and Mother herself was soon feeding in turn on the wildness she had excited among her worshippers. As the clapping became more frantic she shed yet another layer of reserve, contorted more violently than ever, arched over backwards, almost double, like a limbo dancer trying to get under the lowest bar. As she did so she began to ululate, uttering the word "Amma" shrilly and repeatedly with such rapid movements of the throat that even from the balcony it was possible to see her neck throbbing steadily.

Not everyone was intoxicated. Amidst all the frenzy, some of the Western women below and around me were holding themselves in check, unlike every male in sight apart from Joy and me, and unlike every Indian woman I was able to watch. Many white women, too, were prepared to let themselves go on the sensational plateau Mother beckoned from; but others were content to sway a bit, to beat time with their fingers quietly, they were not yet ready to let go. I guessed they were visitors like us, testing the atmosphere and not yet at a moment of truth. They were still holding part of themselves coolly back when the performance came abruptly to an end, with a loud clanging on a gong, a blowing of conch shells, and the wooden doors sliding shut in front of Mother, who was lying prostrate in mid-stage.

There was an intermission, while people sat and talked quietly, or read, or went to the back of the hall to buy things from the stall which had been moved into the auditorium from its customary premises downstairs. It had been arranged so that it was impossible for anyone to pick up a picture of Mother, or a cassette of bhajans, or a bundle of sandalwood incense sticks, or any of the other things for sale; benches had been placed so that no one could lean over them. It was necessary to point to something and hand over the money before being served. The people running Mother's affairs were by no means simple country folk, as she had been. They were as streetwise as anyone from metropolitan India. Her personal assistant was said to be an Australian woman.

She returned to the stage transformed, no longer she but She, in Her divine person as reincarnated Krishna. She was no longer dressed in white but in a golden robe and with an elaborate crown on Her head, which would have sat well upon the king in an extravagant production of *Aida*. She had glittering bangles on Her wrists and a very large garland of flowers hanging round Her neck. She was seated on the leopard skin, and Her face was not animated now but a little haughty as acolytes crawled around Her, prostrating themselves repeatedly and covering Her skirts with flower petals. Another man entered with a brass bowl full of flames, which he passed in front of Her repeatedly, balancing it and backhanding it as deftly as someone performing in a circus.

Joy leaned over to me excitedly. "I've never seen that done in front of a living person before," he said. "Only in front of temple images."

The musicians were now sitting round the stereo system in the body of the hall, and more chanting began, though this time She took no part in it. It was simply the setting for a laying on of hands. Two queues formed, again divided according to gender except in the case of children, who all formed up on the female right. They had been stacked in close order so that they looked like a juvenile chorus line about to break into their routine; and they didn't quite appreciate the great solemnity of the occasion, rushing forward to Mother in turn, instead of approaching with proper humility. The adults without exception fell to their knees when they came near Her and crawled the last couple of yards, very awkwardly in the case of some Westerners. Everyone was treated alike: Mother bent and hugged the submissive head to Her own, patted or stroked the lowly back, letting go only when the other showed a desire to pull away. It was an utterly maternal gesture, repeated again and again for over an hour while we remained there. People came down from the stage with eyes gleaming, but only once did someone seem to be quite overcome by this proximity to the divine. A Western woman in a mauve sari, almost certainly a visitor, mounted the stage with a box of flowers ("Prearranged!" hissed Joy), which Mother passed to an aide, rather in the manner of royalty on a street walkabout. The woman then stumbled rather than crawled into Mother's lap and seemed to be in tears, while the object of her devotion patted her back comfortingly for several minutes, as if to say "There, there!" until the woman had recovered and could disengage.

The queues were still forming when we stole away into the night and crossed the silent backwater, which twinkled with the reflection of distant kerosene lamps, as fishermen upstream tried their luck at the top of the tide.

When we returned the following day the air of anticipation that filled the temple before Mother's appearance onstage had shifted to the vicinity of the thatched hut. People were sitting inside, obviously awaiting another manifestation of the reincarnated and transmogrified god, in pensive rows: some reading, some sitting in the lotus position, others merely quiet and still, with head inclined in thought. Outside, people were dawdling until the event, the Event, began. They kept walking past the entrance to the garden in which Mother's villa stood, to see if they could catch sight of Her, but they went no closer than that: the door to the garden was open, but it still said No Entry as well as bearing the Sanskritic calligraphy meaning OM. Among those waiting there was an elderly white woman in shalwar kameez, with a sweetly vague face and grey hair severely bobbed, who might have been a pillar of the Mothers' Union or the Women's Institute anywhere in the rural English shires. There was also a raw-boned man, something over seven feet tall, with a shaven skull and a beaky tormented face, his skin tanned by both wind and sun I guessed, dressed in a short-sleeved check shirt and lunghi, with chappals on his huge feet. He was reading a manual of some sort, full of diagrammatic photos, and he kept making occult signs with his free hand, extending fingers and thumb in different combinations, varying angles. I had come to the conclusion that he was almost certainly a Slav, and was beginning to construct a fantasy about his emergence from the Gulag, when someone greeted him and he, in an unmistakably cockney voice, informed the other that he hailed from West Ham.

"Hello. Are you waiting to see Mother?" The voice was American, the woman was tall and slim, wearing the white cotton wraparound of the ashram's permanent company.

"Waiting to watch her, actually." I reckoned she was in her late thirties, friendly but with something that hinted at strain. "You belong here, I think?"

"Oh, yes, I've been here four years. I wouldn't be anywhere else." Was there something just a bit too defensively quick in affirming that?

She was open, without guile, perfectly willing to reveal herself. She had been Nancy, a biochemist at Berkeley when she came to India out of simple curiosity and, like so many of us, got hooked. She subsequently returned to join the ashram of Sathya Sai Baba, who was probably the most celebrated of the gurus alive today, but he had failed her in a surprising way. She had spent ten years in his entourage, "and in all that time he never noticed me, never spoke to me, never read anything I wrote, never let me kiss his feet, didn't acknowledge my presence in any way until he heard I was planning to leave him for Mother." It sounded like a very sad tale of love unrequited; but in Mother she had evidently found what she was yearning for.

"Oh, the stories I could tell you about Mother," said this devoted liegewoman, who had herself in a small way been reincarnated, too: no longer Nancy, but Samiti. But the stories were not about Mother's solicitude for, Her recognition of, Her interest in the disciple, but of a wider compassion and approachability. "There was a leper once and she licked his sores, though he smelt horribly." Samiti didn't quite gag on the memory, but her face told how it had got to her in the pit of a sensitive stomach.

"Have you seen our original temple?" She was pointing to the little shrine, with OM Sweet OM above the door. "In the early days, Mother used to sit there surrounded by just a dozen of us, and it was nice . . ." Her voice trailed off wistfully, as though she regretted the loss of the old intimacy and its replacement by something bigger, more successful, which was quite obviously thriving, affluent even, judging by the building works and the plans for a second world tour. I got the impression that Ma Amritananda Mayi's Math, like every other religious foundation I'd ever heard of, had exchanged its first beguiling notions of fellowship, revelation and above all blessed simplicity, for something much more complex and prosperous, structured into hierarchy, subdivided unevenly into a society of Marthas and Marys.

"There's a cave down there," she said inconsequentially, pointing to a hole I hadn't noticed before, in a wall behind the original temple. She said the cave had a slit which let in some light and air, but it was pretty gloomy and must have been like an oven in the heat of the day. Then she added, "An American's been down there meditating for a month now. His wife takes his food in every day. One man spent the best part of three years down there. Mother used to visit him from time to time. When he emerged, he went away."

"In what condition?" I asked. This particular form of mortification, after all, wasn't far removed from captivity in a medieval dungeon. It wasn't the same as a penitential life spent in an open cave beside the headwaters of the Ganga.

"Oh, he was very beautiful. Not beautiful to look at, but beautiful inside. You could see."

The same rustle of anticipation that had preceded Mother's arrival the night before was now heard in the vicinity of the hut. When I looked through the door she was already there, sitting on the low bench with the leopard skin, dressed in her white robes, therefore no longer She but she again. People who had been squatting under the thatch for an hour or more were going up to her; to be hugged, fondled, kissed, smiled upon, whispered to in turn. The harmonium was quietly playing and the atmosphere was very soothing, without the histrionics of the manifestation in the temple, even though some people still found the encounter too powerful for their composure. A girl came away in tears; a strong-looking man in his thirties buried himself in Mother's embrace and his shoulders shook. She herself, I had no doubt, was wholly benign and something more than that. She would have made a fabulous nurse, the sort of woman men thank God for when they are recovering from major surgery on a public ward.

Then something sinister happened. I heard behind me in the

compound the sound of someone speaking loudly and angrily. Clapalong, the bearded Indian who had been so prominent in the congregational responses the night before, was standing over Joy, who was sitting next to an old woman with a notebook and a ballpoint in his hand. He was very clearly berating my friend in Malayalam for conducting an interview and taking notes, and Joy was protesting, explaining, with an uneasy expression on his face. I walked over and stood by them, but Clapalong suddenly turned on his heel and strode into the forbidden garden, heading for Mother's villa.

"What's the problem?" I asked Joy.

"He says journalists aren't wanted here. I told him I'm not a journalist."

Clapalong returned, and with him was a younger man in a saffron robe, one of the brahmacharyn, a member of Mother's Praetorian Guard. Clapalong was untidily, flamboyantly hirsute, but the newcomer's hair and beard were very carefully trimmed. I had no difficulty envisaging him in an expensive dark suit, possibly with a lawyer's tabs at his neck, rather than in these religious robes. He too hectored Joy in their native tongue, but with more control than Clapalong; the English phrases "ask permission" and "good manners" came poking through. He then put a hand on my friend's shoulder but as I stepped forward to intervene, Joy gestured that it was okay. The two of them went through the garden gate and entered the thatched hut the way Mother must have gone in.

I turned to Clapalong. "What is it about this place," I asked, "that you don't want people to know?"

"Journalists always lie about us," he replied. He thrust a forefinger up one of his nostrils and began to excavate energetically.

"Good Lord," I said, "do you often do that in public?"

He glared at me and walked over to a corner of the compound where some men were constructing something. I could see him gesturing, talking rapidly, ordering them about.

I went to the front door of the thatched hut to see what I could inside. Apart from the queue I had watched before, there was also a much shorter line entering from the other end. At that moment Joy came round the outside of the building, not at all strained now, but with a blissful expression on his face. He hurried me towards the gap in the hurdle fence which was the way back to the ferry. "I was taken to head of queue," he said happily, "and I have been blessed by Mother."

"Well," I said, as we were being rowed across the tranquil backwater, "tell me what it was like."

"It was like being hugged by Mummy when I was little boy." He wobbled his head in the Indian manner, from top to bottom and loose at the neck. He looked very pleased with himself. "Also it was like being held by wife when I am getting big."

# *Alleppey*

To most foreigners, Alleppey was simply a staging post on the way from Trivandrum to Cochin. It had left no impression on the great travellers of the past, though it had once been the principal port of Travancore, overtaking Quilon in the eighteenth century. Since its decline, which coincided with the great advance made by Cochin in the twentieth, it had been best known to outsiders as an important junction on the backwaters. Someone doubtless connected with the modern tourist industry had called it the Venice of the East, on the strength of two industrial canals running straight through the little town. This was inflation pumped up to bursting point. The canal banks were lined not with palaces, religious buildings or an Indian version of the Piazza San Marco, but with warehouses full of coconut matting and other products of the bountiful palm. Men spurted sweat as they strained to pull and push carts overloaded with coir ropes past stockpiles of bricks and timber along the canal banks. Once, all such cargoes would have been sent up to Cochin for export along the waterways, but not any longer: now they mostly went by juggernaut along the roads.

Nor was there anything of great interest away from the canals apart from the principal Hindu temple, which promised much with its shingled roof and its wooden gallery above the gateway; and with its notice which advised that "It is strictly forbidden using footwears within the temple compound. Smoking chewing and spitting within the temple compound is strictly forbidden. Wearing shirts banians and lunkey within the temple is prohibited. (Temple Take Care Committee)". But entry even on those rigorous terms was forbidden unless you could acclaim Brahma, Vishnu, Shiva and all the other deities in the Hindu pantheon with a clear conscience. Across the street was the jeweller's shop owned by Abdul Lateef, with the day's going rate for gold chalked up prominently on a board; as it was by Sri Lateef's many competitors in Alleppey. These premises were fitted out with showcases, alarm systems, metal shutters, but most trade in the town was conducted much more modestly than that. A few yards from the temple someone had spread his wares on a small trestle, which was all he required for the sale of spare parts for defective wrist-watches, each item salvaged from other broken time-pieces: a great variety of watch faces, fingers, glasses, winding knobs, flywheels, casings, spindles, straps. Next to this speciality was an even narrower one, offering any of the few bits and pieces that someone might need in order to mend an electric torch. It seemed impossible that anyone could make a living this way, but India defies such assumptions more than any other country I have known: perhaps because the reworking of junk must come more naturally to a people whose principal creed sees life as a perpetually revolving cycle.

I had decided to linger here in order to find out what I could about the origins of Kerala's communism: Alleppey was where it was supposed to have got its first foothold, after India as a whole had been introduced to the doctrines of Marx and Lenin by returning émigrés. These came mainly from the Punjab and Bengal, they wanted the British out of the subcontinent, and to this end made contact with the Comintern in the years immediately after the First World War. The most notable of them was the Bengali Brahmin M. N. Roy, who became Lenin's confidant and in 1920 opened a school for Indian revolutionaries in Tashkent; where, that year, the Communist Party of India was born. Its activists were soon going back over the Hindu Kush to create as much trouble as possible in their homeland and for a dozen years or so the illicit CPI was the sole repository of socialist hopes on the subcontinent, until a ginger group within Congress was formed with approximately the same aims. But even as late as 1964, certified and undiluted communism in India meant the CPI and no one else. That year saw the end of its monopoly with the formation of the rival CPI (Marxist), essentially a product of the Sino-Soviet dispute. Thereafter, other splits occurred at intervals, often locally, especially in West Bengal, where a state election was fought in 1967 by sixteen political parties, ten of which professed allegiance to Lenin and Marx. By then, the CPI(M) had gained the upper hand in the original rivalry, a lead that has been maintained ever since. By 1992, both West Bengal and the small state of Tripura, wedged between Bangladesh and Assam up in the north-east, had long since voted communists into power. But the world's first democratically elected communist government was the one that took office in Trivandrum in 1957.

Communists had been regularly in and out of power in Kerala ever since. It was widely held that they had only been ejected in the summer of 1991 because of a huge sympathy vote for Congress, shamelessly garnered in the aftermath of Rajiv Gandhi's assassination. I had certainly been left in no doubt that Marxism was alive and kicking vigorously here, in spite of the fact that it had been completely discredited in Eastern Europe and that the Soviet Union itself had collapsed after repudiating its founders. In Kerala, the red flag might still be seen flying anywhere, the hammer and sickle was likewise visible on many walls, and there were even hoardings bearing crude portraits of Marx, Engels, Lenin and Stalin. In Trivandrum one day there had been a long procession of the Revolutionary Youth Front up MG Road which lasted for over an hour, two files of young men (but not a single woman) with banners and placards, intent on demonstrating outside the Secretariat; one of its marshals had aggressively tried to stop me crossing the road, and when I brushed him aside he looked as if he would have had me set upon but for the presence of many police who would have been only too happy for such an excuse to use their lathis. In Quilon there had been a notice by the ferry building: "Build up mighty democratic movement on the base political line of anti-capitalist Socialist Revolution by the great leader of the proletariat." Half a mile away a crowd was being harangued, to the inconvenience of the traffic, by a zealot of the Socialist Unity Centre of India, a very handsome young man with thick black well-oiled hair and brilliant teeth, who mouthed obloquy, snarled defiance, screamed for action and generally let himself go in a frenzy of megalomania. If fate had dealt him the best possible hand, he would have been an immensely rich film star, darling of the Bombay studios. As it was, he made the best of his talents to get on a little in the world, emitting the unpleasant and universal sound of the rabble-rouser, whom we have heard throughout my lifetime from every political direction, at home and abroad, always sure of an audience and never silent for long.

And in Trivandrum I had met the world's first democratically elected communist government leader, the legendary E. M. S. Namboodiripad, whose name was a clue to part of his celebrity. His was a classic story of the high-born who turns his back on privilege and wealth to identify with and fight for the poor and the victimised: in his case the Nambudiri Brahmin who rejected caste and his own superior position at the apex of Hindu society, and decided to live instead according to the doctrines of Karl Marx. According to some, E.M.S. was responsible for changing the entire Nambudiri attitude to women, which traditionally had condemned most of them to celibacy in order to minimise the pollution of the race by blood coming from any other source: only the eldest son in a Nambudiri family could marry a Nambudiri girl, and her sisters were not available to the men of any other caste. It was said that he wrought this change first of all among his own people of Malabar, in northern Kerala, and the emancipation gradually spread south down the rest of the coast. His admirers also claimed that he gave away all his property on inheriting it, placing his wealth at the party's disposal. His detractors reckoned that, far from being a saintly, disinterested man, E.M.S. had run an extensive system of patronage for his family from the moment he came to power in 1957, securing jobs, property and other advantages for each in turn. Beyond dispute was his political record. He had emerged from the ranks of the Congress Socialist Party, the ginger group within Congress, to become a CPI centrist in the jargon of Indian communism, later to be the General Secretary of the CPI(M) and its chief theoretician. On the all-India stage his only equal was Jyoti Basu, also of the CPI(M) and for many years Chief Minister of West Bengal. E.M.S. became Chief Minister of Kerala in the first place because he offered socialist policies not much more radical than those being practised at the same time nationally by Jawaharlal Nehru, but which the electors found more appealing than anything the corrupt local Congressmen might serve up. He remained Chief Minister, on and off, for the next twenty years; and since that initial victory in 1957 the communists in one form and another had held office in Kerala much more often than not.

So it was with a rare sense of approaching history in the flesh that I set off for the Namboodiripad domicile one afternoon. Inevitably, it was Kamala Das who had secured an entrée, when my own unaided efforts had come to nothing. She had simply rung up the great man's daughter at lunchtime and the word came back that I should present myself at five o'clock sharp. I was to be allowed one hour with him, provided I submitted no more than five questions in writing the moment I arrived, and gave him ten minutes alone to consider them before we met. On no account was I to ask any supplementaries later on. It was a familiar deal: Jyoti Basu had made similar conditions in Calcutta in 1969, but because his answers tended to be an unamplified "yes" or an unqualified "no" I was in and out of his house in ten minutes flat, vastly disappointed in what I had failed to achieve. I hoped that Basu's old comrade in arms would be a bit more forthcoming than that. The Bengali had been at the height of his middle-aged powers when I met him, impatient of interruptions that came between him and the world's work. But E.M.S. was now in his eighties and with luck he would have developed an old man's flatulence. "Just remember," Kamala had warned before I left, "that he's a cunning old devil who knows all the tricks." Das added another tip. "He has a famous stammer and Monoo says that it only happens when he's telling lies or trying to defend the indefensible."

Kerala's most distinguished living citizen dwelt in one of those Trivandrum suburbs that reminded me so much of the West Indies. The Namboodiripad villa was a substantial and pukka two-storey affair on a quiet side road, standing pink-washed behind a garden wall which had a sentry box built into it, that day without an occupant. The bougainvillaea, the frangipani and the other vivid vegetation surrounding the house was only just on the controlled side of impenetrable jungle, a perfect shield against the equatorial heat of summer and an effective way of ensuring privacy. As I opened the gate and walked into the garden a woman appeared and motioned me to enter a room further along the verandah.

A tiny old man was sitting at a table and appeared to be marking an exercise book; school textbooks in Malayalam were on the table, too, and on the floor, placed together as neatly as if for a kit inspection, were a pair of child's chappals. The historic political figure was evidently a doting great-grandfather, too. He was coffee-coloured, like Jyoti Basu, a shade or two lighter than the auto-rickshaw drivers of the city, and would have seemed pallid next to the old beggar I had followed through its streets, or alongside any of the local fishermen. Caste was a matter of pigment as well as of purity; the two mingled in the Indian mind, though not always consistently. His hair was white but it had receded well behind his forehead, starting very close to the crown. The face was roundly fastidious, almost supercilious, and could have belonged to a prelate or the sort of judge who affects not to keep abreast of the contemporary world. His hands were shapely without lacking masculinity, but they had not done a day's manual labour in their life. He wore thickly horn-rimmed spectacles and a hearing aid was plugged into his right ear; and in the breast pocket of his white shirt were several ballpoints. Behind him were the sort of metal shelves that are standard issue in military establishments and the lower reaches of a civil service. They were not quite crammed with books, but full enough, most of them in English. I spotted three volumes of the *Selected Works of Lenin* and a hefty thing entitled *Against Revisionism*. In one of the spaces left on the shelves was a small bust of Lenin, mass-produced in some Soviet factory for the adoration of the obedient all over the globe. I was subsequently told that if I had been there only six months earlier, I would have noticed a similar effigy of Stalin as well.

E.M.S. Namboodiripad looked startled when I went in: if he had been warned of my coming, he didn't let on. I explained myself and handed him the paper with the questions I'd written down. He took it, glanced at it quickly and handed it back to me. "Well, let's get it done, shall we?" he said. Then suggested that I sit where he was sitting, so that I could have the table to write on. He shuffled round to sit in an armchair opposite. He wasn't yet infirm, but he was certainly becoming frail. When we were both seated he nodded that I was to begin. My first question was blandly designed to extract the maximum response, one that not even the adroit Chief Minister of West Bengal could have dismissed with a monosyllable. "What caused you," I enquired, "to become a communist and when?"

His reply came at dictation speed and sounded as if he was reading from a prepared text, as he very probably was; he must have been asked the question hundreds of times.

"I began my work as Congress man and I was inclined to the Left. I joined the Socialist Party within Congress in 1934. Within a year and a half I came into contact with communists and in 1936 joined the party, even while continuing to work as a Congress socialist. My own experience of political work showed that the communist line was better than that of the Congress."

He paused. I waited for him to continue, even though this wasn't what I had wished to elicit. I already knew all this; I wanted to know about his conversion from Nambudiri Brahmin to rebellious socialist. He didn't continue. He'd just finished answering question one.

"Better in what way?" I asked, making the best of it.

"We now go to question two," he said. He stammered over that sentence.

I asked him what had been the chief achievement of communism in Kerala. "We have been able to unite all the democratic and forward-looking elements in the state in a Left Democratic Front. Working in this way we have become the biggest political force. We were defeated in the last election five months ago only because all the others combined against us. Because they saw that we were better than the others."

I wanted to know why, in 1967, he had outlawed the gherao in Kerala, where he was Chief Minister, when Jyoti Basu was actively encouraging its use as a political weapon in West Bengal, as I knew from uncomfortable personal experience. Gherao is a Bengali word meaning "surround", and in the class warfare of Calcutta, individuals were habitually intimidated by mobs who surrounded them until they submitted to whatever demands were being made. The individual was not molested, but he couldn't get away, couldn't drink or eat, couldn't relieve himself except on the spot, in his office, on the street, or wherever the mob had caught up with him. I was gheraoed twice and the longer of the two lasted no more than an hour or so, but I didn't enjoy it much. One man nearly died from dehydration after being corralled in his factory yard for two and a half days during a wage dispute. So why had Kerala's communist bossman forbidden a tactic that his Bengali counterpart was employing very effectively?

"Outlawing the gherao was wrong. We allowed the gherao because the principle of protest by surrounding peacefully was correct; if it went beyond that it was illegal. But we didn't outlaw it, the law did."

"But if you . . ."

"Question number three!"

I wanted to know why he thought communism had never achieved power anywhere in India except in Kerala, West Bengal and Tripura.

"I put to you an alternative question. Why has communism *achieved* power in Kerala, West Bengal and Tripura. Your question is meaningless. You should read some books. That is all."

I held on to my temper. "I have read some books, Mr Namboodiripad, quite a lot, in fact. But for the moment I'm not much interested in other people's theories. I'm only interested in yours. It's meant to be a sort of compliment."

"That is all." He glared at me, with magnified eyes that seemed to fill his horn-rimmed spectacles.

One more question, the most obvious of the lot: how must Indian communism be modified in the light of what had happened in the USSR and its satellites?

"If it's a matter of questioning the fundamentals we adhere to them and we won't modify. In practice we might correct some distortions that have occurred. We are absolutely convinced that the fundamentals are correct."

"Does that mean that . . ."

"I have nothing more to say on this matter. It is concluded."

I wondered how long it had been since the great theoretician had actually discussed anything with anyone below the level of Jyoti Basu and one or two other seniors in the party; whether he had long ago exchanged the habit of enquiry for the arrogance of power without even noticing his loss. Much more than I was irritated by a fairly futile audience with this Mosaic figure, I was saddened by the transformations that had overtaken him. He and his colleagues had suddenly had their most cherished beliefs damned as unequivocally as if the Pope and the Roman Curia had declared one day that Jesus Christ was merely a decent Jew; and they had obviously been unable to come to terms with this. But the bigger tragedy was that E.M.S. Namboodiripad's mind, once widely and uniquely open in the most bigoted society imaginable, was now demonstrably and irreversibly closed. He had either lost or deliberately thrown away the key.

In Alleppey, too, they were still keeping the faith as aggressively as anywhere in Kerala. In the secondary schools, teachers were resigned to their pupils going on strike up to twenty times a year, because there weren't enough textbooks, or sufficient concessions when travelling by public transport, and on any other pretext that could be invoked; the party was known to be responsible, though people seemed less than clear why its local activists would want to disrupt the system when their own people were ruling in Trivandrum, as they had done in recent years. I had noticed groups of young men loafing on street corners near the centre of the town, flaunting party colours on arm- and headbands, cheerful enough to me and to any other foreigners who walked by, but clearly ready for action of some sort.

"Ah," someone said, "they are the attimari gangs of the CPI(M). They are keeping watch for trucks bringing goods to the commercial centre. When these arrive the gang leaps on board, claiming the right to unload, not allowing the driver or the shopkeeper to do the job themselves. It's an extortion racket."

So were the regular house-to-house collections for party funds, by louts who abused those preferring not to subscribe. The railway line north from Trivandrum still hadn't reached Alleppey because the local party bosses insisted that they and not the Railway Department would choose the labour force; and the railwaymen preferred the indignity of stalemate to the certainty of sabotage. So great was communism's hold on every aspect of life round here that I was surprised not to have heard any rumour of the Naxalites. They themselves preferred the cumbersome title of CPI (Marxist-Leninist), but were more widely known as descendants of rural guerrillas who originated in the Naxalbari district of West Bengal in 1967, adopted Maoist principles, and soon had a reputation for great savagery in many parts of India. Twenty years ago, I was told, they had moved into Kerala and decapitated a number of people, sticking the heads on street lamps, their trademark when they decided to terrorise a region. This so horrified the local communists that a determined effort was made by the Namboodiripad government to see the Naxalites off across the state line, and they had never returned. One of their leaders had since become a lawyer working for the Government of India; another was a prominent figure in subcontinental Women's Lib.

The heartland of South Indian communism was this town and its surrounding district. It had always been so since the 1930s and to understand why, I was told, it was important to know that this was the centre of the coir industry. That was self-evident from the activity along the canal banks and along roads full of trucks heavily loaded with articles manufactured from the coconut. Most of the population who weren't shopkeeping seemed to be involved in some way or other; a common sight was someone cycling down the street with half a dozen doormats lashed behind his saddle, WELCOME beckoning all who followed him.

The man behind the desk in my hotel gave me the name of the biggest coir manufacturer in town and when I rang I was invited round to his home. It stood well back from the road behind a high stone wall and it was necessary to present credentials to the durwan on the gate before my car was allowed to drive in. Inside was the greatest opulence I had ever seen in India outside the princely palaces, a modern dwelling brilliantly designed so that the garden and the interior merged without an intervening wall; the lawn looked as if it was watered on the hour every day and that each blade of grass was separately manicured. Tables and chests of drawers topped with alabaster were artfully deployed inside and out, as were display cabinets full of expensive things in green jade. Some of the surfaces bore vases of black jade, and there was much lacquered furniture. The place was dripping with ostentatious wealth but whoever was responsible had managed to avoid vulgarity. The magnate himself was nowhere to be seen, but his wife punched the telephone to call the factory and announce that I was on my way, that I was to be shown round. She offered me coffee or chai before I left, but I had obviously been summoned in order to pass muster; or not. There was nothing, I reflected as I thanked her and left, like attending to the tiresome but important details yourself.

Another novelty awaited me at the factory. I was shown into the office block, where many people were working in total silence: not a telephone rang, not a typewriter clattered, not a computer hummed. This was such an utterly alien concept in the West, and had been for a hundred years or more, that I stood for several minutes in a stairwell watching fascinated through a window as men and women wrote things on pieces of paper and in heavy ledgers, their heads bent industriously, their eyes fixed on their work, exchanging neither words nor glances with one another, and certainly doing nothing as unprofitable as to gaze out of the window for a minute or two. In the office of Mr Gopal, the manager, there was a telephone, an elderly instrument three times as heavy as the up-to-date model in his employer's house. But it made no sound while I was there. Mr Gopal was as sharp, as in command of his enterprise as any European manager I have known, and a sight more decisive than many. He listened attentively to my preamble, asked a couple of pointed questions, then waved aside my request for a comprehensive description of the coir industry.

"Description, explanation is not what you are needing, sir. Much better that you see whole process for yourself. A day in the field is much better than whole textbook of words."

I nodded assent.

"You have car and driver?" he asked. "You are free tomorrow? Then be here, please, at nine o'clock and someone will be waiting to show you everything." He hadn't, I noticed, even used the phone to find out whether anyone was available. In India, someone was always available.

My conducted tour of the coir industry started with a ten-mile drive along the main road towards Cochin, before we turned off on to a side track which wound through endless groves of coconut palms, growing in very sandy ground. We came to our first stop amid backwaters such as no tourist ever sees, channels remote from the main waterways, so narrow that the trees growing out of either side mingled overhead. Some of them were crossed by wooden footbridges, identical to the ones on Chinese willow-pattern plates. Small versions of the sailing country boats were tethered here and there to trunks or to stakes driven into the mud; they were a form of canoe, but constructed of heavy dark wood. In the side channels, too, were rafts of coconut husks, which were green to start with but rotted into an evil-smelling brown debris after six months in the water. Some wretch then had to wade in up to his chest in order to bring them ashore, where women literally beat the fibres out of each piece with staves. These were then put through something like a threshing machine, which blew them across a shed repeatedly until they were dry. Large bundles of this dried fibre lay beside the little channels like coarse brown candyfloss, or were already piled high in the canoes, for movement to the next point in the operation: which was a cottage industry, with women spinning the fibres into long rough strings behind their dwellings, in a smaller version of the ropewalk that has been familiar in Dorset and elsewhere in Europe for hundreds of years. Finally, hanks of these were shifted to weaving sheds equipped with gigantic looms fashioned wonderfully out of crude timbers which had been lashed together with similar cord, operated manually and requiring all the strength of four or five wiry helots to shift one huge beam back and forth. In this fashion vast rolls of coconut matting were made, while other processes produced the doormats, and others spun multiple cords into hawsers strong enough to hold an ocean-going tanker to her berth.

I was shown all this in stages, at different places some distance apart amid the coconut groves, and it wasn't quite what I had expected. I had anticipated that the coir industry of Kerala would be as appalling as the jute industry of Bengal, which involves the nastiest sweated labour in the most dreadful conditions I have ever known. It wasn't like that at all. Instead of evil, truly satanic mills, with deafening machinery in feeble lamplight which swirling clouds of dust obscured, people here were working in surroundings that the Bengalis might think idyllic. At the start of the process, men separated the husks from the nuts on large spikes set into the ground beside a pleasant backwater; at the end, weavers produced the matting in small sheds with open sides that let in the air and the sunshine, where the loudest sound was the creaking of a beam as it was hefted back and forth every few minutes. In between these operations it would have been disagreeable, even unhealthy, wading around those decaying rafts, not much better for the women beating the rotten husks into fibre, and the atmosphere on the threshing floor was certainly dusty, tolerable only because it, too, was open to the fresh air. But nothing here was as awful as the dark treadmills of the jute industry.

I had been under another misapprehension before that day. I had assumed that the company owned the entire forest of coconut palms and everything that went on in it. This was not the case. Each village, every family, had its own plot of ground, and wealth was measured by the number of palms growing there. No wonder, when *Cocos nucifera* is even more munificent than the nutmeg tree: its trunk is good for many purposes, its leaves for thatch, its leaf ribs for broom handles, its sap for liquor and sugar, the copra of the nut for nourishment and the water for refreshment, the oil of the dried copra for cooking, and the coir of the husk for the world to wipe its feet on. The villagers harvested the coconuts and performed all the tasks I have just described; the weaving sheds were in the main little local co-operatives. Everybody was on piecework: deliver, and the company paid by results; fall sick or have your crop destroyed by the elements, and you would starve. I asked my guide how much these people earned and he said forty rupees a day per man on average, the women not so much. Forty rupees would have bought less than half a pound of seer fish in the Alleppey market place that afternoon. For all that the condition of the coir workers was a distinct improvement on that of their counterparts in jute, this too was the sweated labour of the East; and on the strength of it the communists had come famously to power in Kerala.

I had read about a peasant uprising here just before Indian independence, orchestrated by the communists, who saw the backwaters as an ideal topography for a "zone of liberation".* There had been nothing more than that to go on until I reached Trivandrum, where I heard that not only had there been an uprising in 1946; there had been a massacre of coir workers by the police and the Maharajah of Travancore's troops, acting in concert. My informant added that the communists had deliberately engineered this in order to obtain martyrs for the cause. He reckoned the party stalwarts had assured the peasants beforehand that when the soldiers raised their guns they were not to be afraid: the guns would not be firing bullets, but

---

* *Marxist State Governments in India: Politics, Economics and Society* by T. J. Nossiter (Pinter Publishers, London, 1988) p 39.

pellets of cereal that would do them no harm. Improbable as that story sounded, I was not tempted to dismiss it out of hand. Five hundred rioting Africans were killed in the newly independent state of Zambia, after a religious demagogue named Alice Lenshina told them that if they charged the police with the word "Jericho" on their lips, they would be impervious to bullets.

If there had indeed been a massacre forty-odd years earlier then the local communists would be only too willing to tell me about it. Armed with two more names from my hotel manager, I set off first for the Alleppey offices of the CPI, the only party that existed in 1946. There, I interrupted three men reading the morning papers, who looked at me as if they had never seen a European before, and maybe hadn't on those premises. When I stated my business, one of them courteously began to say that Mr Natesan hadn't yet arrived, but if I'd like to sit down . . . at which one of the others interrupted sharply to tell me that I must make an appointment if I wished to see the party secretary. I bade them good day. Standing on its dignity was maybe one reason why the CPI had been comprehensively out-flanked by the CPI(M) throughout India ages ago.

At the offices of the CPI(M) they were only too ready to be of assistance, a likeable bunch who offered me tea beneath four splendid framed lithographs of Marx & Co, superior agitprop art from Moscow that any day now will be collectors' stuff in the West. After enquiring whether the tea was to my taste, Mr Chellappan, the party secretary, switched on the fan over our heads, apologised for his limited English, and got his young assistant to translate the story he would tell.

"Of course there was a massacre," he said. "It took place in two villages on the 23rd and 27th of October, 1946. In Punnapra, which is only six miles from here, 150 workers were killed. In Vayalar, about twenty miles to the north, 250 died. They were coir workers and agricultural workers, who had gone on strike for better con-ditions. They were shot down by the Maharajah's soldiers, about 1,000 of them, and by the British Resident who came up from Trivan-drum specially."

Mr Chellappan and his assistant both paused to let this last item sink well in.

"Apart from the 400 people killed, many were injured and

thousands escaped. But the massacre didn't dampen the workers' ardour and the strike continued until after getting our freedom in 1947."

They paused again, likeable but not missing a trick.

Would it be possible to go to, say, Vayalar and see where the worst of the shootings happened; perhaps even to meet survivors? Nothing would be easier.

I was driven along the road I had taken the day before. We passed the turn-off I was already familiar with, and eventually ran into a village deep in the palm forest a mile or two beyond. Two streets of tiny shops met in a right angle, all roofed with thatch, though behind them higher buildings had white walls and shallow pitched pink tiles to keep off the sun or the rain. There was hardly any traffic apart from the bicycle. Most of the villagers walked, men with spindly brown shanks exposed by their lunghis being hitched up, women shading themselves under big black umbrellas, identical to the one I might have used at home to avoid getting wet. These Malayalis were such dainty people, slightly built, generally without fat, and their gestures were invariably delicate. As I got out of the car I watched two men standing in a doorway. They had finished their business, had probably said farewell, but something had made them linger a moment more. One held the tip of the other's index finger in his hand and they stood like that for a minute or so, loosely at arm's length but still attached. It was a gesture that would have invited ridicule where I came from; but here it was a perfectly unself-conscious expression of natural gentleness.

Two young men from the party were awaiting us, full of smiles and amiable wobbles of the head. Dilip, moustached and lighter by half a shade of brown, was the taller of the two, though not by much. Pratap had a full beard cut neatly close, and a mannerism that some would have counted effeminate: he giggled as well as wobbling his head, while his body convulsed as if someone were tickling him in the ribs. It was charming, loveable even, but I could see how mutton-chopped Victorians with uneasy memories of their English public schools would think such people pretty wet compared with the Pathans, the Gurkhas, the Sikhs and the other so-called martial races of the North.

The boys led us down a side lane out of the village, telling the local statistics as drearily as politicians everywhere, but one of them I scribbled into my notebook. The average wage of a coir worker, said Dilip, was not forty but only fifteen rupees a day, and the union was trying to get it increased by half as much again. We crossed a bridge over a backwater. "This," said Pratap, "was not here at time of massacre. The shooting took place on island."

"But why would the workers gather on an island to demonstrate their solidarity?"

He shrugged, giggled and wriggled at one and the same time; then became serious again. "Soldiers arrived by longboat and motorboat also and began shooting indiscriminately." He gave every syllable of the last word rather more than it deserved, as though he enjoyed the complex sound it made and the subtleties of his skill in producing it.

A few hundred yards beyond, in the middle of what had once been the island, we came to a clearing amid the palm trees. "And this is our memorial to oppression by the feudal landlords and the class struggle to overcome it," said Dilip, pointing to a bleak object standing in the empty patch of sand. It certainly wasn't much of a memorial to 400 martyrs who were sacrificed in order to bring communist government to Kerala. A bare cube of concrete had been set on a larger plinth and there were rusty iron rods sticking out of the top, as though some addition had been planned but never carried out. Dilip said it had been like that for ten years now and they were still collecting money to finish it. No inscription had been attached. No stranger would have had a clue what it was about. But strangers very rarely passed this way: we were well off the beaten track. Yet it stood over the spot where many of the martyrs were buried; the soldiers took other bodies away and buried them elsewhere.

"What, Hindus as well as Muslims and Christians?" I asked.

Pratap flashed his smile and looked ticklish again. "No religious affiliation," he said. "Come, let us show you celebrated coconut tree."

They led the way into somebody's garden, overlooked by a pukka bungalow. Standing alone was an aged and battered palm, surprisingly still alive. "People sheltered behind trees, which gunfire hit. Here is remaining one." And it had, indisputably, been riddled with bullets. I counted a dozen small holes, made a long time ago, around

a huge one that went right through the trunk to the other side. I
didn't see how the tree had survived all that.

Then I was taken to meet one of the survivors. Sankunny had
been a lad of fifteen in October 1946 but now he appeared to be
more ancient than he was, a battered-looking codger with an old
soak's grin, very dark, which emphasised the thickness of the grey
stubble on his cheeks. He had a pot belly and there was something
wrong with his foot, which was swathed in grubby bandages. He
spoke no English but Dilip translated my questions and passed the
answers back.

The shooting, said Sankunny, started at noon and the soldiers
appeared suddenly in civilian clothes. No, the people hadn't been
demonstrating that day, but there had been agitation against the
Diwan of Travancore, the Maharajah's Chief Minister. When the
soldiers arrived the people were told to disperse but didn't, so the
shooting began.

When I asked whether anyone had told them that the guns would
be firing grain rather than bullets, Sankunny looked as though he
didn't understand what I was talking about. "It's a lie from Congress," said Dilip. He asked Sankunny to bend over to show me
something. There was a blemish of darker skin at the angle of the
neck and shoulder, another further down the old man's back, on
the muscle of his shoulder blade. One was the entry wound made
by a bullet, the other where it came out again.

Our conversation had taken place among a collection of thatched
huts and while we talked some women nearby paused in their day's
work, which was spinning coir, just like the ropeworkers of Bridport,
but not nearly as well paid. They listened while Sankunny told me
his tale standing in the doorway of his dwelling, which was a one-
room shack of coconut timber and thatch, as bare inside as a nomad's
tent. Forty-four years of independence and several periods of communist rule in Kerala couldn't have improved his fortunes by much.

I had one other appointment in Alleppey itself, with the communist bossman of its local government. A misunderstanding made me
arrive much later than Mr Sudhakaran had expected me and at first
he treated me like an infractory schoolboy, though I was almost old
enough to be his father and had apologised profusely. He was a
small and dark man in his mid-thirties, sleek-haired, moustached and

bespectacled, who enjoyed the services of a first-class dhobeywallah judging by his apparel: even at midday and without air-conditioning in his office, the creases down the short sleeves of his shirt were still remarkably sharp and straight. He raised an arm as I entered and pointed to his watch crossly. "I have been waiting all morning for you. I can now give you only ten minutes of my time." His morning had not been wasted, however. He was surrounded by aides with many papers in their hands. He dismissed them as soon as he had finished berating me; and quickly softened when we were alone, without ever allowing the trace of a smile to relax his face.

He talked fluently about the circumstances leading up to the 1946 massacre. The chief adversary of the workers had been the Diwan of Travancore, Sir C. P. Ramaswami Aiyar, a Tamil in the service of a Malayali prince. Mr Sudhakaran allowed that Aiyar was an efficient administrator, "but he was an autocrat who wanted to subvert the people, giving no voice to democracy". He was allied with the landlords in Alleppey, "anti-social wealthy people, who suppressed the people and looted the wealth of the people".

Mr Sudhakaran's mouth and nose were screwed into an expression of deep disgust and his head wobbled passionately. "Women were molested at their whims and fancies," he said.

This state of affairs had been going on throughout the 1930s and so the communists organised the workers, while the Maharajah made friends with the British. It was not E. M. S. Namboodiripad who started the communist movement in the South but P. Krishnapillai, who led the Travancore Coir Workers Union and founded the local party in 1937. As well as coir workers, he also organised the fish workers, the toddy-tappers, "low-caste people, social outcasts, all people who are exploited".

I wondered whether he was still alive. Mr Sudhakaran's head wobbled again, gravely this time. "Alas, he is no more. He died in 1948. We are living monument."

By 1946 matters were coming to a critical point and hundreds of party members took up arms. They made country spears out of bamboo, sharpened lethally, and marched on the landlords; also on the police stations in the Alleppey district, where one or two police were killed. The Diwan declared an emergency and as a result there was the confrontation leading up to the massacre: "Not only 400 were killed, but many, many hundreds." Mr Sudhakaran was positive about that, but imprecise. The troops had a mass burning of bodies in Alleppey, he said, and not all the bodies were dead when they began.

When I put to him the communist fiction about the guns firing harmless shot, he dismissed it contemptuously as "a make-believe story" invented by Congress, who would say anything to discredit their principal rivals in Kerala; which was, indeed, as conceivable as the yarn I had heard in the first place.

"And this is important," he added, striking the desk with his ballpoint at each emphasis, "not a single comrade received a bullet injury in his back. That's a very important point. They were there to do or die." It would have served no purpose to tell him about the position of Sankunny's bullet wounds; and I, too, would have fled in the circumstances.

There was something about this dapper little apparatchik that I found myself warming to, in spite of his need to put me down initially. Not very far under the self-important exterior there was a good and fairly honest man grappling with the first imperative of political life, to win at all costs. He left me in no doubt that he was determined to do everything he could to restore the communists to power in Trivandrum, and he was confident that it could be done before long. The last time they governed it was with eighty seats in the legislature; the 1991 election had reduced them to forty-nine. Mr Sudhakaran waved his finger at me, but inoffensively. "When we have a majority of seats in the legislature once more, we will never lose power again," he said.

"How can you be sure of that?"

"We can be sure. Either by parliamentary means or some other."

"Involving violence again?"

"Violence becomes necessary when the people make such a choice."

I preferred to believe that he didn't mean that; I thought he was striking a pose again, as he had done when I entered late. I opened my mouth to argue with him, but he was shuffling papers on his desk and had pressed a bell that brought an aide running. I was dismissed.

I was at the door when something made me pause and turn to

him. I had sent in my card from the corridor to announce myself when I arrived. On impulse I now said, "If you ever come to England, do look me up. I'd like to continue our conversation there."

For a fraction of an instant he looked defeated; then recovered as he shrugged expressively.

"How can I come?" he replied. "I cannot go without the permission of the party."

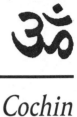

# Cochin

I left for Cochin by the first waterbus of the day, when the only shops yet open in Alleppey were those on the boat jetty, offering the early commuters paan and chai and other things to eat and drink. Also available were several local newspapers, a further index of Kerala's unusual literacy. The journal with the biggest circulation in all India was not one of the metropolitan dailies with an international reputation but *Malayalam Manorama*, which Joy Thomas had once worked for, and which came off the presses each morning in the town of Kottayam. If the display at the boat jetty was anything to go by, there were many other publications in the state which prospered, too.

The jetty was a little downstream from the coir warehouses, and the canal hereabouts did not suggest prosperity. Just below the chai stall a battered police launch was half submerged at its mooring, with a stove-in hull and superstructure, and after it in quick succession were the wrecks of half a dozen ferries, their poor broken timbers infested with the vegetation that was the curse of all the backwaters. The locals called it African moss but I recognised it as water hyacinth, masses of which I had first seen floating down the Congo twenty years earlier. It was a nuisance even in that mighty river, and whoever had introduced it to the more sluggish watercourses of Kerala had much to answer for. It had made the municipal basin at Alleppey stagnant, and all manner of unmentionable sub-

stances appeared to be brewing just beneath the weed, judging by
the number of bubbles and burps that were rising nearby. The night
before I had eaten karimeen, a species of backwater catfish the locals
doted on, though it was too bony for my taste. I now prayed that
it hadn't been caught anywhere near the canal.

By the time our skipper had climbed to his position in the
wheelhouse and given the ship's bell a couple of clangs for the off,
we were almost full, though no one needed to stand. There were
women with parcels and shopping bags and there were men with
their lunches in tiffin tins and there were even people sitting with
briefcases on their laps. A number of fellows had climbed aboard
with bulging sacks or big boxes that got in everybody else's way, but
a couple of huge tractor tyres were manhandled on to the roof;
inexplicably, when I couldn't recall having seen a tractor since arriving in waterlogged Kerala. There was other cargo up there as well,
stowed in close order just behind the wheelhouse, where it would
soon be roasting as the sun cleared the horizon and rose into the
sky. Even at seven o'clock the sweat was beginning to form in the
shade. It trickled down the face of a deckie, who came to collect
fares in exchange for the slips of paper he plucked from a long
ticketholder with clips, such as the bus conductors used at home
when I was a boy.

We emerged from the canal into an open expanse of water, the
Vembanad Lake, which was "infested by alligators of enormous size"
according to the *Travancore State Manual* of 1906, though it was said
that these had since become extinct. Birds skimmed low over the
surface everywhere, canoes plashed across weedy inlets, paddled by
men using very narrow blades, and people immersed themselves
totally in the first bath of the day, whether they had religious affili-
ations or not. Others were standing on dry ground, watching our
approach, among them youths in gaudy shirts, waiting to see what
talent was coming up the water this breakfast-time. A rooster ran
squawking from behind a hut, and a cow trudged nodding along a
path. Some men sat outside a little chai stall, reading yesterday's
news, and it was we who brought them today's. All life was conducted here on very narrow banks of earth, raised above saturated
paddies on one side and the lake or channels of water on the other.
These dykes supported thatched homes, conical haystacks, piles of

bricks, as well as livestock and people; and everywhere coconut palms, growing in isolation or in meagre files, leant this way and that, as though they had never been exposed to a prevailing wind. This was an inundated landscape much like the one visited by disaster year after year in Bangladesh; but in Kerala the elements have generally been more merciful. A line of high telegraph poles strode across the endless levels and under the uninterrupted vastness of this sky I saw a tropical version of the English Fens. Indecipherable birds of startling brightness flew across backgrounds of infinitely varied green. A line of egrets stood vigilantly still, over their ankles in wet paddy, and a kingfisher flashed brilliantly across the mouth of a side channel. Even with an overcast beginning to obscure the sun, this was a vivid world.

Every five or ten minutes the steady *tankatankatankatanka* of our diesel engine dropped to a chuckling *poppetypop* as we came into some new landing stage, with its stump of an old palm tree for tying on. Some passengers disembarked at every stop, while fresh ones climbed aboard, friends and acquaintances hailed each other, some gossiped, others read their papers, several sat glumly as though not much looking forward to the day ahead. It was not all that much different from heading for Liverpool Street or Grand Central on a commuters' train in the West. At the third stop a swarm of small children were waiting for us to appear, with their tiffin boxes and their exercise books, and with freshly applied smears of sacred ash or tilak lines on their brows. Some of the boys fished out combs as soon as they were aboard and completed their toilet publicly before settling to piping gossip of their own; which caused the conductor to rap the back of their bench with his ticketholder, warning them to behave. He didn't have to worry. I'd never known such polite little boys ask so tentatively whether I had a ballpoint to spare. They pressed me only to inspect three-letter words in English, written painstakingly in their exercise books.

A man in a red lunghi, with a bag slung round his waist and followed by his dog, strode across a dyke top empty of everything except a row of palms with much space between each. He ignored all but the last, which had pegs sticking out of its trunk, and these he began to climb: a toddy-tapper starting his day's work to produce the hooch that, according to Marco Polo 700 years ago, "inebriates faster than wine made from grapes". After the next stop we passed a thatched hut fluttering a blue banner which identified it as the State Bank of Travancore and, within a hundred yards, a similar building bearing the flag of the CPI(M). Then came a small temple with OM in Sanskrit on each side of its door, and a makeshift volleyball court with a fishing net hung up strategically between it and the lake's edge. Before we left the shallows of the western shore to cross to the eastern side, our wash had made life even more uncomfortable for a man standing in the water up to his chest. He was dredging mud from the bottom in a basket shaped like a wok, then hoisting it above his head into a boat attached to a stake, and each time he did so some of the slime ran down his arms and into his face.

In a monsoon squall the lake crossing might have been a tricky one, but this morning the surface was so still that it reflected every nuance of the sky, whose mirror image was interrupted only by patches of water hyacinth. Sometimes a small clump had isolated itself, but there were also great platforms of the weed substantial enough for storks and spoonbills to tread upon warily as they peered over the edge in search of fish. Halfway across we encountered a small launch towing a country boat full of people who sat on the gunwales facing each other, showing only blank interest as we passed; nor did our passengers do more than stare as though these were total strangers who puzzled them, and whose every detail they wanted to remember just in case. The lake, it seemed, was nowhere very deep: not far behind the launch and obviously bound for the western side, a man poled a boat with a thatched shelter, well loaded with terra-cotta pots. Similar craft with small sails appeared, makeshift rigs fashioned out of sacking or stitched-together plastic sheets. Not once was a greeting exchanged, but always every eye registered size, shape, contents, build, features, expressions, purposes. This was the guarded vigilance of the countryman everywhere, the universal caste mark that sets him apart from the city folk.

And people had reason to be cautious here, for all that these surroundings were tranquil this morning, in their way idyllic. Only days before there had been a brief news item from this district, reporting that "A CPI worker has been hacked to death allegedly by CPM activists at Samkranthi near here. Gopalakrishnan, alias

Raghu, 26, of Perumpayakkad, was returning home on Friday when a group of persons carrying deadly weapons attacked him."* Nothing more: just a brief paragraph towards the bottom of an inside page. Life could be very bleak in India; and was, for some, every day of the week.

We entered a broad channel on the further shore, with rice paddies behind its banks on either side, lines of palm marking boundaries like hedges in more temperate northern lands. The children scuttled ashore at the first stop and disappeared into a school beside a temple, within a stone's throw of a country boat loaded with hay. A large black cow was munching some of this cargo until a girl came out of a hut with a big tin pot, filled it with water and began to wash the animal, which didn't appear to be enjoying the process much. We moved on, past a file of women marching along the dyke with sickles in their hands while, distantly, a man crossed a field with a large bundle of cane balanced on his head. The channel narrowed and suddenly became choked with weed. At first it yielded easily as our stem cut into it, but then it thickened, the note of the diesel changed as the revs mounted, and the old waterbus began to strain. I remembered that in the nineteenth century a boat full of Italians had disappeared in the Sudd, the enormous swamp that still impedes navigation on the Nile in the southern Sudan. The water hyacinth of Kerala imperilled nobody in that sense, but it was on the way to producing an economic catastrophe unless measures were taken to eradicate it soon. Our speed had fallen from five or six knots to a slow walking pace within 500 yards, and the boat was now shuddering with the effort of trying to butt its way through. We crawled past a canoe loaded with pots of drinking water which was barely moving at all, even though a lad was hauling on a rope from the bank while the boatman made what headway he could, using his pole. And this was on the outskirts of Kottayam, one of the more important communities in the state, headquarters of Kerala's rubber industry as well as India's bestselling newspaper. The dyke tops were even busier now than they had been on the edges of Alleppey. Telephone wires appeared for the first time, and a man rode his motorbike carefully past a line of girls in headscarves, making their

* *Indian Express*, datelined Kottayam, February 9, 1992.

way to school. A Gothic church, a temple and a Muslim Youth Movement hut followed each other in quick succession, and every few yards women were at the waterside, dhobeying the household linen in spite of the encroaching weed, generally watched by goats tied to adjacent bungalows. Soon, as television aerials signalled urban sprawl and most of the graffiti demonstrated support for either the one or the other principal forms of communism, our wash was sucking an evil-smelling black muck out of the banks and into the choked backwater. The last few hundred yards to the jetty were like struggling across a monstrously overgrown lily pond, badly in need of draining.

I took a train the last few miles up to Cochin and arrived in India's fourth seaport unprepared for the hurly-burly of almost metropolitan life. In the first half-hour I was made well aware how much the rest of Kerala lacked hustlers, impudent street boys, rapacious auto-rickshaw drivers and worse. Nowhere else had I seen a bus with a sign in two languages by the door, Beware of Pickpockets, but it was on all the public transport here. At my waterfront hotel there was an air of sleazy opportunism around the desk, with none of the genuine warmth I had become accustomed to everywhere further south, even at a fleapit I could otherwise have done without in Quilon. This place did, however, have a superior rooftop restaurant and from it I watched the maritime business of the day wind down as the sun slipped nearer and nearer the Arabian Sea. Ferries net-worked the harbour as intricately as the craft that radiate outwards from the Golden Horn, to bring Asia and Europe closer across the waters of Istanbul. Huge container ships dominated the long storage sheds of Willingdon Island, where the principal dockings were, and where majestically anglepoised cranes were offloading the last of the cargoes before night shut everything down. A great high-sided merchantman in ballast came buoyantly up the roads and behind it was a curiously ominous shape that I couldn't immediately identify. This passed between the fishing nets standing sentinel on either side of the harbour mouth, squat in the water but with a superstructure of sorts; as it rounded Willingdon and presented a broadside view, it resolved itself into a submarine, coming stealthily home to the HQ of Southern Naval Command.

The streets that evening had a lot of Calcutta's nocturnal energy, with men selling things on the pavement, crying their wares much more vehemently than anyone in the small provincial towns. Others were doing deals that may not always have been legal, noticeable only because the participants eyed the crowds around them urgently, as if they feared authority or the approach of an enemy. The centre of Ernakulam, the mainland and business heart of the port, was hyperactive until well into the night, its shops open, its thoroughfares flowing with pedestrians, its traffic charging ceaselessly along the waterfront. After a month in much quieter, less aggressive parts of Kerala, I found myself slightly on edge with claustrophobia in the midst of all this shouting, this pressure of bodies, this unrelenting racket and turmoil. It wasn't nearly as bad as the culture shock I experienced when I came to India for the first time a quarter of a century earlier, and was intimidated by the roaring impact of Calcutta in particular. I recognised some of the same symptoms, though.

Something else hadn't altered in all those years, as I discovered when I needed to change money next morning. At the State Bank of India in Ernakulam the procedures were exactly the same as they had been at National and Grindlays on Chowringhee, during my first expedition to the subcontinent. I was invited to sit across a desk from a clerk somewhere in the middle of the banking floor, with the open vault only a few strides away, and be hanged to security. The desk bore several ledgers, and entries were made by hand in each. Dockets had then to be completed in triplicate before I was given a numbered brass disc and told to take it to window 5, where I would be given my rupees. But the cashier who was supposed to be manning window 5 hadn't yet turned up, and didn't for another ten minutes. When she arrived, she was preceded by a couple of peons lugging a heavy tin box, and followed by a security guard in khaki, trailing a single-barrelled shotgun. Ten more minutes passed while the box was emptied, another five while its contents were counted; then the cashier raised the grille and indicated she was ready to be of service. A split second before she gave this signal, the man standing behind me at the head of the queue, contorting himself like Houdini, slipped first an elbow on the counter, then a forearm, which almost at once supported a shoulder, followed quickly by his chest, until he had interposed everything above his hips between me

and the waiting girl. It was the move Lytton Strachey presumably
had in mind when he was invited to contemplate the pacifist defence
of a sister threatened with rape. I left some time later with my
money, thinking wistfully of high-tech banking in Bombay.

No one but a trader could have been excited more than briefly
by Ernakulam, or by Willingdon Island, which had been created
artificially between the two world wars after years of dredging and
landfill. The tongue of land beyond Willingdon, forming the
southern arm of the harbour entrance, was another matter
altogether. Here was the original Cochin, which owed its existence
as a seaport to a phenomenally heavy monsoon in 1341. The rains
that year so flooded the River Periyar that it changed course and
forced its way into the sea here, several miles south of its established
estuary. At one and the same time, the major port of Cranganore,
once the Roman Muziris, was left virtually high and dry, while
shifting sandbanks created a perfect alternative anchorage; and here
old Cochin steadily grew to become, eventually, the most prosperous
haven for shipping along the whole of the Malabar coast. In its lanes
and within its warehouses, along its waterfront and among its other
buildings, were the principal clues to the particular sophistication of
Kerala; and something more than that. Here also was the key to the
European exploitation of the entire subcontinent, which culminated
in the British Raj.

The harbour entrance symbolised Kerala's openness to the world
outside. Often enough already on this journey I had been struck by
various things that did not feel indigenous, that were surely grafts
implanted from some place further east. The pinnacles of the Kaudiar
Palace were one, glimpsed from the road in Trivandrum, and so
were other styles in the local architecture: a tip-tilted end to the
roofline of the temple in Alleppey, a similar touch on a market hall
in Quilon, the shallow pitched roofs, the deeply overhanging eaves,
the finely fretted galleries. The headcloths worn by the country
coolies and boatmen were unlike anything I'd seen elsewhere on the
subcontinent, where the usual pugri was several feet long, wound
round and round to give total protection from the sun; the head-
clouts in Kerala, again, originated further east. And here, in the
harbour of Cochin, whose traffic included innumerable fishing
canoes, the crews wore straw hats shaped like small inverted woks,

whose copyright belonged in Shanghai and the rice paddies of Sichuan.* At the harbour mouth were those sentinel fishing nets with the same pedigree, legacy of a trade with China which went back to the time when Rome had its staging post in Muziris. The meshes were suspended from a primitively ingenious arrangement of timbers and pulleys, with boulders hanging in counterbalance. At the bottom of the tide, when they were raised and idle while the fishermen were mending nets, these looked like the terrifyingly enlarged insects of science fiction, waiting to lower themselves on to their prey. They were also a good working definition of contraption, as illustrated so memorably by Heath Robinson.

Within a cockstride of those nets was another legacy from afar, the first European church in all India, which the Portuguese built early in the sixteenth century, and where Vasco da Gama was buried for a few years until Lisbon required his remains to be shipped home. A Dutch gable had subsequently been added to the west front of St Francis, and the building still later passed through Anglican hands before fetching up in the ecumenical embrace of the Church of South India; a local sub-plot in the story of colonialism on the subcontinent. Its bare interior still contained one conspicuous relic of the Portuguese time: the punkahs ranged down both sides of the nave, fringed for greater breeziness and swung to and fro on ropes, ever ready to be brought into service again in the event of a power cut and the overhead fans ceasing to turn. Outside the churchyard was a maidan on which, when I was there, the ameliorating influence of the British could still be enjoyed: a cricket match, with the players in immaculate flannels, the umpires in total control, and the spectators much more decorous than they have been sometimes at Lord's.

The Portuguese were also responsible for a lovely palace a mile away which, again, the Hollanders acquired and renovated in due course. It had been built as a gift to the Rajah of Cochin in 1555 and was notable for some of the most beautiful Hindu murals I had seen anywhere. I particularly liked two paintings empanelled in the women's bedchambers. "Lower: a remarkable portrayal of the Brindavana Forest, abounding in deer, birds and other animals,

---

* The name Cochin, suggestive as it sounds, does not in fact have a Chinese connection. It's a Portuguese corruption of Kochchi, which is Malayalam for "a small place".

giving themselves up to merry enjoyment. Upper: Krishna represented as lying in a pavilion spread with flowers, with the gopis
crowding round him in different attitudes and postures." Not all
these merry enjoyments and different postures would have been
deemed edifying by seventeenth-century Dutch Calvinists, though
they tolerated them, as their contemporaries in Cromwell's England
surely would not have done. The attendant, who was there to ensure
that the paintings came to no harm and were on no account to be
photographed, knew an appreciative audience when he saw one,
however. When he and I were alone in the room at last he indicated
that, for a small consideration, I would be allowed at least one
discreet flash.

The key to these foreign incursions could be inspected along
Bazaar Road, one block over from the Mattancherry Palace. The
road was narrowly winding and on working days it was blocked
every so often by heavy Ashok trucks, with the usual admonitions
of the subcontinent – Horn SOUND Horn, Keep Distance, and so
on – painted across the back. Wherever a truck was parked, a line
of coolies would be staggering between it and the nearest doorway
under the weight of sacks and boxes which were either bound for
the docks on Willingdon and destinations anywhere on earth, or
which had just arrived from cultivators scattered the length and
breadth of Kerala, and even across the Western Ghats. The doorways
led into godowns where precious commodities could be stored until
agents from all over the world had inspected samples and bought.
Beside the doorways and lining both sides of Bazaar Road were small
rooms, entirely open to the street, where the samples were displayed.
Here were the Azhikal Brothers, almost barricaded into their office
behind a new consignment of wooden chests which had just arrived
full of the best Nilgiri tea. Here were Ambal Traders, who specialised
in bidi leaves and other tobaccos, and next to them was a place
overflowing with sacks full of garlic, stockpiled beneath beams
inscribed with pious sentiments: Service Is Our Motto and Your
Custom Is The Life Blood Of Our Business. Across the way, where
the Jai Trading Company had established itself, three men sat beside
a table on which were a dozen bowls containing rice, all crucially
different to the portly Sikh from Long Island, who was scrutinising
each intently before deciding which he wanted in what quantities

for his import-export business in the States. The shops along Bazaar Road were almost identical, with their small domestic rooms tucked under the eaves, and their more ample business space down below; which was wood-panelled and painted blue more often than not, with a single strip of neon light and a fan overhead, a calendar invariably and a religious picture sometimes on the wall, a large table for the main business to be conducted across, and a smaller one where a clerk doggedly worked his way through endless invoices and files.

But the transactions in one particular commodity were of more historical significance than all the rest put together. It was spices that brought the Europeans to India and sharpened their appetites for even more of her natural wealth. This was so even in the case of the Portuguese, who were also propelled by the instinct to proselytise and to find out what lay over the horizon; which caused their half-English Prince Henry to found his school of navigation on a windy clifftop at Sagres in the fifteenth century, where da Gama and Columbus learned their skills. But like the Romans before them, the Dutch, the English and the French afterwards, the Portuguese were attracted to India in the first place and above all by the profit to be made out of spices grown in the hinterland of this Malabar coast.\* The profit was there because the spices sometimes acted as a preservative and always disguised the taste of rotting meat; a problem that would not be solved in the British Isles until Squire Townshend of Norfolk in 1730 discovered that the turnip made excellent winter cattle feed, so that most beasts no longer had to be slaughtered the moment the grass died in the autumn of each year. The need for these exotic flavours was nowadays not at all what it had been in the days of the early European ventures to the East. Yet here, along sweltering Bazaar Road, merchants from afar still examined and fingered and sniffed and tasted judiciously, while men in spotless white lunghis awaited their verdicts with confident expressions amid a tantalising pot-pourri of bulging sacks, whose openings had been

---

\* The Venetians had long enjoyed a monopoly of the European spice trade from their sources in Syria and elsewhere in the Levant. The Portuguese undercut this with their Indian adventure from the beginning of the sixteenth century. In 1503, five Portuguese vessels sailed from Calicut with 380 tons of pepper and other spices, which they unloaded in Falmouth much more cheaply than anything the Venetians could supply, and at a bigger profit.

carefully rolled down a little, to expose chillies and cardamom seeds and peppercorns, knobs of ginger, lumps of turmeric, cloves and cinnamon and nutmeg, and all the other spices that had irresistibly brought the foreigners here for centuries.

Where Bazaar Road petered out, Jewtown began: the word was written plainly on an official sign. It marked the boundary of an ancient ghetto and a modern tourist attraction, which was also signalled by a shop festooned with panama hats, succeeded shortly afterwards by Krishna Handicrafts and Curios, the Madonna Art Gallery and similarly irrelevant premises, each hoping to cash in and be rewarded in US dollars and other hard currencies. The street became even narrower than Bazaar Road had been, more obviously an old Jewish quarter, with the Star of David inscribed on the stucco of several walls, including that of the Sassoon Building of 1949: outpost of an illustrious Bombay mercantile enterprise which began more than 130 years earlier, after one branch of the great Sephardi clan of Sassoons had migrated from Baghdad, where they had dwelt since being ejected from Spain in the fifteenth century. That made them, in the long history of Jewtown, nothing more than *arrivistes*. Jews had been settled here since 1567, along the Malabar coast for much longer, though no one is certain when they arrived.

According to one of the traditions they arrived in Kerala aboard King Solomon's merchant fleet; by no means impossible when traces of Malabar teak have been identified in the ruins of Ur, not so very far from Solomon's kingdom. Another source reckons that they were descended from Jews taken to Babylon by King Nebuchadnezzar. There is also a story that when St Thomas landed at Muziris in AD 52 he was greeted by a Jewish girl playing a flute, and he is said to have baptised some Jews living in the town. The Cochin Jews themselves have always believed that 10,000 of their forefathers fled from Palestine after the destruction of the second temple in AD 135 and were welcomed by the Hindu ruler, who allowed them to settle wherever they pleased, most of them choosing to make their home at first in Muziris, later known as Cranganore to Hindus, as Shingly to the Jews. And in that district the Jews eventually enjoyed a small independent principality from the fifth to the fifteenth centuries, ruled by one of their own. A fourteenth-century itinerant Hebrew poet, Rabbi Nissim, wrote:

> I travelled from Spain,
> I had heard of the city of Shingly.
> I longed to see an Israeli King.
> Him, I saw with my own eyes.

The tranquillity of the Jews in Cranganore ended in a massacre by Muslims in 1524, and they fared little better wherever the Portuguese held the whip hand along the Malabar coast. Their first settlement at Cochin, after abandoning Cranganore, was sacked by the Portuguese and they survived only because the Rajah of Cochin befriended them. They recovered their old prosperity when the Dutch overtook the Portuguese as the dominant Europeans in this part of South India. In 1686, Moses Pereira de Paiva, once of Lisbon, lately of Amsterdam, counted four synagogues and 128 Jewish families living in Cochin, with umpteen other synagogues and their supporting congregations elsewhere in Kerala.

And now there was only this. As I paused at the end of Jewtown Road, it struck me how very Central European rather than Indian it was. There was something about the style of the houses that was familiar from some place other than Kerala and distinctly not on this subcontinent; they had the local tiled roofs and the local jutting eaves, but it was the fenestration that was out of place, and the wooden shutters that opened like doors. Also the fact that these dwellings were built in one continuous terrace on both sides of the street, even though these swerved a little and dog-legged once to form a tiny square. At the far end was the last surviving synagogue with its sturdy white tower, its clock face, its delicate bellcote balanced above the roof, and its ornate weathervane rising above that. I could almost believe I had seen stuccoed streets like this in the old ghetto areas of Warsaw and Prague. And yet, if the Cochin Jews were right about their pedigree, there was no obvious reason for the similarity.

I have no idea what instinct made me look up before I moved on down the narrow street. I was still standing at its end, outside Allied Trades of Jewtown, when I glanced at the upper windows, which were protected from intruders by elaborately wrought iron grilles. In the centre of each, as carefully painted as the rest of the ironwork, was a swastika: sixteen of them in all. For a moment I was too stunned to see that this was the ancient Vedic symbol of wellbeing, not the diagonal Nazi variant, and that it had therefore never represented anything but sanctuary and protection to the Jews of Cochin. The fact was that in childhood I had been conditioned to regard any swastika as accursed, and to encounter one in such proximity to a synagogue, of all places, briefly shocked me as much as if I had come across a truly evil thing.

I walked on and paused again at the entrance to the synagogue, where a notice warned "Visitors not allowed on Saturdays and Jewish holidays". A paved courtyard lay beyond, with plantains and shrubs growing against the outer wall, where gravestones leant as if they had been brought from somewhere else and parked here for want of a better place to put them. The wooden shutters had been flung back from some of the synagogue's windows in the middle of the yard and a babble of voices came from within, pierced every few seconds by the shouts of over-excited children. The place was crowded with Indians and Westerners and an old man with a plum-coloured yarmulka on his head was standing in front of the open Ark, trying to explain the significance of its sacred scrolls. His voice was not strong and kept trailing off as if he had forgotten what he wanted to say, though it may have been in dismay at the behaviour of his audience, which was awful. Hardly anyone was listening to him, most seemed keener on taking photographs than anything else, and the parents clearly hadn't the slightest intention of stopping their children from running wild. Eventually, having taken their souvenir pictures, and without a word of thanks to the old man, the visitors attended to their leader's call and trooped out into the street for the next stop on their afternoon trip round Cochin's sights.

The synagogue was very beautiful when the tourists had left. Light was reflected from its white walls to its chandeliers and to the row of coloured glass globes that hung under a gallery. Light rose from the floor, which was covered in tiles with blue willow-pattern motifs and no two alike, it was said; eighteenth-century work from Canton, brought here by the trader Ezekiel Rahabi. Light twinkled from the polished brass railings of the bimah, which stood like an orchestral conductor's podium in the middle of the room. I sat on one of the benches that ran round the walls except under the Ark, whose doors

Mr Cohen closed with the air of someone who dealt in mysteries. His hands caressed the gilded red panels reverently.

I apologised for the uncouthness of his departed guests, but he only moved his head slightly, as if to indicate that it was normal and out of his control. I asked him things about the synagogue and his replies came after pauses, as though it was an effort to collect his thoughts. He told me that there were now only twenty-five people left in the congregation, most of them his contemporaries, or nearly so. The birth of Israel in 1948 had dealt a mortal blow to the Jewish community in Cochin, for many young people had left India then for the great fulfilment in the Middle East. The reasons they all gave, other than the obvious one, was better job prospects in the new nation and a bigger choice of partners in marriage.

Mr Cohen went to a cupboard in the narthex of the building, between the way in from the courtyard and the main chamber of the synagogue. He came back with a large, leather-bound book, the Register of Marriages, which had a small cavity where a worm had eaten its way through from front cover to back. Entries began in 1947 and didn't even fill the first page. Just fifteen weddings had occurred in the next forty years, and there hadn't been one since. Rachel Simon, Leslie Salem, Rachel Sassoon, Elias Roby, some Cohens, Koders and Halleguas, were the last Cochin Jews who would ever be joined in wedlock in this place.

"Have you ever been to Israel yourself, Mr Cohen?"

The tired old man moved his head fractionally. Silence for a minute before he came out of reverie. "Hoping to go inna coupla months." I couldn't tell whether that was an arrangement or merely pious optimism. He was a man, I sensed, who saw the end of all things not far away.

In spite of the forbidding notice outside the gate, I asked whether I might attend the service the following day. "Are you Jewish?" he asked.

"I'm afraid not," I replied; wanting to add, "I would have come over once, if you'd have had me, a long time ago." But I held my tongue. Jackie Cohen was already back with his thoughts of the Israel he might or might not see; and quite possibly his contemplation of eternity.

I returned nevertheless very early on the morning of Shabbath, unsure when the service began. I had myself ferried across the lapping waters of the harbour in a canoe with an outboard, and walked the length of Bazaar Road without seeing another soul; just dogs scavenging in the gutter garbage, and a cow sauntering placidly, with the shell of a whelk tied to one of its green-painted horns. The trading posts were shuttered, and when I turned the corner near the swastikas, I was struck even more by the resemblance to medieval Mitteleuropa. Jewtown Road was as deserted as a shtetl just before a pogrom; or immediately after. There was even a cart, identical to an old bydlo, parked outside someone's house, with its shaft upended to the sky. I walked down to the synagogue but no one was there, so I sat with my back to the clock tower a few yards from the gate. The fingers above me had stopped at six o'clock.

Just after eight two old men approached, each carrying a book well bound in black leather. Like Jackie Cohen, they wore shirts and trousers, with chappals on their feet. One had a yarmulka on his head, but the other wore a little pillbox affair, rather like the cap that distinguishes the Sindhis in Pakistan. They went inside the synagogue without looking at me. Then a bearded young man came along, calling for Jamie in a loud voice, suddenly giving himself away with a gesture that belongs to one race above all, a frustrated shrug with arms outspread and eyes raised to heaven; a caricature that can bring the house down for any comedian who inherited it at birth and times it perfectly in the middle of his act. The young man, too, disappeared inside the synagogue. Meanwhile, from a house fifty yards back, an elderly woman in her Saturday best, with a scarf tied round her head, had started to peer anxiously up and down the street. A third old man came by, carrying his book in one hand and reaming his ear with the other, and entered the synagogue. Ten minutes later he came out again, wearing a tasselled prayer shawl now, and shouted through the open window of the house next door before withdrawing. The old man in the Sindhi cap reappeared, also shawled, and strolled off down the street. Two matrons arrived, one of them the woman who'd been waiting anxiously. Then a group of young people, who marched straight into the synagogue without so much as a glance at the notice; and one of the girls only just remembered to stub her cigarette out on the doorstep. All four of them were very conscious of their virility. Their complexions ran from blond to swarthy and they were well accustomed to the sun: they had Israel written all over them. Yet another shawled old man began to make scolding noises up and down the street; and eventually Jackie Cohen came out of the house next door on very careful legs. No sooner had he gone to worship than the elder in the Sindhi cap returned from his errand, came straight up to me and asked what I was doing and whether I was Jewish. I told him I was hoping I might at least watch the service through the windows from the synagogue's courtyard. At this he motioned me inside and indicated that I could sit in the narthex, where all the women were, and watch through the opening in the wall that divided it from the principal chamber beyond. "But you don't take any photographs," he announced, before going to join the other men. I wasn't even carrying a camera.

The service had already begun. The two Israeli boys, now in yarmulkas and shawls, were standing on the willow-patterned tiles, intent on their books. The bearded young local man was aimlessly strolling about the floor. Two of the elders were on the bimah, reading aloud from scripture, the others sitting around as informally as if they were in a tea shop. Periodically one of these would haul himself to his feet and take his turn at the reading. In the narthex the womenfolk and I sat and listened to these intonations obediently. Then they stopped, and two of the men went out to the street. The lady in front of me turned and explained that they'd reached the point at which they couldn't continue unless they had a quorum of ten men. "That's because we follow the Babylonian Talmud," she whispered. "In Jerusalem they only need seven. We appealed to the Chief Rabbi in London to reduce to seven but permission was refused." She gave me the look that comes naturally to all manner of provincial peoples, inside and outside the United Kingdom, after dealings with London on almost any topic under the sun. We smiled at each other understandingly. I realised why I'd twice been asked whether I was Jewish. It wasn't the ghetto mentality: they were clutching at straws.

The deputation of two returned, accompanied by an invalid, who could barely shuffle even with the assistance of his zimmer frame. And then, like manna from above, a stranger strode into the synagogue with the panache that only a born and bred New Yorker can exhibit in all circumstances anywhere on earth. He was handsomely bearded, in his forties, with a short pigtail down his back, he was already wearing his prayer shawl and when he took off his straw homburg his yarmulka was carefully hair-pinned underneath. He settled on to a cane-bottomed pew beneath the bimah, placed his homburg beside him, crossed his white-flannelled legs, and looked around him with authority: possibly an East Side medical practice, but more likely teaching at the New School and home to a brownstone on Brooklyn Heights. And he had rescued the service for that Shabbath. The young woman who turned up five minutes later didn't count.

The men had begun to chant in a nasal monotone, while in the narthex the women passed the time variously. Two were holding a silent conversation, mouthing the words to each other without making a sound. The other matrons patted their hair, adjusted their dress, or attended to other aspects of their appearance; then one began to rummage in her handbag. The Israeli girls looked as if they were simply waiting until their virile young men could return to them. One of the boys covered his head with his shawl at one stage and immediately afterwards the women rose to their feet and chanted a response to the singing on the other side of the interior wall. Everyone kissed their books and the service entered a new phase. The chanting was briefly mournful and one of the men began to sway from side to side as well as bobbing forward simultaneously, just as devout people do at the Wailing Wall in Jerusalem. An elder climbed into the bimah and spoke informally, but so quietly that he was inaudible in the anteroom. Then the curtains before the Ark were drawn aside, the doors were humbly opened and the bearded young man took in his arms one of the scrolls, crowned with gold and encased in silver, and carried it gently to the bimah. There he removed the crown, unlocked and opened the case, exhibited the scroll to the congregation. He then took it to the gallery upstairs, out of my sight.

At that moment, a woman's face appeared at the barred window to my left. It was a very Indian face, dark and Malayali, not Jewish. She said something to the woman in front of me and a brief conversation then took place, which I couldn't understand. The face disappeared again. I had a feeling that the servant and the lady of the house had just settled something important about the cooking of lunch.

The service continued, rambling untidily. Men went upstairs apparently as whim took them and came down again haphazardly. A different Hebrew chant was now heard from the gallery, which sounded much like a Christian hymn. For several minutes there was no one in sight on the blue tiled floor below. Books had been left open on the benches around the walls, and their pages were riffled by a faint warm breeze. In the narthex, the three women who occupied the pew in front of me were now gossiping openly, not bothering to lip-read each other. The Israeli girls looked extremely bored and one had caught the eye of her boyfriend so impatiently that, just before he went up to the gallery, he had responded with an exaggerated shrug of helplessness; so what can I do about it, Esther? The New Yorker appeared to be completely at home, but carefully watching as well as participating confidently, savouring every moment for the improvement of dinner parties when he got back to the American metropolis.

The sacred scroll was brought down from the gallery while everyone in the building sang, apart from me and the impatient Israeli girl. With the same tenderness as before, the Law was encased and crowned, and borne to the Ark and there restored to its place beside the other scrolls. After the doors had been shut, and when the curtains were drawn across the Ark, a prayer was said; and the chief act of worship was finished for another week. The last handful of Cochin Jews made their way slowly into the light of day, renewed in their faith, as their forefathers had been in that place for over 400 years. They had dwelt again in the house of the Lord, and they had once entertained the hope that generation upon generation might also do this after them. But the book eaten by worm said otherwise, with its one incomplete page of promises and the rest a heartbreaking emptiness.

I spent a great deal of my time in Cochin crossing its harbour, usually by ferries that were almost always overloaded and in other ways courted catastrophe several times a day. The skippers had no concept of awaiting their turn to berth at the stopping places or at the terminal in Ernakulam, any more than their passengers had when disembarking or climbing aboard. The vessels converged simultaneously, and there was invariably a free-for-all of people swarming in all directions from one boat to another and the landing stage. I saw no one fall in the water, though there were several near misses, and I soon understood very well why the capsized ferry disaster is a regular item of news coming out of this subcontinent.

It was while I was waiting for a ferry one day that the young buskers turned up, to make what they could of the opportunity presented by a growing crowd of commuters. One was a pretty though petulant-looking girl on the edge of puberty, dressed in shalwar kameez, with a long pigtail down her back. She carried a drum. With her was a snotty-nosed, raggety tot of two or three years old, possibly her kid sister, carrying a grimy drugget and a plastic hoop. The little one spread the rug and went into the most remarkable parody of belly dancing, complete with pelvic gyrations, to the beat of the drum; which was then dropped, the dancer being shoved firmly aside in the same decisive move. Big sister did a couple of backward arches, handstands, cartwheels; then grabbed the tot so roughly that she squealed in protest, dumped her up and down in various uncomfortable postures, hauled her through the plastic hoop (more squeals at this), flattened her on the drugget and finally walked all over her. By then several of the watching women were doubled up with laughter and men were smiling indulgently. We didn't applaud but we gave generously, before the elder girl marched away, swinging her bottom provocatively, the little one with the begging bowl stumbling along behind like the toddler she actually was.

I was also waiting for a ferry when I encountered Mr Anthony; though much later I was to conclude that Mr Anthony had carefully intercepted me. I was reading a flybill pasted to a wall. "Be First and Get Best," it declared. "You Can Only Speak English by Speaking it. Spoken English Classes (by Bombay Professionals) For Professionals, Employees, Housewives and Students." I had just decided that this catch-all excluded only paupers, who would be of no use whatsoever to Bombay professionals, when a balding, sharp-featured man in his thirties edged up to me.

"What is your name and which country are you from?" It was, curiously, the first time anyone in Kerala had asked me that by way of introduction, though it is the most common approach of all throughout the rest of India. The man was well turned-out in shirt and slacks; he wore tinted sunglasses that did not conceal his eyes. I identified myself and he smiled brilliantly, then asked me if I were alone. By the time we clambered aboard our ferry we were in full conversation. Before we reached the Ernakulam terminus I had learned that Mr Anthony was in insurance, married with three children, a Malankara Syrian Catholic by faith. He told these things with enough reticence for me to find him very agreeable. He was not a pushy man. He charmingly asked me to have lunch at his place before I left Cochin, and we agreed that Saturday would be most convenient to everyone.

Would it, I asked, bearing in mind that I was hoping to attend the synagogue service that day, be too late if he picked me up at two o'clock? "Not at all. You are most welcome at whatever is your convenience," he said. We parted with assurances of mutual esteem. His last words were, "At two o'clock, then, I shall come to the hotel and take you to my home." I hadn't thought to ask him where that was; somewhere in Ernakulam, I assumed.

How wrong I was. On Saturday I hurried back across the harbour from Jewtown, badly in need of a shower and a change of clothes in the sticky heat of midday. I had almost finished dressing when Reception rang to say that Mr Anthony was waiting for me. Mildly surprised, because it was not yet 1.30 and punctuality is not an especially notable characteristic on the subcontinent, I went out to greet him. As we were walking out of the hotel, he dropped bombshell number one. "You have eaten?" he asked, in that tone of voice which assumes you have.

"Well, no. I thought I was having lunch with you."

An agitation crossed his face. "There has been small difficulty," he said, wobbling his head. "I had some work to do this morning and was not able to help my lady, and so she has planned a meal for this evening. I hope that is agreeable to you."

"Of course. But I really must be back here by eight o'clock. I have some work of my own to do this evening." I wondered why he hadn't phoned about the change of plan, why he had come even earlier than expected if everything at his place was running so late.

Mr Anthony looked slightly uncomfortable, but gave the wiggle of assent. He led the way to the ferry landing and, uneasily, I at last asked where his home was. "It is on Vypeen Island. We go there by boat. Then we take bus." My heart sank a little then. Vypeen formed the northern arm of the harbour entrance; it was going to take us three-quarters of an hour to get even that far, with a bus ride to follow.

My host wanted us to climb aboard the bus that was waiting when the ferry berthed, but it was standing room only. I had ascertained that the ride would be ten miles long, and that the buses ran at frequent intervals, so I demurred. I was beginning to feel faint with hunger and dehydration, having been on the go since six o'clock and nothing at all inside me yet: I'd been so anxious to get to the synagogue early that I was away before the hotel breakfast was served. Mr Anthony was all concern and sympathy when I told him this, and insisted on buying me a soft drink and some biscuits from a stall beside the bus stop.

Refreshed, I looked forward to the ride up the island, but instead of being allowed to enjoy the scenery I was now subjected to interrogation by my host: about my work, my home, my family, my pastimes, my possessions, my future plans. So intensely was he interested in the minutiae of my life that I was unable to slip in any questions of my own. By the end of the ride, it had dawned on me what I had let myself in for. Mr Anthony, kind and well-meaning man that he obviously was, had been looking for a Foreign Friend whom he could take home one day and show off to his family, his real friends and his neighbours as evidence of his own worth, his own respected place in the firmament. And I was the chosen one, the stranger from afar, the touch of distinction who would hold My Own New Friend in equally high regard. My role that day was to symbolise something that mattered a great deal to Mr Anthony's self-esteem. I was to demonstrate that he was a cut above the run of insurance salesmen in Cochin.

We got off the bus and then we walked for another twenty minutes down a series of country lanes in a temperature of 95°F and high humidity. Mr Anthony was now chattering as relentlessly as he had been questioning on the bus, and I was close to the point where I couldn't even grunt. We passed a well-founded bungalow. "That's where my Mummy and Daddy live," said Mr Anthony. "You'll be meeting them later." Inwardly I blenched. We walked another 500 yards and turned into the gate of an almost identical bungalow. As we did so a large and fierce dog, tied to a not very strong-looking cord, flung itself in our direction, coming as close as the cord would allow. It bared its teeth and snarled at me, and if I'd had enough energy I'd have done the same in return. If that creature comes within six inches, I promised myself, so help me I'll kick its balls straight into the bloody backwater.

It was three o'clock when I was introduced to Mrs Anthony, a warm-looking woman in her twenties, who smiled a lot but didn't seem to have any English. Her husband, without consulting her, I noticed, announced that afternoon tea would be served at four. Meanwhile, perhaps I might like a glass of lemon water . . .

"It's boiled water?" I asked anxiously, no longer caring whether this might offend My Friend. Very seriously, not *quite* taking offence, he said, "Of course", so rapidly that I wondered whether it were true.

Mr Anthony indicated that I should sit in a basketwork easy chair, while he took station in a swing made of basketwork and shaped like an opened silk cocoon. He swung gently to and fro and began to talk at me again, about the insurance business, and my business, about his children, one of them sick, his wife, who had also been sick, his Daddy, sick as well and sleeping at present, but later on . . .

A shy little boy of six or seven kept quietly popping in and out to inspect the stranger. Mr Anthony got up and left the room, returning a few minutes later, just as I was nodding off to sleep, with a tiny girl who was squalling horribly. He carried her like exhibit C/2 and announced proudly how he'd told her that if she didn't stop making such a noise Mr Anthony's Friend would be very angry with her. Not surprisingly, this intelligence made the poor scrap roar with trepidation. Exhibit C/2 was thereupon removed and a minute or two later My Friend returned with a fairly new baby, mewing fractiously with a temperature. It occurred to me that Mrs Anthony might soon be worn out with so much childbearing and enforced hospitality.

The phone rang and, left alone at last, I dropped off to sleep properly, waking a few minutes later to the sound of an all-too-predictable suggestion. "Shall we go for a walk? I should like to show you my village." Perhaps after we'd had tea, I countered; and

Mr Anthony was so anxious to please that this event was brought forward fifteen minutes. Revived by some good gingery cake as well as chai, I allowed myself to be chivvied outside again where, within the first quarter of a mile, we stopped four times so that I could be introduced to acquaintances. It was all so utterly amiable, and Mr Anthony was so very happy to be showing off his Foreign Friend, that I felt churlish in my inability to return his enthusiasm. I could only manage polite hellos and howdyedos, and I writhed as I heard myself sounding more and more like the constipated Englishman abroad, as faithfully recorded in all the caricatures.

And then, for fifteen minutes, the afternoon was redeemed most wonderfully. We walked into the main square of the village, an expanse of compacted sandy earth with small, shabby bungalows and shops on three sides. The fourth was occupied by a large white Dutch-gabled church, with pale blue doors and louvres. Opposite the main door, not quite in the middle of the square, was a remarkable likeness to an English medieval market cross, complete with figure in vestments standing under the canopy.

"This is your church?" I asked Mr Anthony.

"Yes. I think we should go inside." He was so proud to be showing me the important things in his life.

We stepped into an interior that I would have assumed was Roman Catholic, had I not been told differently. The white and blue colour scheme outside was repeated on the inner walls, which were hung with framed devotional prints that looked cheaper than the ikons of Orthodoxy. There was a sumptuous reredos behind the altar, crammed with plaster figures in niches, including a Christ hanging from the cross, dripping with more gore than is normally the custom outside Spain. What gave away the church's true location was its pulpit, which balanced on the tip of an elephant's upturned trunk: I thought it had been carved from ivory but Mr Anthony said it was white-painted wood. I was mystified by an absence of stairs or any other way a preacher might get into it: was a rope ladder dropped from above, as in the old whaling church in *Moby Dick*?

Mr Anthony had been stroking his moustache reflectively. "Steps were taken away some time ago." He pointed, grinning, to a loud-speaker dangling from the front of the pulpit, then to a microphone beside the altar. "Labour-saving device," he said. "Priest can now stay up there and speak. Doesn't need to come all the way down here."

The perambulation continued. Asked if I would like to see where prawns were farmed, I cautiously agreed, provided this wasn't too far away. We crossed a footbridge over a backwater whose salinity was high enough to keep it free of African moss, a soothing place with people paddling small country boats, and others strolling the banks. After walking another mile I could feel myself beginning to flag again, and when Mr Anthony suggested we go as far as the seashore I firmly declined. We turned on to another track, recrossed the channel, walked yet another mile and came to a road. "Here," he announced confidently, "we take auto-rickshaw home." Three went by, overloaded with people returning from the beach. We began to walk again.

By this time I was not only whacked: I also had a blister on my heel, having left my socks behind in the hotel in my haste to finish dressing when Mr Anthony prematurely arrived. I was getting tetchier as my companion continued to babble non-stop; he was now nervous and although his English was good his articulation was becoming incomprehensible, so that I had to keep cupping my hand to my ear and saying "Eh?" repeatedly, which made me crosser still. It wasn't a happy limp down that road to the nearest village and the relief of an auto ride home.

Where I was allowed to collapse for only a couple of minutes before being hauled off to meet Daddy, after Mr Anthony had consulted his watch for the fifth time in the past half-hour. Daddy, a bulky and beaming man half naked in a lunghi, turned out to be much better news than his son. As soon as he saw my face he ordered Mummy to make a lemon drink. We then discovered we'd both had heart trouble, and that in consequence we each took the same enteric-coated aspirin a day to prevent a recurrence: we got along famously. But after ten minutes, bless the man, Daddy leaned forward and said in tones of authority, "Mr Moorhouse has now had enough for one day. He needs rest more than talk. So off you go." He put a firm hand on my knee and pressed it with understanding. Mr Anthony wobbled his head dutifully and led me back down the lane for the last instalment of his hospitality.

Mrs Anthony had gone to a great deal of trouble in preparing that meal. I had been asked to state my likes and dislikes in some detail and she had therefore cooked fish in three different local ways, serving it with several vegetable dishes. It was good food, but it was cold by the time it got to me. It also became apparent that I was going to have to use my fingers to eat. They didn't have a fork in the house and offered me a spoon, which I dislike as much as I can't abide hot food gone cold. I was going to have to make the best of it with bare hands.

This is an art form in India, more than anywhere else I know, probably because there is so much more variety in a meal on the subcontinent than in Africa or any other place where eating is a manual as well as a gastronomic exercise. There are little piles of this and that, together with messes of which and what, with subtle shades of taste, different colourings and contrasts in texture, whether the food has been prepared in Kashmir, or Bengal, or Rajasthan or any one of the other nineteen states of the republic, all of which have extremely distinctive local cuisines. Enormous variety is the attraction of Indian cooking, above everything else, just as variety is the key to the country's wider appeal: this is what holds outsiders in thrall, even when all else fails. The art of eating there consists in the way people move things on their plate, their thali, their banana leaf, or whatever they are feeding off; the way they move things, pick and choose their preferences and convey these to the mouth. The fingers that enjoy this exercise – and any Indian will tell you that the tactile enjoyment of food is quite as important as the digestive pleasure – are as supple as a potter's, as they press food into the desired shape so that this will be a perfect offering to the palate; as they push that unwanted fragment of ochra to the edge of the mixture; as they drag this titbit of sambhar to the rice so that it, too, can be moulded into a blissfully satisfying sphere. Some young girls, delicate eaters, will bring a morsel to their mouths on the lobe of one finger, and remove it with a pucker of the lips, a gleam of teeth, a barely detectable ripple of the throat. Many older people, greedy or hungry or both, will scoop up a handful of food like primitives and then lick each finger clean when done, with all the noisy gusto of a calf sucking at its parent's tit.

I, alas, didn't come anywhere between these two extremes of eating food the Indian way. I simply didn't enjoy the messiness of using fingers very much, though often enough I'd tried to, as I did now once again.

It didn't help when I realised that I was eating alone; even less when the doorbell rang almost as soon as I'd started and, before going to the door, my host announced that he had guests. Two men and a woman arrived, and after being introduced said not another word, but watched me handling good food clumsily. Mr Anthony actually stood with his hands propping him against the table, following every move I made with eyes that weren't going to forget anything.

I looked up at him and grinned through a mouthful of fish. "Bit like watching the animals at the zoo, isn't it?" I said when I'd got the mouthful down. I smacked my lips loudly to show how much I was enjoying it. Then sucked my teeth for emphasis.

Embarrassed, the others began to talk to each other and after fifteen minutes, when I was finishing Mrs Anthony's generous meal, the visitors left to see the sunset from the beach. I didn't doubt that they had dropped by only because they'd been invited to come and see the Foreign Friend.

I knew what was coming before I left, and the good Mr Anthony did not fail me, with protestations of eternal friendship, his desire that I and my family – the lot presumably, including a forthcoming grandchild – would come and stay here in his home before long, and the hope that he and his clan would do likewise in my abode at the earliest possible opportunity. "We wish to maintain precious friendships like this above all things," he finished with a last, and this time passionate, wobble of the head.

I squirmed; as I did all the way to the bus stop, one and a half miles away, with Mr Anthony enquiring more than once whether I was sure I'd got his address correctly, and pressing hard to extract a firm promise that I would write to him from time to time. I tried to be as non-committal as possible because I hated the idea of raising hopes that I knew were doomed from the start, but he didn't begin to notice my equivocations in his own blind enthusiasm for his Foreign Friend. We were both imprisoned by something in our cultural differences as immutable, as fraught with misunderstandings and mutual incomprehensions, as laden with potential hurt on the one hand and with reluctance on the other, as anything that passed between Miss Quested and Dr Aziz. I was bored stiff by him, for reasons that had nothing to do with his being Indian, but tried not to show it simply because I didn't want to hurt his feelings. He was insensitive to me, yet wished to come close at all costs. Through all my testiness and my lack of his warmth, his fundamental decency never flagged. After I had climbed aboard the bus he followed so that he could tell a young man to make sure that I got the right ferry back to Ernakulam; and the lad did, when we reached the landing stage. My last sight of Mr Anthony as the bus drew away was of his eyes shining up at me through his tinted spectacles, his white teeth flashing beneath the moustache, his hand waving as demonstratively as if I were a blood relative leaving on the first stage of a lifetime's emigration. I waved back, a constipated Englishman's token gesture, knowing I would never see him again.

I have wondered ever since whether he realised that.

# *Madurai*

It took the Mail over three hours to climb from the coast to the summit of the Western Ghats. At first it had rumbled across the backwaters at speed, but as soon as these were left behind the diesel settled to a steady plod as it hauled the long train round one sweeping bend after another, and now it was always rising ground. The hills on every side were bush-covered and deeply ravined, their ridges and peaks seeming to swerve off in every direction, though the main lie of the land was distinctly from north to south. Only now and then was the bush peeled back to reveal bare rock, perhaps where some fire had got out of hand. From time to time a cloud of smoke rose from a distant ridge, or drifted down a slope to drape itself across a gully. Mostly the view was of thick rain forest, a primeval growth of many different trees, with coconut palms now well outnumbered by neem and peepal and jackfruit and other varieties.

"Not Western Ghats to purists," said Mr Fernandez. "They would say Western Ghats come no further south than Palghat. These hills you see here have different local names but really that is nit-picking." He made a pernickety gesture with his hand. "To all intents and purposes these are Western Ghats also. They are the big barrier between Kerala and rest of country." He looked pleased to have clarified this taxing point of topography.

"Lindsay, be*have!*" said Mrs Fernandez to one of their sons, both of whom had behaved pretty well, I thought. Lindsay, who was merely tickling his younger brother on the top bunk, but not getting in anybody's way, had been improbably named after the great Australian cricketer Lindsay Hassett. Mr Fernandez was only too pleased to explain that puzzler, too. "You see, he was hero of mine ever since my Dad told me about seeing him in Madras before I was born. He scored 143 against All-India for Australian Services just after the war. One of the great, great innings according to my Dad."

Truly, I reflected, there is no cricket nut on earth like the great subcontinent's cricket nuts. I didn't for a moment doubt that this one had the score precisely right. He probably had all the other details of the match off by heart, too.

"Hazare caught him brilliantly in the end," Mr Fernandez added, "off the bowling of Sarwate." His beard fairly bristled with pleasure now. He looked even happier than when teaching me Indian topography.

The Fernandez family had carefully explored the length of the train before joining me in an otherwise empty compartment. It soon became clear that the choice was made because I was a Westerner as much as because there was plenty of space for the four of them. They were part of that significant Indian minority which owes its existence to 500 years of European settlement on the subcontinent. John Masters, who was one of them, wrote eloquently in *Bhowani Junction* about the insecurities of being Anglo-Indian at the time of Independence, when people of mixed race felt that they might be victimised in the new democracy because of their alliance with the British during the Raj. In fact, they never were victimised, though some of them had lived uneasily, always looking over their shoulders, ever since. Mr Fernandez owed his light brown complexion and his aquiline good looks to a combination of Portuguese and Indian blood, which had mingled in Goa during some generation long past. Neither he nor his wife, in fact, had ever lived anywhere but in Tamil Nadu. He worked for an American company in Madras, and she taught in a private school. They were on their way home after a holiday with relatives in Kerala.

Before the Mail left the coastal levels and started its long haul up the Ghats, we had finished our obligatory cricket conversation and turned to more serious things. The family were trying to emigrate, but already Australia had turned them down because, in spite of Mr

Fernandez's degree, probably because of it, they didn't have enough qualifying points. Australia evidently wasn't interested in anyone from India except as labourers and artisans. This seemed to me a poor return for his long devotion to Hassett's 143 in Madras, with a son marked for life as a result.

Mr Fernandez grinned. "But we have very good chance of getting to USA in nine years' time. I've been with the company now for five years and I've pretty well made myself indispensable." I could see where his great patience originated; he was an ardent cricketer, after all. But whence came all that optimism? And why were they so determined to get out? They were obviously quite well-to-do by Indian standards; employment by foreign companies, especially those headquartered in the States, was more highly coveted than anything apart from a successful business of one's own.

"It's the corruption more than anything," he said. "It's just too much nowadays. It's in everything. We bought a new apartment last year, which cost us one and a half lakh of rupees." Mrs Fernandez rolled her eyes, to tell me she didn't know how he did it, but wasn't she the lucky one? Her husband simply looked grim. "We've had to pay another one and a half lakh to get its deficiencies put right, plumbing and wiring that was all wrong. No redress whatsoever against the builder. We have golden retriever with a little room of her own. She pees in a special place and instead of it going down the drain it floods back into our part of the house. It isn't right, you know."

I told him that he could hear stories like that all over the Western world, too. It was the sort of thing that happened in cities everywhere.

Mr Fernandez held up his hand to stop me going on. "Okay, I'll buy that one. But you don't have our moneylenders, do you? Do you know the latest dirty trick they're playing here? They now change the title deeds to stiffen the repayment terms, so that the borrower will never be able to pay the original loan, only the interest."

He looked aggrieved; then suddenly started laughing. "Some people have started hitting back by signing their names in ink that vanishes after a few hours. One genius borrowed vast sums from several sharks, and distributed the money among all his friends and relatives, just before he and his entire family vamoosed to Australia."

We had started to run downhill, the ravines now further apart, the ridges flattening into slopes, the bush beginning to thin out. Somewhere just before reaching Sengottai, we crossed the state line from Kerala and entered the land of the Tamils. Before we had even come to a standstill in the station, bearers were rushing along the platform, selling pakoris on banana leaves through the barred window openings of the carriages, and other lads brought trays loaded with glasses of coffee and chai. A number of people got down from the train to stretch their legs, among them a sophisticated-looking fellow wearing impenetrable shades, well-cut shirt and slacks. He took a paper from the station newsboy, scanned it from cover to cover in the next five minutes, then handed it back in a disordered mess. The boy remonstrated, the man waved him away, turned his back and roared with laughter to some companions who had been awaiting his next move. They laughed with him, obsequiously. I heard Mr Fernandez suck in his breath. "That's another thing I can't stand about this country," he said. "The way people behave contemptuously to the underdogs." He might have been talking about some nationality other than his own.

Among the station staff awaiting the train was a middle-aged woman with a plastic bucket, a ladle and a steel beaker, there to provide drinking water for all who wanted it. The trick was to pour the water straight down your throat without the beaker touching your lips, and several people did this deftly as I watched. The woman stood by patiently, in two different sorts of uniform: blue garments provided by the Railways, and her own personal accoutrements – a gold disc pinned to each nostril, a red bindi on her brow, a vermilion smudge in the parting of her hair, a silver ring on the middle toe of each foot. When the piece of old railway line which served as a station bell was struck to announce our departure, she poured the remaining water in her bucket straight on to the platform, where it steamed on the hot stone. There was a drinking fountain nearby and a passenger left its tap running. As the train began to move, an old man with a white walrus moustache and with a large headcloth wound round his head strode crossly towards it and turned it off.

We left the bush-covered hills behind and began to cross the great plain of Tamil Nadu, which stretches unbroken to the east coast and almost all the way up to distant Madras. Gone were the endless coconut groves and the abundant waters of Kerala. Instead there were immense spaces dotted with thickets of palm and other trees, and regularly dominated by some huge outcrop of rock which rose alone in the hazy heat. One of these became a ridge, spiky like a dragon's back, with a small white temple perched on a platform of stone; and it would have been a penance to ascend those rocks any time the sun was in the sky.

We came to Tenkasi Junction, a small railway settlement such as John Masters described, this one dominated by the immense gopuram of a temple. The younger Fernandez boy pointed to a steam engine puffing up and down the sidings with a rake of trucks. "Those Anglo-Indian railwaymen," said his father, "really were something else. They could bring a train lickety-split up to a water tower and stop it exactly alongside the hosepipe. The Indians who took over the driving after Independence never got it quite right. They used to overshoot, so that they'd have to back up." I wondered whether there had ever been the slightest truth in that bit of racial mythology, and whether Mr Fernandez had ever dared tell it within earshot of any Indian who was not of mixed blood.

There was another temple at Sankarankoil where, said Mr Fernandez, the people worshipped live cobras kept by the priests. At Sivakasi, he pointed out some factories at a small distance from the railway line, the centre of India's considerable fireworks and match industry. "They use child labour and every so often some kid gets his hand blown off." He shook his head gloomily. He was a man whom history had stranded on the wrong side of the tracks.

I could think of one reason why the firework barons would prefer to exploit children in Tamil Nadu rather than try to in Kerala. The hammer and sickle was not often to be seen on this side of the Ghats. The most obvious political symbol now was the rising sun of the Dravida Munnetra Kazhagam, the party that had sailed to power by tapping the electorate's highly volatile feelings of Tamil nationalism.* The DMK emblem was everywhere: in the towns we passed through and on convenient surfaces throughout the countryside, among fields of rice, bananas, sugar cane. The life of this plain was much more like that of the India I was familiar with outside

* Dravida Munnetra Kazhagam means "Dravidian Progressive Organisation".

Kerala. People were winnowing grain as we thundered past. Others were washing water buffaloes in small ponds. The earth was burnt sienna and there was no longer an infinite variety in the shades of green. As we cruised slowly towards yet another station I gagged at an appalling stench that had attached itself to us: then realised that the last half-mile beside the track before the platform began was the local latrine, whose ordures were left for the flies and the dung beetles to remove. Just beyond, a yoke of bullocks stood patiently, harnessed to a cart. Their horns were handsomely painted, one red and one green on each beast, whose necks were garlanded with little bells. There wasn't another country in the world that could be so unappealing and then so swiftly captivate.

Darkness fell, and Mrs Fernandez began to arrange the bedrolls for her sons on the top bunks. As soon as the family had bade me goodbye when the train pulled into Madurai, I heard them locking the compartment door, to ensure their privacy during the long journey through the night to Madras. I climbed down from the carriage on to a platform heaving with multitudes who struggled with each other and their possessions to get aboard. People elbowed their way to the steps, levered themselves upward, bruised with the hard edges of their baggage all who impeded them. There was no question of anyone standing aside to let the very young, the very old, the obviously infirm get through first, and the most vigorous elbows belonged to women of all ages. They were even a match for the station coolies, who battled to reach the first-class carriages with great boxes and bundles balanced on their heads. All was noise, confusion, a matter of survival and devil take the hindmost. Under the yellowy, underpowered glow of the station lights, it looked like an exodus of refugees, frantic to put distance between them and a stricken town.

I had come, as all those departing pilgrims had come before me, for one thing alone: to visit the great Sri Meenakshi Temple at Madurai. The city had been important since the time of the Pandya dynasty, which ruled the Tamils intermittently between the sixth and the fourteenth centuries, and made this its capital. The authority of the temple, however, originated long before those Middle Ages, with a mythology in which fact and fiction are mingled even more startlingly than in the Old Testament of the Jews and the Christians.

Once upon a time, according to this account, the Pandyan King Malayadhwajan conceived a daughter who was a reincarnation of the goddess Parvati, consort of Lord Shiva. The child had another distinction, a third breast, but the king was told that this would disappear the moment his daughter set eyes on her future spouse. Meanwhile he was to bring her up as if she were his son, and was named Thadadhagai. Not surprisingly, she became a warrior, a subcontinental Amazon, mighty and victorious in battle. She was optimistic enough to take on, for reasons that are indistinct in the popular account, Lord Shiva himself in his Himalayan abode, Mount Kalias. What's more, she defeated the army sent against her by the god.

The story was told in a paperback for pilgrims (Sixth – and badly smudged – Edition) that I picked up at the station bookstall on my way into Madurai. It went on:

Seeing this, Shiva Himself came to fight with the undaunted queen. But, no sooner did she see Lord Shiva than her third breast disappeared. The queen threw down the weapons and stood abashed. She was glad that her wars had given her husband. The marriage of the divine couple was performed in Madurai on the eighth day with all pomp and splendour. The Lord ruled the Pandyan Kingdom under the name of Sundara Pandyan (meaning Pandyan of great beauty) for some years . . . After accomplishing many marvels, Lord Shiva made His divine son Murugan to be born as His mortal boy. This boy was christened Ukkirapandian (Pandyan of valour). After the coronation of this prince, the Lord in His mortal form and His consort, Thadadhagai, entered the temple and changed Themselves into Sundareswarar and Meenakshi.

In depicting the reincarnated Parvati, who dwelt among mortals before again becoming Shiva's consort under another name, this tale classically exemplified the central belief of Hinduism: in which the universe and all life is cyclical, the gods reappear in different forms and with different names, and mortals themselves are liable to transmutation from one existence to another. This is a world with six heavens above the earth, seven purgatories below the earth and seven hells below them. It is a world in which time is calculated on the basis of the kalpa, the single "day of Brahma", of unimaginable duration. It is a world in which the most blessed fate for any living creature is not an improvement in the next existence but moksha, liberation from the endless cycle of renewal, release from existence itself. In this world the deity who is worshipped more fervently than any other is not Brahma, the creator, to whom only one temple in the whole of India is dedicated; nor is it Vishnu, the preserver, from whose navel grew the lotus which gave birth to Brahma, and who rules the world after Brahma has performed the creative act. It is Shiva, who is both the destroyer and the reproducer, and who appears in one of his 1,008 manifestations as half-man, half-woman. He is the God of Paradox. And every Hindu coming to Madurai was intent on acknowledging Shiva's omnipotence. Each might have a personal deity – the benign elephant Ganesh, the terrible blood-stained Kali, Hanuman the monkey, Garuda the celestial bird or any of the other figures in a bewildering pantheon – to be adored daily, petitioned regularly, invoked at all times and in all places. But every true pilgrimage to the Sri Meenakshi Temple would above all else involve humble prostration before the linga, the phallic symbol of Lord Shiva.

Pilgrims were walking away from the city next morning as I was being rickshawed in from its outskirts. A long procession of men in saffron lunghis strode behind each other in a disciplined file, their naked torsos smeared copiously with ash, every man carrying a bundle on his shaven head; but it was impossible to tell whether these were penitential burdens or merely belongings borne conveniently. They were eccentric figures in an urban landscape marching steadily off into the countryside, quite possibly to another holy place. People made pilgrimages the length and breadth of this vast nation, very often the hard way in order to increase their virtue, and because they had one day made a simple vow, on impulse, in gratitude, or because it seemed expedient to do so. In Trivandrum I had watched two men, dressed in a style alien to Kerala, striding purposefully along with staves, obviously heading south; they were from Andhra Pradesh, probably on their way to Kanya Kumari. People would travel in similar fashion from South India to the great Gangetic plain, simply to bathe in the sacred river then to bring back some of its precious water in a garish plastic bottle. Many of them hoped they might die beside Ganga Mai before they turned for home again; for such would be the best assurance of all that moksha would be theirs.

Across the unbroken flatness of the city the four great wedges of the temple's chief gateways beckoned, rising so high above the surrounding buildings that each gopuram was pinnacled with a red light, to warn off low-flying aircraft after dark. Eight smaller gopurams also stood out from the lesser buildings of the temple complex, but they lacked the majesty of the principal four. Each of these rose in tier upon tier of carved figures, the most sumptuous display of fantasy I had seen in India or anywhere else, of a variety and inventiveness that made the gargoyles and other images of the greatest Gothic churches in Europe seem sparse, inhibited and grey. A plaque on the wall of the West Tower, which went up early in the fourteenth century, just as the building of Exeter Cathedral was getting into its stride, said that there were 1,124 sculptures on its façade; and all the other gopurams were as richly endowed. On one tier alone there were multi-headed personages facing three ways at once, a moustachioed godling in knee-breeches flexing his fourteen arms, mermaids reclining suggestively within the open lips of conch shells, sixteen sprites struggling to control a serpent which had coiled itself round the building, androgynous creatures bestriding bulls and horses and swans, characters wearing crowns or tiaras or haloes or vaguely pharaonic diadems, and figures that appeared to have been frozen in the middle of some elaborate choreography whose every dancer was performing an unrelated movement of its own. All this was delicately coloured in pastel shades of pink and green and yellow and blue, with an artfully blended fleshy tint that made even the most grotesque apparition seem to be endowed with a disturbingly human personality. And this vividly crazy carnival of goblins and satyrs, nymphs and genies, demons and heroes, with glaring eyes and posturing limbs, with hands that beckoned and shunned and implied every conceivable emotion in between, this monumental hallucination reproduced itself again and again as the gopuram rose higher above the ground; until, at the very top of the building, an enormous and devilish face looked down with wide open mouth, from which every creature on the four walls had been disgorged in a magnificent, astonishing, terrifying and tumbling extravaganza.

Here was the gaudy repudiation of Islamic sobriety. In place of severe religious abstractions, here was riotous and carnal piety. This was one measure of the division between rival fundamentalists.

The temple was nothing less than a small township in its own right, whose surrounding walls kept a tumult of traffic at bay. Wiry helots pedalled cycle-rickshaws everywhere in the direction of Sri Meenakshi, pestering me so relentlessly for a whole week with wheedling cries of "Master" that even at my most doggedly pedestrian I eventually gave in from emotional rather than physical exhaustion. And in the swarming streets immediately outside the temple walls, all the commerce of pilgrimage was conducted vigorously by people who offered everything from footwear to charms. A greybeard took post each day at the corner of the eastern and southern walls and set out on a cloth an array of talismans and cures that not even the ayurvedic medical practitioners of Madurai would have advised. He had large jars containing pickled snakes and lizards, together with substances that looked still more disagreeable, and periodically he drained the juices and the oils in which these fermented and stewed, pouring them down a tin funnel into small bottles and phials, which were then added to the carefully graded collection at his feet. He also had a tub in which, among many unrecognisable objects, I identified a snakeskin, a mummified fish with a gaping mouth, two empty tortoiseshells, the desiccated head of a monkey and the bill and jawbone of a pelican.

The temple had its own bazaar on its eastern side. Here the temporal and the spiritual worlds immediately came to terms, the one flowing into the other without the slightest hesitation or difficulty. I stepped off the street into a stone-flagged hall as delicately sculptured and as vividly painted as the nearest gopuram. Its pillars were formed by voluptuous figures nearly twice the height of any Tamil, and these were the only images left undecorated. They upheld a gallery in which chubby celestials sat at intervals in niches, surrounded by frescoes of adoring humans; and the roof high above was also covered in mythological creatures, interspersed with mandalas, yantras and other diagrammatic pictures devised to interpret the cosmos or merely to assist the struggling believer's meditation. Below and among these rhapsodies were stalls selling almost anything that might be found in the shops of the city outside. Every kind of obvious religious artefact was here: florid posters, portraits framed in gilded tin, soapstone effigies, brass incense holders and the sticks of bathi and cones of dhoop to go with them, mounds of coloured powders dizzying in their intensity, and garlands of flowers to festoon the deities, hanging in such quantity that they sweetened the air and cleansed it of all staleness. There were also bowls of halwa, bunches of bananas, coconuts and other foods that would be offered in propitiation of the gods. There were stalls selling stuff that seemed irrelevant to this holy place, like cheap plastic footballs, cricket bats and other toys, woollen satchels, hold-alls, suitcases, umbrellas and metal vessels for carrying water or cooking rice. Standing restlessly nearby was the temple elephant, with its keeper sitting cross-legged beside a huge shackled foot. The animal was bored and swayed from side to side to shift its weight, regularly doing what it had been carefully trained to do. It accepted coins in the tip of its trunk, touched the vibhuti chalked on its forehead, then deposited the money in the keeper's hand. To some pilgrims this would be a transaction with Ganesh himself.

I sat on a ledge beside a stall to take all this in; and the score or more of men sitting at trestles along a colonnaded aisle, fingers deftly stripping flowers from stems and entwining them along a string so that they would make a fragrant decoration fit for a god. Almost at once a little elf of a man with a heavy grey stubble materialised in front of me and sat down at my feet. He all but laid his head on my knee, looked up sweetly and made eyes at me like a faithful Labrador.

"You are nice man," he said, very gently; then, pointing to each of us in turn, "You are my father. I am your son." He was at least as old as I and two small boys nearby broke into uncontrollable giggles when they heard this.

He paid no attention; his world for the moment was me. He rubbed his bristly chin on my knee and began to stroke my arm affectionately. I put a finger to my lips and quietly hushed him while I continued to make some notes. He stopped stroking and smiled beatifically. Some of his saliva dribbled on to my slacks, but much worse had happened to me out in the street. A leper had insisted on showing me the raw stump of his right foot, where his toes had recently been; an old crone had grabbed my wrist as I tried to sidestep her without paying ransom, grasping it so fiercely that I deliberately trod on her when she wouldn't release me.

"I must go now," I said, as I disengaged myself from the old elf and stood up. "I will see you later, then," he replied. He had not asked me for anything.

The transition from the bazaar to the temple proper was signified by a low enclosure in the middle of the floor where the stalls came to an end. It was painted in the same pink and white candy-stripes that decorated the walls of Sri Meenakshi's courtyard and gave it a curiously English festival air; they hinted at marquees somewhere in the vicinity, where cucumber sandwiches might be served, and possibly cream teas. The enclosure inside was occupied by a squatting representation of Nandin the bull, The Happy One and Lord Shiva's steed as He travelled the universe. This Nandin was sculpted in black stone, but had been smeared with coloured powders so often by the faithful that he had a ruddy and piebald appearance, as well as acquiring, the day I first saw him, a garland of white flowers which hung lopsidedly from his horns and covered his right eye. A heavy metal safe with a slot in the top stood at one end of the enclosure, and approaching pilgrims did not fail to make an offering. They then paused by the bull, to press their fingers in a tray of powder, then to his already stained body, and finally touched their own foreheads with the powder that remained on their fingertips. They marked Nandin and themselves with rapid gestures, like Christians making the sign of the cross.

The doorway that separated bazaar and temple was so massive, with deeply grooved sides, that it could have been the entrance to a castle. I looked up to see if there was a portcullis that might be dropped if the place were besieged in a religious war, but there was only a heavy bronze door, which was closed each night and during the time of rest in the early afternoon. Beyond was a long high corridor whose mighty pillars, carved and with heavy capitals, supported a painted roof. The details were indistinct in a gloom broken infrequently by strips of neon light. Beyond that first corridor were others in every direction, all with little illumination and all confusingly alike, distinguished only by the shrines that appeared at intervals. It took me two full days before I was confident of navigating from one part of Sri Meenakshi to another. Before that I got myself lost in the temple's murkier corners more often than not. It was much like trying to find the way round a maze in the last half-hour before night falls and darkness is complete.

The pilgrims appeared to have no such difficulties. In parties, in families and individually, they strode with unerring instinct to the shrine whose deity they were particularly devoted to, especially to the two chambers in which the Lord Sundareswara and Sri Meenakshi herself were separately quartered. These were out of bounds to all who were not Hindu, though I briefly entered the former by accident. Arriving at the temple very early one morning, when neither I nor the priests were properly awake, I wandered through an opening I was unfamiliar with and found myself confronted with Lord Shiva's linga, a brass column which had sheaves of corn sprouting from its base like pubic hair, and which stood gleaming above an intricate metal arch, and even above the massive stone brackets of the walls, to disappear through the painted roof. Hanging from the ceiling over each corner of the dais from which the linga arose, was a long and colourful fabric tube, a kind of Chinese lantern. These four cylinders, decorated vividly with elephants and lotus flowers and abstract signs, hung motionless around the sacred phallus in that airless chamber, as I stood and gaped and realised what I had blundered into; then quickly turned and withdrew before I was seen and challenged embarrassingly.

Many other gods besides Sundareswara and Meenakshi were also honoured in the temple. Behind a high iron fence there rose a bronze representation of Kali, covered from head to toe with dabs of white ash and red powder and spattered liberally with little pats of melting ghee, so that she looked as if she had broken out in some unseemly rash. Congealed ghee floated in a tub of water nearby, where Kali's worshippers could buy it in minute quantities and flick it devoutly through the railings at that terrifying bronze. Then they raised their clasped hands before their heads, stood silently for a moment, murmured their prayers and left, their faces shining with something close to ecstasy. There was also another shrine to Nandin, much more elaborate than the one in the bazaar. The bull here crouched on a high pedestal from which four heavy pillars rose to support a richly carved canopy of stone. I watched two of the priests spend twenty minutes swilling him down with bucketsful of milk, then with the liquid of coconuts, then with ghee, before anointing him with turmeric paste. Fresh marigolds were then hung in ropes around his neck and a clean white cloth was tied there like a bib. The priests were as matter-of-fact in their sacramental duties as roadmenders mixing tar, and the purifying liquids poured off the bull through ornate rainwater heads into the temple's drains. On the other side of the railings that surrounded the shrine stood the pilgrim who was paying for this rite: a thickset man with an alert face and a northern dhoti wound tightly between his legs, whose eyes followed every move the priests made and never blinked in all that time. There were many, many shrines smaller than these, all protected in some way from the possibility of defilement and all inviting donations in an adjacent safe.

I repeatedly walked down corridors that seemed to be empty of anything except massive columns; until, rounding a corner, I would come upon a solitary figure who had wedged himself into the angle of two walls, where he could best adore the stone or bronze figure wrapped in a winding sheet behind a grille; which he did by sitting motionless for an hour, with his legs crossed awkwardly and his head held on one side. It was while I was trying to find my way around this tremendous and echoing maze that I happened upon the shrine dedicated to Mars, Moon, Venus, Mercury, Saturn, Jupiter and Sun, according to a notice in three languages posted by its side. It was a strangely unimpressive structure, a pedestal, a canopy and nothing in between, yet always it was venerated by people who bought little lamps of oil and coconuts, placed these on special holders beside the shrine, then walked round it briskly two or three times, muttering as they went. A pregnant woman, who looked refined and was expensively dressed, circled it many more times than that.

After my early explorations to familiarise myself with this sprawling and complicated place, I took to frequenting the area near Meenakshi's own shrine, partly because this was on the main axis of the temple but also because there was more natural light than in most areas: the shrine was close to the great open-air tank in which people should have ritually bathed before making puja, though it was almost bone dry as a result of a long water shortage in Madurai. A profitable trade in washing facilities was flourishing as a result in all the nearby pilgrim hostelries, but many preferred the less expensive Vaigai River some distance away, where the locals dhobeyed their clothing, slopped out their trucks, watered their cattle, their sheep and their goats.

The entrance to Meenakshi's shrine was on one of the most richly decorated corridors, an extension of the cloister running round the water tank. Its ceiling was painted with a mixture of abstractions and figurative scenes and it had recently been restored, with every brush-stroke glistening and clear. Immediately below came heavy stone brackets featuring animals from some Vedic bestiary, grotesques that were not quite in the semblance of dragons nor yet that of lions, all coloured blue. Below them came the columns of unpainted stone, each with its more than lifesize carved figure that echoed one or other of the statuettes posturing outside on the gopurams. Pandavan princes and other epic characters from *Mahabharata* were here, and so were gypsies, eunuchs, devadasis, hunters, musicians, as well as divine figures in many forms. Their numbers and their variety throughout the entire complex of Sri Meenakshi were beyond my computation: in one chamber alone the roof was notoriously supported by nearly a thousand columns such as these. The temple authorities had made the chamber into an art gallery which, because it had no direct religious significance, was ignored by the pilgrims and usually empty. To stand quite alone among its massive pillars was to be intimidated as well as enthralled. Those endless figures with unyielding expressions seemed to be protecting some secret that might be lurking in the bowels of the earth – or even in the shadows over there! It was warm and close, the light was subdued, and when my eyes fell on yet another Nandin it took little imagination to sense that this was the very labyrinth Daedalus built at Knossos for King Minos, and that the frightful Minotaur was prowling just out of sight, hungry for his annual tribute of Athenian youth. So powerful was this illusion that, in spite of myself, I turned and rapidly retraced my steps away from that deserted chamber, happy to find my way out again and to reach the amicable hurly-burly of the bazaar.

I spent hours of that week sitting on a ledge of the cloister nearest the opening to Meenakshi's enclosure, which was announced by a businesslike frosted glass sign, illuminated from behind. Opposite the opening was a stone lotus flower, railed in like every other object of veneration, and most people acknowledged this before passing into the sanctuary. Some did press-ups beside it, facing the doorway, though females usually knelt and bowed low. A woman with an appalling growth on her nose, which looked like an ant-eater's snout twisted out of shape, prostrated herself for several minutes in silence. A man raised his clasped palms in greeting to the goddess, then slapped his face with them twice. Another twirled round several times, hands together high above his head. A fellow in shirt and slacks bustled up, as though he were snatching a break between business appointments, tapped his forehead three times, crossed his arms round his neck and bent his knees thrice so deeply that his buttocks touched his heels. A tall, white-bearded figure, gorgeously wrapped in a scarlet cloak and with a scarlet toque on his head, strode up and flourished something like a field marshal's baton which rattled as he waved it at the sanctuary before going in. A little old lady stood with head tilted towards her god and sang with great passion a chant that sounded weirdly like an Indian adaptation of "Alouette". There was as much individuality in the acts of devotion as there was in the personality of the devotees. There was none of the regularity that characterises the rituals of the Muslims, the Christians and the Jews.

The priests of the temple were recognisable because they were uniformly stripped to the waist and each had the three horizontal lines of Lord Shiva's mark in ash on their foreheads and both arms. The pilgrims came in too many different guises to count. A well-dressed girl had plastered her face with a powder that had turned her a bilious green. A child-mother who couldn't have been more than sixteen had her baby in the crook of her arm, its head shaven like her own and also coated in yellow paste. Another young woman was clad like a bride, with flowers in her almost luminously black hair, as she hurried past with a basket of flowers and fruit for some god. Some men seemed to have grown their hair to extraordinary length out of religious conviction, while others had been totally depilated in their ardour for the same deity.

I gradually discovered that there was a distinct rhythm to the life of the priests and pilgrims each day, which was divided into two halves, with a long siesta in the middle, when the important shrines and the bazaar closed and people took their rest. They lay sound asleep, dozing or merely watchfully prone all over the temple's stone floors: a crippled beggar who pushed himself around the bazaar on a low trolley with four wheels dismounted at this hour and used the trolley as a pillow for the next two. In the shaded cloisters around the tank a couple of old men squatted and engaged in what sounded like fierce argument full of animus, with climactic gestures and harsh voices that pierced the ears at fifty yards' range. Three other men sat with them, their heads turning from one protagonist to the other, like spectators at a tennis tournament, attending closely to what was almost certainly nothing more than a discussion of some fine theological point, conducted vigorously but without any real acrimony.

As the heat began to go out of the day, worship resumed its normal patterns and fresh pilgrims again flowed in through the eastern gate. Soon the whole temple once more echoed to the sound of many people talking with animation, much more loudly than the sound made by a theatre audience before curtain up, though it contained the same note of keen anticipation. The West knows similar noise only before a football or a baseball match. In late afternoon a drummer emerged from Meenakshi's shrine, followed by half a dozen priests with mincing steps, including one who was short and balding with an air of pert reliability that would have sat well on a provincial bank manager or possibly someone in the civil service. They disappeared down a gloomy corridor and were succeeded by my elfin friend, who waved at me and said "Happy New Year" as he passed.

I had by now found steps leading up to a Broadcasting Studio (Admission Restricted), as good as any place from which to watch the comings and goings near the shrine. I was sitting there when men began to move about with kerosene lamps, held like flambeaux on the end of poles with an air of ceremony. They had just become necessary as darkness fell round the tank when a procession arrived, led by a red-skirted drummer with a shaven head and lithe movements that might have made his reputation in Kerala as a Kathakali actor.* The procession had formed round a man who was swathed and tightly hooded in a deep saffron robe, who carried a wand with a saffron ribbon tied to it. He was plump, aloof and had a gormless

* Kathakali ("story-play" in Malayalam) was first devised by a Rajah of Kottarakkara in Shakespeare's time as a form of people's theatre. Its plays are mimed by male actors and all tell tales from Hindu mythology in highly stylised performances which traditionally begin at 8 p.m. and go on till dawn.

smile but he was unquestionably regarded as an important holy man, judging by the way his acolytes busied themselves to make him comfortable in a low basketwork chair before a microphone, which was connected to the Broadcasting Studio (Admission Restricted). A large and ornate bell hung over his head. He chanted briefly to the gathering of maybe fifty people, then swept into a sermon which was delivered in a voice that was somewhere between contralto and tenor; it reminded me of a comedian, popular among the English fifty years ago, named Wee Georgie Wood. After a while the delivery became more strident and was accompanied by gestures that belonged to the stock repertoire of every political and religious tub-thumper: the finger that wagged, and jabbed and pointed, the dis-missive hand, the open palm which purported to weigh matters reasonably. Most of this guru's audience sat riveted by his oratory; but a woman changed her infant's nappies nearby and another, lacking such expensive material, wiped her own child clean with a cloth then went looking for somewhere to wash it out.

Bored by a diatribe I couldn't understand I wandered off, to dis-cover that by the temple's east door a dozen men were manhandling a heavy cart with rubber wheels, on which were perched two dolls representing Sri Meenakshi and Lord Sundareswara, virtually indis-tinguishable beneath their concealing gaudy robes. This was trundled through the bazaar, preceded by an assortment of mace-bearers, drummers, trumpeters and men carrying flambeaux. People became agitated as the procession went by, clasping their hands in salute to the gods, pushing and shoving each other to get close enough to warm their hands in the fire and the smoke. A mother passed a hand quickly through flame and in the same movement brushed the warmth across the face of the infant sleeping in her other arm. The contraption was pushed down a corridor and into a fenced-off area, where many helots appeared and lifted the float from the cart like a sedan chair, with heavy bamboo poles. They set it down and people began scurrying back and forth with brass dishes full of food for the gods, who were soon conveyed through a doorway and out of my sight, led by a drummer and a man playing nadaswaram, a South Indian woodwind instrument with the tone and range of an oboe.

The next episode of the drama was played at Sundareswara's shrine late in the evening, when the temple crowds had been reduced to a sprinkling, who hung about like autograph hunters at a stage door or a players' entrance, waiting for the stars to appear. They stood near a doorway almost identical to Meenakshi's, except that this one had wispy stalks of corn strung up above the opening. From somewhere within came the banging of drums, before the procession of mace-bearers and other acolytes emerged, this time attending a small palanquin with a solitary pole running through it from end to end, carried by two priests fore and aft. The palanquin was an unwontedly plain gravy brown and without decoration, but curtains had been drawn across its sides to conceal its occupant, who was fanned on one side by a man bearing a peacock's tail, and on the other by a priest carrying a large feather duster. To the beating of the drums, the god was borne down the gloomy corridors slowly, followed by a straggle of pilgrims, the flames throwing spooky light and shadows on the walls, the smoke hanging pungently in the stale air. The procession paused by each shrine it reached, where the palanquin was set down by its bearers, the flambeaux were waved in set patterns and people prostrated themselves ardently. When we reached Meenakshi's shrine these devotions were lengthier and more complicated before Sundareswara was hoisted shoulder high again and taken through the doorway; but only the priests and acolytes accompanied him inside.

A man who had followed this progress with his wife and child turned to me with a smile that radiated enchantment. "The Lord must always spend the night with his lady," he explained. "That is as it should be. That is good example to us all." His head wobbled emphatically. "But at dawn he must go back to his own place in reverse order and without delay."

I returned just before five next morning, when the streets around Sri Meenakshi were deserted apart from scavenging dogs. I almost tripped over several prone figures on the flagged courtyard, and other people were sleeping elsewhere inside the temple proper. A number sat dozily close to Meenakshi's shrine but were not encouraged to follow a priest who opened the heavy doors and went inside. Minutes later he reappeared, ringing a handbell vigorously; to be swiftly joined by the woodwind player of the night before, who struck up a duet with a drummer who had also materialised from the dark tunnel of the nearest corridor. Another priest appeared, his head, arms and torso all generously smeared with Lord Shiva's triple ash marks. He carried an urn from which flames and smoke came forth, and he swung it through the air on extended arms. At this, the dozing people shook themselves properly awake, wiggled their heads at each other amiably, exchanged jests and pleasantries and smiled at the new beginning to a day. The atmosphere suddenly became charged with sheer happiness: it was like being in a Christian church on Easter morning. The waiting pilgrims shuffled quickly through the doorway, while pigeons cooed to each other from the stone brackets above our heads.

From the sanctuary came a loud clanging, like the sound of demented firebells: outside the entrance, the drummer paddled a tune with the fingers of his left hand while beating time with a stick held in his right. Then silence descended, broken only by an occasional cough somewhere along the adjacent corridors, and by the pigeons above. Through the opening I could see that the worshippers within were standing in orderly ranks with their hands upraised, facing a stout brass column which looked much like the linga I had seen in Sundareswara's shrine. When they emerged they seemed equally refreshed; including old men of Madurai who had probably never missed this first puja of the day in half a century, and small girls from all over India, whose parents had dressed them in their finest frocks for the moment that they might never repeat but would remember for the rest of their lives. Refreshed too was the little woman who had arrived out of breath, went through her preliminaries rapidly before disappearing inside, smiled at me warmly as she came out again and raised her clasped hands in a greeting that I returned. Then she went off to earn her daily bread somewhere in the awakening city.

The woodwind player, who had disappeared, now came back and blew a couple of practice blasts as his next cue approached. A flock of worshippers hurried out of the sanctuary just before six o'clock, followed by the palanquin conveying Lord Sundareswara back to his own place; but this time there were no footmen fanning him, his ardour having presumably been cooled somewhat in the past few hours. Nor did the procession move at the stately pace of the night before: this time, with musicians and flame-bearers once more at their head, the priests carrying the concealed god were almost trotting with their load. They did not pause until they reached his threshold, and there but briefly, before they trotted inside, whereupon the faithful round the doorway slowly dispersed.

I took myself to the cloister above the tank. Its surrounding steps ought to have been filling with pilgrims ready for the ritual bath, but now led to nothing but an empty floor, where a man began to push dirt into neat piles as a peach-coloured dawn came over the temple walls. A solitary star could still be seen high above the eastern gopuram, whose carved figures from now on would be imperceptibly transformed from dark outlines to three-dimensional shapes and finally into polychromatic grotesques more fanciful than anything Walt Disney ever dreamt of. A high thin baritone was skirling from the other side of the empty bath, and when I strolled in its direction I saw it belonged to a bearded old man sitting with his back to the cloister wall, his white cloak not only concealing his body but also hooding his head. He held before him in both hands an open book and from this he was singing his rambling, rising, dipping chant with all the unaffected innocence of an English cathedral chorister. I watched at a distance until he came to the end of his canticle, saluted the changing sky with clasped palms, closed his book and bound it with a cord. Then he sat upright and recollected himself. I waited a little while before settling down next to him, which caused him to open his eyes and smile at me. He ferreted in his satchel and brought out a notebook with a plastic cover picturing Sylvester Stallone as Rambo II. It was apparent that we didn't have two words to rub together between us, but this was only a small impediment to communication. He pointed to his name, Mr S. Palanimuthu, of Kumanay District, in the notebook and indicated that I should add mine. There wasn't a hint of asking anything more of me but I still gave him a coin, which he accepted with a gracious little bow; it was no less than I would have done for a busker who had entertained me in the London Underground.

At that moment an old woman came along and also gave alms, in spite of the fact that he waved her on beforehand, as if to excuse her from such charity. She then turned on me and began to beg for something in her turn, drawing on an impressive armoury of piteous gestures. Had she not done this I would probably have tipped up without demur, but I shook my head briskly against her wheedling, which caused her to become more strident and obviously to start denouncing my meanness loudly. When she squatted in front of me and prepared to lay siege seriously, Mr Palanimuthu spoke to her sharply for several minutes and then gave her a larger coin than she had offered him. She walked away, grumbling, and he turned to me with a great laugh of male solidarity. He slapped his thigh in high humour and said something that I translated as "You get 'em in here all the time."

I went back to Meenakshi's shrine, drawn by the sound of music again. Three priests were sitting by the broadcasting microphone, with tabla, harmonium and small dome-shaped cymbals, and I squatted on the steps again to listen, while the percussionist keened away in a voice that sent high-pitched crescendos echoing down far corridors. Others came to listen with me and a man from Delhi approached after watching me steadily for several minutes.

"You are studying our culture?"

"Yes I am. I'm enjoying this music just now."

"It touches our soul. That is the beauty of it."

He said this with great earnestness, very anxious that I should not miss the point. He was telling a simple Indian truth to the stranger, completely unaware how close he was to self-parody. Having spoken, he began to clap hands in time to the singing, so that I should not be left in the slightest doubt that his soul was perfectly in tune that day.

Two policemen came down the corridor with a basket of fruit for the gods, doubtless a gift from the local station and a way of staying on the right side of the temple authorities. They were followed by a man who had allowed two nails of his right hand to grow so long that they were contorted into ugly and twisted talons, which he was anxious to protect by holding the wrist carefully in his left hand. He wanted the world to know that he dwelt on some rarefied spiritual plane which did not include the pollutions of manual labour. The next pilgrims in this sequence wanted all bystanders to realise that they were men of power and substance before they were anything else. They came with police and plenty of staff in tow, all scurrying to keep up with the visiting politicians from Madras, all treated with huge disdain by men well accustomed to obsequiousness trailing for ever in their wake. They were escorted into the two principal sanctuaries, went through whatever motions were deemed appropriate to men of their stature, and hurried on to the next item on their agenda, leaving lackeys to settle whatever dues the priests exacted for services rendered. By the time they were bound for more politicking in the city outside, the sun was coming up so fiercely that the flagstones of the courtyard were too hot for my bare feet; and by noon, as siesta approached, they were blistering enough to practise firewalking on.

Day after day this rhythm was repeated at the temple of Sri Meenakshi in Madurai, as was the rich variety of its ever changing congregations, and the way that the secular and the religious life of the city mingled so naturally in this sprawling community beneath the fantastic gopurams. More than once it struck me that it would have been something like this in the cathedrals of medieval Europe, with their painted walls and their often grotesque statuary, their bustle of commerce somewhere in the precincts, their endless pilgrimages to the relics and the shrines, their mendicants and their self-appointed preachers, their pardoners, their summoners, their manciples, their reeves and all the other Chaucerian characters populating that world and flavouring it distinctively; all long since vanished, like much of the piety that had brought it together in the first place. But not here, in India. Where, in all that week in Madurai, I saw only one thing that utterly offended me.

I was watching the activity at Kali's shrine one day when a crowd of foreign tourists came through. Their guide had not even finished explaining the significance of the goddess and the form of worship practised by her devotees, when one of the party went to the priest in charge of the water tub, bought two pats of ghee and with caricatured movements hurled these in slow motion at the bronze, so that his wife could capture his bravado with her cine-camera. Many of the foreigners roared with laughter, while the nearest Indians managed to look disdainful and disapproving without moving a muscle or uttering so much as a sigh.

I hurried away, shamed by the man's vulgarity and the colour of my skin, to sit on the steps near Meenakshi's shrine. A small boy came past with a basket of flowers on his head, and when I smiled at him he tried to wink at me by closing both eyes at once. Shortly afterwards he returned with a girl of about the same age. She thrust

a flower at me and I, mistaking her purpose, declined it as gently
as I could.

She held it out more urgently. "No money," she said. "Take."

So I did, and prayed that she and her brother might have a long
life.

# Shantivanam

Long before the train reached my next destination, it was obvious why Trichinopoly – as the idiosyncratic British used to call it – had figured in the Anglo-French struggle for supremacy in eighteenth-century India. Across the plain of Tamil Nadu a luminous dot became distantly visible in the late afternoon haze, shimmering just above the blur of the horizon. As we rocked and swayed towards Tiruchirappalli upon a clatter of bogies, the dot slowly enlarged, rearranged its shape, acquired other dimensions, became massively substantial, finally dominated the skyline and the city sprawling under it. The Rock was destined to be a fortress from the moment people settled around its base, a huge bastion of sandstone with natural terraces around its summit, on which buildings could now be seen, and where trees had somehow managed to take root. Two hundred years ago it had been the perfect refuge for Muhammad Ali, the British puppet in the war of the Carnatic succession, which also made it a handy vaulting horse for young Robert Clive's enormous ambition. In modern times it had been perpetually under siege by pilgrims, making the laborious ascent to a couple of temples situated there.

The beggars were awaiting them not long after dawn the next day, squatting in two orderly lines beside the entrance, where the first of several hundred steps leading to the summit had been cut in a tunnel through the living stone. Halfway up, the larger of the temples had also been hewn from the cliff itself, but the principal object of pilgrimage was attained only after clambering up the final flight of stairs, which swerved unevenly round the shoulder of the Rock, with nothing but a handrail between the zealot and a sensational drop straight into the streets below. Having negotiated that, the pilgrim was received by priests at a little shrine perched on the summit, to which only the faithful were admitted. Another universal impulse, besides the religious urge, had left its mark on those topmost boulders. They had been whitewashed with hearts and conjoined names by lovelorn ecstatics who had dared to climb outside the safety of the rail, presumably at the dead of night.

The view from the summit was spectacular. Immediately below was the bustle of midtown Tiruchy, from which the noise of traffic arose, clearly audible halfway up the sky; the fort on the crag above Jodhpur was the only loftier vantage point of this kind that I knew. On all sides the city sprawled until its suburbs faded into the scrub of the relentlessly encompassing plain. The flatness extended so distantly, there was such an immensity of space in what was visible of both heaven and earth, that it was almost possible to believe one could detect the curvature in the surface of the globe. But it was an uneventful view, except to the north, where the colossal gopuram of the Sri Rangam Temple poked high above its great compound in the middle of the bush. This stood upon an island whose general outline was lost to me amidst the concealing vegetation of the Tamil flatlands; only the nearer banks were clearly to be seen on the other side of the wide bridge which crossed the River Cauvery. Such was the scale of this vast landscape that it seemed as if no more than a trickle of water was making its way across a great expanse of sand. The river was much lower than I had expected at this season of the year, scarcely four months since the last of the rains, and not yet halfway to the next monsoon. It was difficult to envisage the July inundation reported by the Abbé Dubois early in the nineteenth century, when the Cauvery's floodwaters spread freshness and fertility far and wide, and devout people travelled great distances

in order to congratulate *the lady* (the water) on her arrival and to offer her sacrifices of all sorts, such as pieces of money, which they throw to her that she may have something to defray her expenses; pieces of linen to clothe herself; jewels to adorn herself; rice, cakes, fruits and other eatables, lest she should suffer from hunger; household utensils such as baskets, earthen vessels, &c, in order that she may conveniently cook and store her provisions and have everything which may procure her an easy subsistence.*

The Cauvery was one of the seven rivers most sacred to Hindus, the holiest waterway of the South, and indirectly the reason for my coming to Tiruchirappalli. Some distance upstream was the ashram that had developed around the person of a remarkable Englishman, whose teaching I first came across a quarter of a century ago, when I was studying contemporary monasticism rather intensively, but whom I had never yet met. Bede Griffiths had been reared in the Church of England, had drifted into a sympathetic agnosticism at Oxford just after the First World War, had recovered his faith as a Roman Catholic, and had been professed as a Benedictine monk at the age of thirty-one. Almost twenty years later, having been Prior of an English abbey and then Novice Master of a Scottish house, he was invited by an Indian of his Order to found a Benedictine community on the subcontinent. After two years in Bangalore the attempt had come to nothing so Bede Griffiths began his collaboration with a Belgian Cistercian, Francis Mahieu, who had also gone to India with the intention of starting a new community. Together, in 1958, they settled in the hill country of Kerala, where they were soon joined by a couple of novices and before long had fifteen men living in their Kurisumala Ashram, following the Rule of St Benedict but under canonical obedience to the local Syrian bishop.

Meanwhile, on the banks of the Cauvery in Tamil Nadu, a similar effort had been made to establish an ashram by two European priests, the Frenchmen Jules Monchanin and Henri Le Saux, though it attracted no native vocations in its early days. Monchanin died not long after they had settled down; Le Saux remained at Saccidananda alone for a while before leaving for a hermit's existence in the Himalaya, where he, too, died within a few more years. The ashram was saved from dereliction on his departure by the arrival of Bede Griffiths and some other Kurisumala monks, though Francis Mahieu stayed behind in Kerala. The new venture represented something

---

* *Hindu Manners, Customs and Ceremonies* by the Abbé J. A. Dubois, translated by Henry K. Beauchamp (OUP, Oxford, 3rd ed, 1959) p 551.

more than a change of scene for the Englishman: it marked a subtle shift in his philosophical emphasis. Kurisumala in Malayalam means Hill of the Cross. He was exchanging this for a Tamil location, Shantivanam, which means Forest of Peace: the name the French fathers had already given to their ashram, moreover, was rooted in the teachings of Sankara, the great guru of the Vedanta, who held that God was at one and the same time absolute Being (sat), absolute Knowledge (chit) and absolute Bliss (ananda).

Bede Griffiths had turned his back on a life which was pivoted on a traditional Christian liturgy in order to embrace one that was, above all, contemplative. The community that now began to take shape beside the sacred Cauvery still acknowledged the spirit of St Benedict's great monastic Rule, but saw its own pedigree more particularly in the congregation of hermits that St Romuald founded in the eleventh century at Camaldoli, in Tuscany. Yet the life of the Saccidananda Ashram was not only flirting with paradox by combining the communal and the eremitical: it was also deliberately and finely balanced between two vastly different religious traditions. After several years in India, Bede Griffiths had written a book in which he held that Christ was the fulfilment of all religions, but from something I had read since it seemed that this was no longer his position; at least, that this was no longer the way he would express his belief. Much more recently he had owned that all religions were complementary: "that beyond all the differences of ritual and doctrine in the different religions there is yet an underlying unity. This unity is not found in any formal doctrine but in an experience of transcendent reality, a reality which may be called God, or Brahman, or Nirvana or, as with Mahatma Gandhi, simply Truth, but its essential characteristic is that it cannot be properly expressed in words. It is a Mystery . . ."* I had long looked forward to meeting this man, who had placed himself so carefully on one of those spiritual frontiers that for ever beckon the restless and the inquisitive. If he wasn't altogether in the line of Teilhard de Chardin or Charles de Foucauld he was at least a potentially awkward freelance, a migrant version of his old Benedictine kinsman Dom David Knowles.

* *Bede Griffiths and Sannyasa*, by Jesu Rajan (Asian Trading Corporation, Bangalore, 1989) p xii.

He had become Swami Bede Griffiths, saluted as such by Indian Catholic priests who were close to him.

I hired a car to take me to Shantivanam, and from the moment we left Tiruchy our road ran alongside the river, which looked even more depleted at close range than it had from the top of the Rock. It was maybe half a mile across but contained nothing more than meagre streams of water which flowed sluggishly round numerous and towering sandbanks. It had occurred to me that this desperate condition might be the result of the long-running dispute over the Cauvery between Tamil Nadu and neighbouring Karnataka, which controlled the river's source; a dispute about water rights which had been marked by bloody-minded intransigence in both state governments, and by a great deal of bloodshed among Tamil and Kannadiga peasants living near the state boundaries. But presently the road began to run between the dehydrated river and a fast-flowing, evidently deep canal, which clearly tapped the Cauvery further upstream for purposes of irrigation; exactly the cause and effect that also deprives the Ganga of its natural majesty except in the monsoon and its immediate aftermath.

For well over an hour we drove through a lush and well-tilled countryside, scattering fowl and causing cyclists to swerve in alarm as we blared through villages on the horn, leaving a wake of brown dust in the air where our wheels ran off the narrow strip of tarmacadamed road. A sign which combined the Christian cross and the Dharmacakra, the Hindu (and Buddhist) Wheel of the Law, eventually pointed to a side turning in the direction of the river and we rolled down a dirt track between wire fences whose posts were massively made of granite. If the Cauvery had been in flood, Saccidananda Ashram would have been within a stone's throw of the spate; as it was, the treeline of its banks gave way to ridge after ridge of sand, smothered in a succulent-looking weed, occasionally separated by large puddles and all but motionless rivulets. The sands were beginning to shimmer with heat, turning from their natural colour to white in the aching glare, but the ashram was almost wholly shaded by trees. Dapples of sunlight fell upon roofs of pantile and thatch, scarcely flickering in the still morning air.

The place seemed deserted and it was a little while before I was able to make any enquiry. A young Indian in a saffron robe came out of a hut and crossed a patch of well-trodden earth, but paused when he saw me standing indecisively. Feeling unusually awkward, I asked him whether Bede Griffiths was there, and if it would be possible for me to see him.

"Father is in the hermitage today and can't be disturbed," he said. He nodded to the south, along the treeline of the river bank, implying some fair distance away. "He will be coming later this afternoon, though." A long pause, in which I fumbled for a visiting card: it had not occurred to me to use such a thing until I began to travel in India and discovered that there it was expected of me by virtually everyone on first acquaintance. I'd never yet managed to produce mine with the appropriately casual panache, however, and disliked the performance, which made me feel pompous, though I saw the point of it well enough. The young man studied the card carefully. "I'll take this to Father later," he said. "We shall be having coffee shortly. Do join us." He swept on and disappeared behind a line of someone's laundry hanging next to a herbaceous border. "The flowers are only for use in the temple," a notice said.

People appeared out of different doorways, simultaneously, as though the place were wired for the announcement of mealtimes and other seminal points in the day. Many of them were Indian, including a pair of nuns, but these were slightly outnumbered by the Westerners. I sauntered with them to a thatched rotunda in the middle of the compound, in time to hear a white girl with a European accent ask a coffee-coloured girl of indeterminate nationality, "Is that your natural skin colour?" As at the ashram of Amritananda Mayi in Kerala, young women were much more numerous than any other group of people in sight. I sat down next to a middle-aged Dutch couple and asked them why they thought this might be. "Because women find it easier to say what's in their hearts," she replied at once. Her husband nodded vigorously. "It's true. We men are trained from birth to be uptight, never to weep. Eventually we're crippled by it." I wasn't sure that this answered the question. What struck me was the number of young Western women who were in pairs, walked hand in hand and in other ways demonstrated great and mutual affection. Why were *they* so drawn to spiritual manifestations in the East? Why were they not hooked on the Camaldolese hermits in Italy? Or the Carthusians up above Grenoble? What *was* the essence of the failure in the West; and the obvious magnetism of the ashrams?

As quickly as it had assembled, the coffee break was concluded and people dispersed. Not one of them had questioned my purpose in being there. Left to potter undisturbed, I began to establish some bearings. The buildings of the ashram were all in pink-washed concrete, including a low-walled cowshed whose thatched roof sheltered a score or so of very healthy-looking Friesians munching grass, next to it a row of well-scrubbed flush latrines. As well as the rotunda, there was another circular construction which housed a decent and catholic library in several languages, ranging through some rigorous Christian and Hindu spirituality and theology, paying attention to other religions in passing, before relaxing into poetry and other forms of literature which extended from John Galsworthy to Lloyd C. Douglas. Deployed on all sides were dwellings, some of them rudimentary bungalows, others little more than thatched sheds. A number of these were dotted among the trees on the other side of the lane leading to the river, eremitical cells semi-isolated in the Forest of Peace.

And then there was the temple, approached from the lane through a gateway which was dignified by the title gopuram. It was, in fact, a small pink-washed arch proclaiming entrance to the Ashram of the Holy Trinity, which was topped by pastel-coloured plasterwork in the Tamil style, including two distinctly Renaissance angels with hands together in prayer, on either side of a three-headed and bearded Hindu figure representing the Creator, Preserver and Destroyer of the universe. The synthesis was even more apparent some yards beyond the gopuram, at the temple itself. This was mostly covered by a rectangular tiled roof with a shallow pitch, but the sanctuary rose to a highly ornate confection of plaster figures, a jolly affair painted in the manner of a Tamil vimana, which could very well have been the work of someone captivated by the riotous gaiety of the Madurai gopurams. At its base were the four beasts of the Apocalypse, lion, ox, man and eagle, separated by the figures of St Paul, St Peter, St Benedict and Mary Queen of Heaven. Above them were four representations of Christ, facing the cardinal compass points in different roles as priest and contemplative, prophet and king. The whole reached its apogee in the throne of God, depicted as a dome covered by peacock feathers, surmounted by a blossoming lotus and ultimately by a finial pointing to infinite space. Employing as it did all the more sickly colours in the spectrum, the entire effect was a visual equivalent of suffering from a surfeit of marzipan.

The interior was more controlled and more soothing. Pillars alone supported the temple's roof, so that it was virtually open at the sides. Apart from rattan mats which covered the floor, the interior was almost bare – until a token chancel step was introduced; but just in front of that a polished slab of floorstone had been decorated with an elaborate star of flower petals, from whose centre a tall brass incense holder arose. To the left of the step a couple of tablets were inset into the far wall: one to Jules Monchanin b 1895 d 1957, the other to Henri Le Saux b 1910 d 1973. Beyond the step was the narrow opening to the sanctuary, surmounted by the cross and wheel of the roadsign that linked three religions, the letters KYPIOC XPICTOC (The Lord Christ) and a Sanskrit quotation from the Upanishads which translated as "You are alone the supreme Being: there is no other Lord of the World." The semi-enclosed sanctuary had a stone-slab altar which put me in mind of the one de Foucauld built in his Saharan mountain hermitage at Assekrem, which had rung like a bell when I struck it sharply with my knuckle; but the altar at Shantivanam was mute and it was decorated not only with a crucifix but with the Sanskritic characters which spell the most sacred word of the Hindus.

The temple was scarcely ever empty: almost always at least one person was in there, squatting or kneeling on the mats, or sitting on the low boundary wall. Such initiates meditated in a silence that suffused the entire ashram, only emphasised by birdsong and by the occasional small country sounds of an oxcart lumbering slowly along the lane, and villagers wending their way to the river's pools. These, I noticed, spoke in low voices as they passed, deferring not only to a holy place but also to a local patron. Saccidananda's activities extended to a nursery school and two small spinning enterprises in the district. It owned ten acres in all and had cultivations there.

I myself sat beneath a palm between the temple and the gopuram, relishing the quiet stillness, which was the antithesis of almost every-thing I associated with people in India, secular and religious, whose characteristics are above all vibrant, restless, vivid, loud, dramatic;

and excessive. The one penetrating sound of that day came when someone strode up to a tree outside the temple and rang the bell hanging from a branch, as if to mark the end of a forenoon watch aboard ship. People converged from all directions, two score of them or so, until the shrine was filled with sitting or kneeling figures: who in unison at once intoned the sacred O ... M ... M ... M ... M ... M ... so that the building thrummed with resonance, as if a bow had been slowly drawn across a double bass.

As the choral note died, the sacred word was taken up solo by a saffron-robed priest, to begin a chant which the congregation then repeated.

> Om Jagadishvara sadapi chinmaya
> Jagadishvara vande ...*

For the next fifteen minutes the dialogue continued in the same way, with intonation and response between priest and congregation following each other like small waves rolling in from a tranquil sea. A passage of scripture was then read, and after another exchange of chants everyone stood with hands clasped above the head. The priest then performed aratti at the Blessed Sacrament, where this was reserved within the sanctuary, by flourishing a flame there before passing it through the congregation, so that all could warm their hands over it. This was a variant of the ceremony I had watched at the temple in Madurai, when the Lord Sundareswara was being made ready to spend the night with his consort Meenakshi; but to these people the flame symbolically manifested the hidden Christ in the sanctuary, its warmth then taking His light to their unseeing eyes. In India you could interpret almost anything in any way you wished.

It was the final act of midday prayer. The people filed out of the temple and headed for lunch – leaving me, a deliberate bystander from the outset, to lean against the palm tree and wonder what on earth I was going to say to Bede Griffiths if I were granted audience later on. I was feeling tongue-tied, oddly apart from this community, though in many ways it was more nearly my natural habitat than

* "Lord of the universe, O eternal consciousness ..."

anywhere I'd yet been on this journey. The car that had brought me after breakfast was returning to take me back to Tiruchy at teatime, but almost certainly I could stay the night or even a day or two here if I wanted to; yet I knew that unless something totally unforeseen happened now I would be leaving in a few hours. I couldn't bring the why into focus, though. Restlessly I went down to the riverside, but the villagers had left its pools and its sandbanks to the noonday heat, which throbbed unpleasantly out in the open. I retreated to the shade, where crows exchanged raucous confidences about what they could see from their lookouts in the trees above. Beside the ashram's boundary fence I discovered a small cemetery I hadn't noticed before. It contained four graves, three of them indecipherable. The other was marked in memory of Swami Amaldas, born 20.1.48, ordained priest 18.1.86, died 8.6.90.

Halfway through the afternoon I saw the tall figure in saffron coming along the river bank, the young acolyte who'd intercepted me hurrying to keep up with the older man's strides. I stood as Bede Griffiths came through the gopuram and we greeted each other like parodies of clubbable Englishmen. We didn't actually shake hands, but it was close.

"Mr Moorhouse, I'm so sorry to have kept you waiting. I'll be with you in five minutes."

"Please, not at all. I'm very sorry to have barged in on you without warning."

The voice was light and cultivated, would have been unexceptional in the cathedral close or the senior common room. But whatever its owner had been in the past he was now distinctly his own man, something between ascetic and patriarch. Hair and beard were long and silvery, body was spare and whippety, nose was vertical and hooked, eyes were both gentle and icily blue. His saffron kavi had fallen away from one thin shoulder, to expose a breast that was in contrast almost femininely full. I remembered seeing images that portrayed the Buddha like that.

He came looking for me shortly afterwards and led me to a thatched hut at the back of the compound, offered me a wicker chair and reclined beside me on a bed with his legs up. "Forgive me, but since the stroke in '89 I find this is the best relief for occasional numbness below the knee." He apologised again for having kept me waiting, and explained that he had been preparing lectures he was shortly to give in Australia, after going home briefly to England. "I have to speak at an environmental conference in Winchester, and I'm to be a lunchtime preacher at St James's, Piccadilly." I could visualise him easily in that most fashionable of Anglican pulpits, but I wondered how he would dress for the occasion.

The little room was unremarkable in its austerity. As well as the bed and the chair I was sitting on, there was a stool at a table under the window, a couple of cupboards, no other furniture. There was no glass in the windows on two walls of the room; only bars, and shutters which had been thrown open to admit the air. An ikon of Christ hung above the bed, a Maglite torch rested on the nearest window ledge. This was a traditional anchorite's cell, but its incumbent had not utterly abandoned the world, nor had it forgotten him. A stack of unopened aerogrammes from many countries awaited his attention on the table. The Dutch couple, not even knowing his name to start with, had tracked him down by, first of all, ringing their local telephone exchange in the Netherlands and asking the operator to help them find the English swami in South India.

We were chatting aimlessly about this and that, and I was beginning to feel fraudulent, though Bede Griffiths showed no impatience at my small talk, in a way even encouraged it. He told me about his impending trip to London and then I asked him how long he had been in India before he realised he would spend the rest of his life here. "From the moment I arrived," he said, "it never occurred to me that I would go home except for brief visits . . ."

"Are you any nearer to understanding the great mysteries of life and death as a result?" I asked. Much later, I wondered whether the question had flummoxed this wise old man by its very simplicity. He looked at me blankly, as though he hadn't a clue what I might be getting at.

And suddenly it all tumbled out, though it had not consciously crossed my mind until I opened my mouth again. I found myself telling him about my increasing difficulty in coping with the fact that my younger daughter had died just as she was beginning to realise how marvellous life could be, whereas I had been brought back from the dead when I had already had more than my fair share of fulfilment and good fortune. She was the third of our four children, sharp and vivacious, wilful and goodnatured, well aware of boys and how they were to be played, otherwise besotted with her horse; and in her seventeenth year she contracted an inoperable sarcoma which was first discovered in her lungs. She fell ill in the summer and she was dead before Christmas. For much of that time, with the help and encouragement of good doctors, her family nursed her at home because there was nothing any hospital could do for her that we could not do better: her parents and her step-parents, her sister and her two brothers. It was not a good back end to that year, but it wasn't all terrible: there was laughter as well as pain, and we all had the time to say things we needed to say to each other. And when December came, the boys and her step-father and I carried her to her grave in the village churchyard which faced, across a stream tumbling straight off the fell, the cottage in which Charles Kingsley wrote *The Water Babies*. That day, I thought I would never smile again. But gradually we all came to terms with losing Brigie, and got on with living as I believe we were meant to, with laughter as well. That had been ten years ago.

Four years later, out of the blue, I had a spectacular heart attack and crashed my car in the process. But for a couple of flukes, that would have been the end of me. A policewoman just happened to be coming down the road and at once radioed for an ambulance which, by preposterous coincidence, was only a few hundred yards away. When I was hauled from the wreckage, surprisingly undamaged by the crash, my heart had been stopped for a couple of minutes: which is about the time limit allowed under the Geneva Convention. The policewoman told the ambulancemen they could forget about me, because I had obviously gone; but they said they'd give it a go, and got the heart pumping again. They had to do this five more times before they trundled me into intensive care, where I remained in a coma for the next thirty-six hours. And eventually, after surgery, I was made whole again: with very small adjustments, I continued my life as before.

But why? Why had I been brought back from the dead to enjoy yet another helping at the age of fifty-four, when Brigie had scarcely been allowed time to appreciate how wonderful life could be – for everyone but her? I was unable to escape a feeling that I had been given, had virtually robbed her of, what was rightfully hers. The longer I lived the more I was tormented by a profound feeling of guilt, sometimes breaking down embarrassingly on hearing a tune, reading a phrase, seeing a gesture that connected these two terminals in my life and shattered me. There was music I dared not listen to any more. The small boy who tried to wink at me in Madurai had reduced me to tears. It was his innocence, of course; and the thought of all the hazards that awaited him.

I gave Bede Griffiths the bare bones of all this, and added that I was tormented as much as anything by the line from the Second Commandment about the sins of the fathers being visited upon the children; nothing to do with worshipping graven images in my case, but there were far too many other sins that I did plead guilty to.

He watched me gravely as I stumbled through this threnody, his blue eyes never leaving my face, his hands resting motionless upon his lap. I said that although I would gladly be relieved of the burden I needed even more to see, at whatever cost, some meaning in the conundrum of my gratuitously renewed life and my daughter's cruel death. At this he began to shake his head.

"But there is no meaning in the sense that troubles you. And you really mustn't think that you're enjoying life at her expense: that's simply the result of a particular philosophy we have inherited in the West, our logical minds trying to impose a pattern on everything, with certain expectations arising from particular circumstances. The fact is that there really is no such pattern. Life is a mystery and unless we approach it in that light we confuse ourselves and waste far too much of our spiritual energy."

There were voices outside, others who wanted his attention. Time for confession was over. As awkwardly as I had come, I got up to go. Bede Griffiths spoke once more in the voice that had been so carefully cultivated so long ago at the Blue-Coat School and Magdalen College, Oxford. "I've found, y'know, that it's not a bad idea to live each day as if 'twere thy last." His blue eyes searched me anxiously as he nodded, slowly, in dismissal. He had not once enquired about my faith or whether, indeed, I had any.

As I reached the door, I paused and looked back before going outside. He had raised his hand, and I think it was in blessing. "I shall pray for you," he said. I was thankful for that, too, though I did not believe Father Bede had just absolved me by indicating the limitations of Cartesian logic. My problem was not an intellectual one.

# *Tiruchirappalli*

Next day I met the Thondaimans, quite unprepared for what awaited me there. A young reporter from All-India Radio had interviewed me in Trivandrum and, on learning that I was expecting to be in Tiruchirappalli, gave me the name and telephone number of a friend of hers. I had asked whether she knew anyone who might talk to me about Tamil nationalism, which was said to be especially strong in and around Tiruchy. Meenambal Thondaiman, she said, was just the person I needed; a highly articulate and educated woman who knew everything that went on in the city and surrounding district. All-India Radio did not elaborate; so that I was a little mystified when the voice at the other end of the phone said it lived in the Pudukkottai Palace, "just up the road from your hotel". When I asked the girl on the desk whether that meant it was within walking distance, she looked amused and said that Pudukkottai was thirty miles away. Only because I was sure I hadn't misinterpreted the instructions did she go and check with her boss. She returned to tell me that the palace was just past the local Army barracks. Her expression said she'd never heard of it before.

I wasn't all that surprised by her ignorance when my auto-rickshaw had to cruise three times round a road junction before the driver was able to make up his mind which way to proceed. Two gateposts, but no gates, were almost lost in a welter of advertisements that someone had erected along the walltops on either side. The

Pudukkottai Palace was completely hidden behind gaudy billboards extolling TV sets, kitchen equipment, ceiling fans, cement and cigarettes, in both Tamil and English. We trailed blue smoke between them into a compound containing a lot of stray-looking dogs which loped among dusty trees, growling and barking at each other in the saturating heat. Beyond them I could at last see a three-storeyed building of undressed stone, which appeared more penal than palatial, with a crenellated roofline and bastions along the wall facing us, each pierced by slits that archers might have used. There were thirty or forty windows on that side of the building, all deeply inset in the stone, and I was only surprised that none seemed to be barred. It looked to me as if someone in nineteenth-century India had designed it after being given an imprecise description of castles and dungeons in medieval England. We swept round the other side, where the architect's imagination had been flexible enough to incorporate a porte-cochère, in which an Ambassador and a motorbike were already parked. As I paid off my driver, Meenambal Thondaiman came down the steps to greet me. She was an attractive woman with a wide smile, just filling out into her forties. "Come," she said, "let's go and have something cool to drink."

She led me from powerful sunlight into a hall illuminated by the spastic glare of colour television, which issued from a corner next to an empty pram. Stuffed heads, buffalo and tiger among them, had been mounted on the walls, with the guns and spears that had presumably been used to kill some of the animals. There was also a pair of elephant tusks curving up from the floor. We walked on into a sitting room with furniture that looked as if it had come out of a Gorringe's catalogue in the 1930s, deployed around bearskin and tigerskin rugs which still had roaring heads attached, all dominated by two huge paintings in heavy gilded frames that were beginning to disintegrate. In one, a young man in court dress was sitting on a throne, while a white-bearded fellow stood behind him, a complicated turban on his head and a royal blue sash over his shoulder, every inch the state chamberlain. I looked at Meenambal Thondaiman enquiringly. "Who's he?" I asked.

"That's the eighth Maharajah, Martanda Bhairava Thondaiman, the one who got into all that trouble with his marriage."

A penny suddenly dropped and she laughed at the expression on my face. "Yes, we were the only princely state in Tamil Nad', and he was our ancestor. We rated eleven guns in the old days."

That put Pudukkottai in the sixth tier of the Indian principalities, but most of the independent states weren't saluted with ceremonial British gunfire at all. In this case it would be partly to acknowledge the fact that the Thondaimans had allied themselves with the Raj at every conflict in the South from the time of Clive onwards.

I paused in front of the other oil, which pictured a blindfolded figure walking on fiery coals, watched by a man in a mitre who was making the sign of the cross.

"It's the Inquisition," said Meenambal. "We're not sure but we think it's Goya." I certainly couldn't tell, but it was well within the bounds of possibility; this subcontinent was full of priceless things from Europe that everyone but the owners had lost track of. Whoever the artist, his painting was in a desperate condition, the canvas having corrugated in the blistering climate of South India.

A servant came, bearing a tray of lime sodas, and with her came two snub-nosed and thickset men, also in their forties, whom Meenambal introduced as her brothers Raj and Ram. We started to talk contemporary politics and they told me much that I didn't know, including the origins of the Cauvery dispute, which began when a piece of British legislation expired. It had been designed to ensure that Cauvery water was shared throughout the area of the old imperial Madras state, and Karnataka had outsmarted Tamil Nadu in 1974, when the original terms might easily have been renewed by Delhi. "They were very careless," said Raj, who made it plain that he had a low opinion of politicians generally; "men who create false issues, simply to raise themselves on high."

"Our people," said Meenambal, "are moved by emotions much more than by thinking."

Yes, I thought, that was quite close to a royal "we".

As curious now about the Thondaimans as I had earlier been about the Tamils, I asked Meenambal what she did with herself all day in this large building. The answer seemed to be nothing very much except make the best of widowhood, though she had degrees in both English literature and zoology. Raj was also a zoologist, Ram was a botanist, while a third brother was a mechanical engineer. I wondered how many people, including whoever needed the pram, inhabited this considerable dwelling.

"I suppose there must be a dozen of us living here all the time," she said, "but there are others who come and go." She giggled at the untidiness of it all.

"Classic extended family," I exclaimed. "Who has been the head since the Rajah died?"

"Oh, but my uncle is still alive. Would you like to meet him?"

My earlier failure to inspect the royal house of Travancore on its own patch was no longer even a matter of regret. And this man, surely, must be the only prince still alive who had ruled his people in the traditional way, who had wielded feudal powers, before Indian independence brought that period of her history to an end. He must be extremely old by now, a living antique.

One of the brothers got up and went to find out whether the last ruler of Pudukkottai was prepared to receive a visitor that day. While he was out, his two siblings outlined the history of the Thondaimans, from the accession of the young man enthroned on the wall behind them.* Martanda was descended from the Kallars, originally a caste of robbers who had seized a great deal of land and ruled its population like any other medieval princes. The Thondaimans specialised in catching elephants and bartering their tusks for grain. They achieved respectability in alliance with the Nawab of Arcot and eventually with the British East India Company, when this needed all the native friends it could muster in its rivalry with the French. In the eighteenth century the Thondaimans could very usefully raise 1,500 cavalry and 3,000 footsoldiers, sometimes putting as many as 8,000 troops and camp followers into the field, with every horseman accompanied by his personal grass-cutter.

By the time Martanda ascended the gadi in 1886, when he was eleven, the old martial glory had gone for ever and Pudukkottai was merely one of 500-odd client states of the British, unique only in the land of the Tamils. Its army by then consisted of nineteen horsemen who formed the royal escort and 110 infantry who guarded the

* Some of what follows I culled from *A Manual of the Pudukkottai State*, by K. R. Venkatarama Aiyar (Pudukkottai, 2nd ed, 1938), which the Thondaiman family kindly lent me that week; and some material I gleaned from official papers in the India Office Library when I returned to England.

palaces and the royal treasury. But its new ruler had inherited a domestic establishment almost ten times that size, including no fewer than five bands of musicians, one of them described as "a Mohammedan orchestra of cymbals, pipes and drums", which played every morning and afternoon at the entrance to the New Palace in Pudukkottai city, to the south of Tiruchy. This contained a kitchen manned by Brahmins who cooked vegetarian food and another staffed by non-Brahmins who would handle meats. There was a separate Menial Establishment headed by a major-domo known as the Pan-servai, because it was he who handed the betel leaf and areca nut to His Highness after a meal. And a Dignity Establishment consisting of umbrella-bearers, torch-bearers, bearers of javelins, victory drums and figures of two-headed eagles; a Chowri and a Chamaram, who carried the Yak-tail and the Whisk respectively; the Kattiyakaran, who recited laudatory verses on public occasions; and a court jester who was also the royal story-teller.

Martanda eventually turned his back on this sumptuous anachronism and in doing so discountenanced the British, who allowed Indian princes to be independent of imperial rule only up to a point. Their requirements certainly included reliable alliance, and after the Indian Mutiny this was never tested; the Nizam of Hyderabad, indeed, gloried in many extravagant titles but in none more than Faithful Ally of the British Government. Martanda had already disturbed the imperial equilibrium in his late twenties when he had an affair with the wife of a Major Reid, whom the authorities identified as a cad who was using the lady as bait in order to blackmail the young ruler; the British believed in the stability of their allies, and they preferred them to lead lives that would not offend their own subjects. Martanda was not quite measuring up to expectations, even after Major Reid had been rumbled and the affair was stopped; the ruler was spending too much of his little realm's substance on jollies around Europe and even further afield, and he was neglecting affairs of state at home. His people were beginning to talk. The British did not like disaffected populations on the subcontinent, even outside the areas of their direct rule, when the disaffection was against native princes and not against themselves. Inflammation had a disobliging habit of spreading uncontrollably in this part of the world.

Eventually, the Rajah of Pudukkottai went too far: he fell in love with Esme Molly Fink, the daughter of an Australian lawyer, and in Sydney in the summer of 1915 he married her. No less a person than the Secretary of State for India, Austen Chamberlain, went out of his way to tell the Viceroy, Lord Chelmsford, that "the lady is of irreproachable character and belongs to a respected family in Australia, known to the Governor-General . . ." This was not allowed to impede prejudice on the subcontinent, however. Memoranda were soon shuttling to and fro between London, Delhi and the British Resident for the Madras States, as members of the Indian civil service, the India Office and their political masters wrestled with this appalling new threat to the status quo in a small and obscure corner of South Asia. Someone ordained that the former Miss Fink must not be styled Her Highness in either official or unofficial communications; someone else decreed that Viceroys, Governors, Lieutenant-Governors and Residents "are debarred absolutely from meeting or receiving the lady, even on unofficial occasions . . ." The British Resident reported from Pudukkottai that "Enquiries showed there was reason to believe that, although such a wife might be received in the State during the Raja's lifetime with respect, yet the marriage would probably not be regarded as valid by orthodox opinion in the caste to which His Highness belongs; that the idea of the Raja being succeeded by a child of such a marriage would be strongly resisted and disliked, and that on the Raja's death the succession would probably be questioned by the other members of the ruling family." At least the Resident had a point.

The game was finally up when Martanda Sydney Thondaiman was born in his mother's home town eleven months after the marriage, though the dénouement took a little longer. Given the climate of opinion in India, it is scarcely surprising that the beleaguered little family continued to spend a great deal of their time abroad, where they now had several homes, though they were always given due homage by the Rajah's subjects on their infrequent visits to Pudukkottai. The British writhed with indecision until 1921, when the Government of India finally ruled out the possibility of the wife and son being recognised. Plaintively, the Rajah noted at about this time that "My son's succession is barred and I am given to understand that I cannot adopt as I have a natural heir." He then offered his imperial patrons three solutions to the predicament they insisted he was in: the annexation of his state and its incorporation into British India; his own abdication; or his withdrawal to England and the establishment of a regency. "In some respects," the Chief Secretary of the Madras Government observed, "annexation might provide the simplest means of escape from the unfortunate position in which His Highness is placed, but it would arouse a good deal of local opposition and . . . the Government of India and the Secretary of State will probably be unwilling to consider it until the other possible methods have been examined." Shortly afterwards, Delhi chose the third option and the Thondaimans went into exile. Seven years later Martanda was dead, leaving twenty lakhs of rupees and the proceeds of a villa in Cannes to be divided between his wife and son, who spent the rest of their lives in Australia and England. Sydney died in London in 1981.

The regency lasted as long as the eighth Rajah was alive, but in November 1928, six months after his death, the government of India "after anxious consideration" announced that he was to be succeeded by a collateral descendant, a great-nephew who was then a child of six living with his parents in the Western Palace at Pudukkottai. There was, of course, no question of his assuming real authority straight away: and for most of the period until he came of age the affairs of the state were conducted by an Administrator, who was a member of the Indian Civil Service, an Englishman. In the meantime, the young prince was to be educated – again by people from Great Britain – in the regal arts and the craft of government. To mark his long-delayed accession in the penultimate year of the Second World War, he presented an aeroplane to the RAF, "in token of my loyalty to His Majesty King George VI". If his upbringing had been in the hands of Jesuits rather than the ICS, they couldn't possibly have schemed a more predictable outcome.

Ram returned to say that their uncle would be very happy to see me straight away. I was led out of the palace and across the compound at the back, where the dogs now lay prone and panting under the trees. We walked towards a low range of buildings that looked as if they might be stables, with a Land-rover and what could have been the original Willys Jeep parked outside. A number of men seemed to be waiting for something to happen, but stirred involuntarily as we approached, then saluted and grinned at one and the same time, with the mixture of affection and subservience that usually characterises the inferior greeting his master in India. Ram gestured to an open doorway, then turned and left me to fend for myself. I walked into a spacious area where a nondescript figure in slacks was bent over a piece of machinery under neon lights. I was about to ask him where I could find His Highness when he heard my step, straightened up, wiped his hands on an oily rag and came forward to greet me.

It was not quite the setting I had expected for an encounter with Sri Brihadamba Das Raja Rajagopala Thondaiman Bahadur; nor did the ninth and last Rajah of Pudukkottai look at all like an antique. This elderly Indian, with grey stubble where a beard might have been, was slender and supple, and he moved easily across the floor. He was surrounded by lathes, jigs, drills and all the tooling that would have fitted nicely into any small industrial workshop in the Black Country of the English Midlands. The maker's name on the biggest piece was, in fact, Willson of Birmingham. The place smelt of engine oil and warm iron filings.

"It's amazing," I said. "This is your hobby?"

His head wobbled fractionally, almost apologetically. "I get a great deal of pleasure from it." He spoke perfect English with the merest trace of accent, but very softly and diffidently. Every gesture he made was restrained, until he touched his machinery. Only then did he seem utterly sure of himself.

"Come, let me show you," he said, leading me out into the yard with something approaching authority. He raised the bonnet of the Jeep and contemplated the engine with a gleam in his eye. "Yes, it is one of the first production models. I have restored her and converted the engine from petrol to diesel. That is more economical." We went back inside. "And that is a four-kilowatt generator I have just finished for the estate up at Kodaikanal. It will run when my windmill is becalmed. I installed that last year." He really was proud of having made these useful things. He was the very model of the shy and obsessive inventor, the one who is teased for blushing if a girl so much as speaks to him, but is pursued by the most attractive and the kindest of them, who is desperate to mother him and gets him towards the end of the script. I couldn't imagine him behaving regally anywhere, certainly not issuing edicts from the throne to a council of apprehensive courtiers. Gandhi used to call him Rajah Rishi, the Ascetic Prince.

He led me to a corner of the workshop, where a number of Hindu deities in gaudy bazaar colours were framed in tin on the wall. An incense holder stood on a toolbox before them. His Highness bore Lord Shiva's mark in grey ash on his forehead. He indicated that I should sit on a wooden chair after he had laid a clean cloth there, then drew up another one opposite.

I dared to say what had gradually been dawning on me. "You really would rather have been a mechanic than ruler of a princely state, wouldn't you?"

A sweet smile crept over his face, and for a moment his eyes seemed less tired, less pouched with wear and tear. Then came the diffident inclination of the head again. "My mother was a very old-fashioned lady and it would have broken her heart."

His mother had a lot to answer for; or so the British invigilators of the Thondaimans reckoned. Widowed the year after the child-prince was chosen to succeed his kinsman, she emerges in the official correspondence as a manipulative neurotic who dominated her eight children and whose chief priority was to secure the best possible terms for herself by exerting all her crushing influence on her eldest – and now most valuable – son. She suffered from nothing worse than mild anaemia, but went into deep melancholia whenever she was crossed, claimed to be maddened by hallucinations, or simply threw hysterical fits; as when she learned that her personal allowance was not to be increased by as much as she had hoped. On one occasion, when the adolescent prince had to go to the hills for the sake of his none too robust health, she berated him for cruelly leaving her to die in the palace. One official said plainly that "the Raja does, in my opinion, labour under one special and serious disability, namely, that he is under the thumb of his Mother, an illiterate and ignorant woman who is really not a whit superior in any way to any ordinary coolie." He was also of the opinion that the young Rajah ought to have more money to spend: "in itself a form of education, though I fear that most of it would find its way into Mother's coffers." The same man also despaired of her attempts to influence the Rajah's native ministers, concluding that "if he married, that *might* help to solve the problem presented by

Mother . . ." Janaki Ayi was herself hoping that a royal alliance might be arranged for her son and fruitlessly canvassed the kingdom of Nepal. But the British Resident reported that when a Patiala bride from the Punjab was suggested as a distinct possibility in the Rajah's twenty-first year, "he showed no desire to marry". And a bachelor he remained, marked for life, no doubt, by the mother who did not die until he was thirty-three.

I asked him what it had been like to be reared by the British as much as by his own family, and for a moment I saw caution in his eyes. There was first of all an Englishwoman, but he had almost no recollection of her. An official account recorded that "As soon as Miss Thompson joined duty as Lady Tutor to HH, there was general apprehension that, under European training, HH might lose his faith in the Hindu religion and adopt Western manners and customs when he comes of age, as it was believed that training under a European Tutor was mainly responsible for the late Ruler adopting European habits of life, staying abroad most of his time and marrying an Australian lady." Nevertheless, the tutelage went ahead and after the young prince had outgrown Miss Thompson he was taken in hand by Captain Harvey, in 1932.

"He was very good cricketer," the Rajah told me. "All-England player, I believe. He coached me and made me quite a useful all-rounder." There were small calluses on two fingers of his right hand that could have been caused by spinning the ball long ago. He had been good enough to play for Tamil Nadu.

Captain Harvey was also charged with matters much more serious than cricket. "Sir Alexander Tottenham intends the Raja should study the system from top to bottom beginning with Village Accounts," according to another memo, which was composed as the prince's majority – and his responsibilities – approached.

From September, when the weather is cooler, the Raja will go out in the mornings for some months with the Village Accountant in the fields and see how cultivation is recorded, encroachments booked, extra charges levied for unauthorised irrigation and so on . . . Captain Harvey will study with him part of the Darbar's Standing Orders and the Settlement Report, and various other Manuals and Rules . . . The Raja will also study the Indian Penal Code, the Criminal Procedure Code and selected State Regulations . . . It is also proposed to arrange for him to try some criminal cases at Kodaikanal next year. Meanwhile, Captain Harvey will continue his instruction in English, concentrating on conversations, elocution, and the writing of letters on various subjects ... His Highness will read the English newspapers and record his impressions of important events, political occurrences and so forth. He will continue to study Sanskrit, Tamil and Urdu ...

"Ah, Sir Alexander Tott-en-ham," said the Rajah, faintly smiling at his memory. "He was a very capable Administrator."

No doubt, but he was also regarded by some of his British colleagues as not much less of a trial than the young prince's mother: the two, in fact, probably recognised each other on sight as competitors, if not sworn enemies. He came out of a familiar mould which had long shaped many of the men who were to rule India: Clifton College and a good Oxford degree before passing the difficult ICS exam. He had just retired from the service when he was appointed Administrator, and when the prince came of age he merely stayed on as his Diwan, Chief Minister of Pudukkottai. Just before that happened a confidential memo from Delhi to London noted that "it looks as if Sir Alexander Tottenham is arranging to keep all the powers in his own hands when the Raja has taken over the reins of administration ... I am also to ask you kindly to make it clear to Sir A, that from now onwards his principal duty will be to put the Raja forward as Ruler of the State and to do everything in his power to develop any capacity he may possess." Sir Alexander had just recommended that the Rajah's accession should be delayed until after the war. His recommendation being rejected, the Administrator simply changed hats and carried on as before. Someone in Delhi then remarked that "Sir Alexander is a remarkable man who recalls the earlier type of Company's Political Officer, such as Sir Mark Cotton in Mysore ..." This was not a fulsome compliment. Another voice added that "The Resident will have to keep a close eye on Sir Alexander Tottenham, who will submit with reluctance to a self-effacing ordinance. He has maintained his vigour and efficiency to an unusual age in India. But the Raja must have his powers and learn the exercise of them if he is ever to be more than a figurehead."

Sir Alexander was seventy-one at the time and had spent half a century in India, with only occasional home leaves in the land that had long since ceased to be his home. Three years later he went to

England on sick leave, had terminal cancer diagnosed, and caught the next boat back to Bombay. When he got off the train at Pudukkottai he said he'd come to lay his bones where they belonged; and did so, only two days afterwards. His royal protégé gave him a state funeral, and had him buried at the Lutheran church with every honour that Pudukkottai could bestow.

The British Resident, who stood apart from the life at court and the politics of the state but kept an official eye on everything that happened there, characterised the young Rajah at this time as "not a very attractive young man, and seems to be somewhat apathetic". Eighteen months later the same man wrote that "The Raja has grown in knowledge and experience and seems to have found his feet. He now shows a much greater degree of confidence and self-reliance, and is readier and more able to discuss affairs." An overwhelming incubus had been removed from his life; but it was nine more years before he was free of the other one.

"Do you spend much time in Pudukkottai these days?" I asked.

"Very rarely. I no longer have land there and the New Palace became the Collector's Office; the old one was pulled down. The temple still belongs to me but that is all." He gestured towards the compound buildings. "There is just this place and my property at Kodaikanal. It is very beautiful up there. Have you been?"

No, I hadn't. And hill stations didn't figure in my plans this trip.

"I am going tomorrow. You are most welcome to come."

I returned to the palace, where Meenambal was awaiting me. "Did he tell you that he was the only prince who paid what the government demanded when the settlement was made after Independence? All the others made sure their treasuries were empty when the collections were made – they'd salted everything away somewhere else. But he paid sixty-three lakhs." No, he hadn't told me that; and it would have been a tidy sum in 1947. "Did he not even tell you how the people rioted when they heard that we were going to be ruled from Delhi, the only independent state in Tamil Nadu, and that he jumped on top of the palace wall and told them to stay calm?" No, he hadn't told me that either. She shook her head in mock despair. "Then he certainly won't have told you that he was asked if he would be Governor of Madras a few years after Independence, but refused."

"No, Meenambal, he didn't tell me any of these things. I'm afraid I had him talking mostly about the British time."

She laughed aloud. "He's such a modest man," she said.

I could see that, and more. He was a very unusual man; possibly unique among princes.

We set off just as light was beginning to creep towards the Rock above Tiruchy, our small convoy going before it through the almost deserted streets. His Highness, his face freshly shaved and with a new mark to honour Lord Shiva on his brow, sat beside the driver of the Land-rover, with Ram and me behind him and three retainers with iceboxes and other tackle in the back. Buzzing sturdily in our wake came the Jeep, carrying other men. Our vehicle obviously belonged to someone with a mania for useful devices: not only was the Land-rover air-conditioned but the dashboard was equipped with a number of gadgets that had been owner-installed, including a barometer and a compass mounted on gimbals that might have been expected to spend its life at sea. As we emerged from the suburbs of Tiruchy and struck the highway beyond, the needle steadied on a course of 240 degrees, and the light began to overtake us from the east.

I soon realised that it was not going to be a conversational journey. The Rajah sat with his hands on his lap, rarely moving except to make a small restraining gesture when the driver wanted to overtake someone riskily. He seldom took his eyes off the road in front, but once half turned to me and, pointing out of the window, uttered the word "Peacock". Nearly an hour later, as we rumbled round the outskirts of a town, he did the same thing, but this time it was "District Headquarters". Wishing at all costs to keep my end up, I nodded intelligently, cleared my throat suggestively, and released an "Ah" into the atmosphere. Ram clearly knew the form for expeditions with his royal uncle and spent a lot of the time dozing off beside me. We would have been wrapped in an amiable silence if it hadn't been for the excruciating traffic noise of India, where klaxons and horns never fail to blast the eardrums whenever people pass or overtake each other. Our man gave that peculiarly offensive tantivy that is aimed at the fellow in front and means "Get out of the way, mate." The truck driver ahead deliberately took his time before moving over and waving us past with a soothing motion. It underlined the caustic message painted in gypsy colours across his tailboard: "We Two Have One".

I settled for watching our progress across an unfamiliar part of the Tamil flatlands. This was well-cultivated ground, and almost every field that didn't have a standing crop of maize or sugar cane or vegetables was being worked by tractors or by oxen yoked in pairs. The crops were guarded by the most imaginative scarecrows I'd ever seen, dressed as elaborately as ambitious representations of Guy Fawkes on Bonfire Night at home. A female figure in a sari was crossing one field without moving an inch, and shortly afterwards a man could be seen hanging from a tree with a very broken neck. On the edge of another cultivation, two brown horses in terracotta stood side by side on a patch of ground that deliberately hadn't been sown: these were not scarecrows but ayyanars, guardian angels who protect the villages of Tamil Nadu from thieves, evil spirits, sickness or natural calamities, and are worshipped fervently by devotees bearing gifts. We had been travelling for well over a couple of hours by then.

The hills gradually hove into view, and through the haze of mid-morning their jagged ridges became more distinct as we closed in on them, their flanks were more obviously covered in scrub. We left the main road and turned towards these highlands, but stopped when we had gone no more than a mile. Everyone dismounted to pump ship and everyone, I noticed, chose a separate spot among the bushes, where he wouldn't be visible to anyone else. When I regained the road, His Highness strolled over to ask whether I'd like some fruit or a cold drink; just as he'd enquired whether I'd care to take some breakfast before we set off. At that moment our driver called him sharply back to the Land-rover, unlatching the bonnet as he did so. The first head under it when it was raised was the Rajah of Pudukkottai's, and when he straightened up he had the dipstick in his hand, and a piece of cotton waste. I could see what the problem was: we'd lost a lot of oil, some of which now lay in a puddle on the ground.

A consultation formed round the royal mechanic, and Ram came out of it to indicate that I should board the Jeep. "We'll go on to Kodai in this," he said. "Highness will fix that himself when it's cooled down." It occurred to me that Highness might have quite a wait in the mounting heat of nine o'clock.

We roared off into the hills and a drive which had become a little tedious was now exciting and spectacular. The plain fell away to our left as sharply as if we were in a bucking light aircraft which had just taken off. What had seemed mere scrub at a distance was revealed as thick afforestation, which the government had liberally plastered with environmental propaganda: "Trees mean Rain. Rain means Food. Food means Prosperity" was a typical hoarding. As we wound our way up steep gradients and swivelled round hairpin bends the hills enclosed us tightly and the air became more deliciously cool than anything I'd known since leaving home six weeks earlier. There were also many more monkeys than I'd yet seen on this journey, Nilgiri langurs according to Ram, which broke off picking nits out of each other's fur to scrutinise us as we zipped past, or bounded across the road as soon as we had gone. The invigorating climate had also attracted the educationists, with one private school after another perched on little plateaux, most of them evidently run by Christian religious orders; but the biggest establishment of all was a Jesuit seminary just before we reached Kodaikanal.

The little town was draped across a couple of ridges at something over 6,000 feet, high enough for it to be above a cloud which was fingering its way along a valley before feeling the nearest hillside and then stroking the very top, so that part of Kodai briefly vanished in a dank swirl of mist almost as soon as we arrived. When this cleared it was apparent that almost everyone who lived here enjoyed stunning panoramas across deep clefts in the hills: the dwellings were made of stone or clapboard and most of them were poised where no one else could block the view. We slowly beat the bounds, dismounting a couple of times so that I might get some sense of the place. The town centre stood beside a small expanse of water with boating sheds on one side and a hill curving round opposite. On the outskirts Ram wanted me to admire a famous waterfall, but by the time we got there it, too, was hidden in mist, so we went instead to see the drop straight to the valley floor from the edge of Suicide Leap, a name now discouraged locally because it had evidently become an incitement. Kodaikanal was nearly all ups and downs, much more exposed than, say, Ootacamund. The air was not only clean and – now that we weren't charging through it in the Jeep – pleasantly warm just after noon, but it was scented with pine and the fragrance of woodsmoke rising from domestic hearths. There were gardens full of colourful trees and shrubs, and it reminded me a little of the English Lake District as it was before the modern tourist industry disfigured it. We might have been somewhere high above Borrowdale forty years ago.

"It is much more beautiful than the other place, don't you think?" said Ram, wrinkling his snub nose at the mere thought of Snooty Ooty. "But the tourists are beginning to come in quantity here also and there is growing litter problem as a result." He hadn't waited for me to endorse or reject his preference. "There are developments we are not completely happy with." He pointed to an area on the hillside opposite, which had been staked out for holiday homes. "If you come back in ten years, this may be as crowded and dirty as Ooty."

We were by this time standing on a terrace in front of a house named Nutshell, one of several bungalows spread across the Thondaiman compound. Ram led me on a tour of inspection through rooms that had obviously radiated comfy wealth once, but now reeked of moth-eaten neglect. There were flyblown lithographs of Kodai on the walls, and on one of the floors a huge tigerskin was stretched, looking much the worse for wear. A conservatory sheltered a stuffed and standing tiger which had also seen better days.

"Were they hunted by the same gun that provided the rugs down in Tiruchy?"

Ram's head wobbled assent. "Highness was crack shot in his younger days. He was always in demand to get rid of dangerous animals, rogue elephants and man-eaters and so forth." His hand rested on the stuffed trophy. "He was called out to pursue this one after it had killed a cow. He spent a night in a tree above the fifteenth green at the golf course here, and he shot it when it came to take the tethered goat. He also dealt with fourteen rogue elephants in the course of time. But then he started taking pictures instead."

I wondered why, as Ram led me past the tiger and a quantity of freshly dhobeyed clothes that were waiting to be ironed. "Let us go for lunch," he said.

We crossed the compound to another bungalow, to be greeted

there by a young man to whom I was not introduced but who was clearly part of this extended family. His wife appeared and apologised for the meal we were about to have, saying that the telegram announcing us had only arrived two hours earlier, though it had been despatched the night before. "It is common occurrence," said Ram.

My young host, after I'd casually mentioned an interest in sport, talked shooting throughout the meal, which meant that he was conducting a monologue, and I switched off after he'd complained, for the second time, that shotgun cartridges now cost thirty-five rupees apiece, which was indeed stiff: it would have taken the average Indian wage-earner the best part of three days to raise that.

"Duleepsinhji spent a whole year in this house," said Ram, trying to remove the glaze from my eyes, "when he was convalescing from illness. He and Highness were great friends, united by their love of cricket."

I looked at my watch. I was thinking that Highness was now worryingly delayed by the Land-rover's oil leak. Tentatively, I enquired when he was expected to catch up. "Oh no," said Ram. "He is not coming *here*. He's gone to his estate over the other side of the hill. He has some business to attend to there."

I communicated my second "Ah" of the day, and hoped it didn't sound too baffled.

We said farewell to our young hosts amid expressions of mutual esteem, and returned to Nutshell, settling into deep armchairs beside the tigerskin rug. Whereupon a new character appeared on the scene, approximately the same age as Ram, with something of the same looks, who introduced himself as – I thought – Weearti. This was not a name I had come across before on the subcontinent and I must have looked puzzled, because he grinned and whipped out of his pocket a visiting card:

V.R.T. Dorairaja B.E.
Proprietor
Sri Brahadambal Industries
(Govt Approved)
Automobile & General Engineering Workshop

So this was the third of the brothers, and the one most closely following in the royal footsteps; using Highness's first name, indeed, as a hallmark for his business. His entrance was the cue for a general exchange of cards, from which I learned that Ram was not only a botanist, but a building contractor and a local pillar of Rotary.

I asked about the young gunslinger's position and was told that he was a great-nephew, quite likely to finish as head of the family one day, if certain matters could be satisfactorily resolved. "It is very complicated," said Ram. "Genealogists in London are trying to sort out the question of inheritance. They have been working at it for years." He sounded wistful. Another legacy from Martanda's marriage and subsequent issue, no doubt.

And then there was the matter of compensating all the Indian princes for the assets they lost after 1947. "We have had very raw deal from our government," said V.R.T., his head wobbling adamantly. "Since 1971, Supreme Court has been reviewing our claims, and it could easily be another twenty years before they publish their findings." Ram nodded his agreement vigorously.

"Let us take boat out on lake," Ram said, in a way that brooked no dissent from me. "Everyone in the family is a member of the boat club," he went on, "and we may have craft any time we wish." He made it sound as if this was one of the more rarefied privileges in Kodaikanal.

What we ended up in was an ungainly little tub, with Ram and me in tandem, pedalling maniacally. I hadn't felt so exposed to ridicule since I was ten years old and my mother insisted on sharing my intrepid voyage across the boating lake at Morecambe. Side by side we sat, with our knees revolving under our chins, our noses stuck haughtily in the air so that we resembled a pair of amphibious camels. As we plodded across this placid pond, kneecaps cracking like castanets whenever we put on a spurt to avoid some heedless oarsman, my eyes fell upon a line of pony-trekkers who were wending their way round the water's edge, watching us intently. A middle-aged and overweight Indian in a toy boat, I imagined, might not have excited more than passing interest. But when he was shipmates to a bald and woebegone European, this was a more complicated form of arrested development and merited careful study. It was the stuff of intriguing rumour.

"This is very agreeable," said Ram, pedalling contentedly. At which I let loose my third "Ah" into a declining afternoon.

We returned to Nutshell and a cup of tea. It was by now five o'clock and, faced with a return journey of well over four hours, I wondered aloud when we might be setting off back to Tiruchy. "I am staying here for night," said Ram, "but arrangements will be made for you presently." I stifled another "Ah" before it could even think of saying so.

The two brothers and I finished our tea, but conversation continued, in my case haltingly. Ram excused himself and left the room, returned after ten minutes, and sat down again. Would I like some more tea? he asked. No, thank you, I said. I thought I ought to be on my way, if that was okay by them. "Of course," said Ram. "It will be very soon now."

Fifteen more minutes passed and I was fidgeting. What on earth were we waiting for? Ram left the room once more, and when he returned his head wobbled happily. "The vehicle is ready now. Driver had to get tank topped up."

It was dark by the time the jeep reached the plain again, with me hanging on to a stanchion beside the driver, and an old retainer crouched at my back; and even our speed could not cool the sticky night air of the flatlands, as this gusted through the open sides of the vehicle. It wasn't far off midnight by the time we reached Tiruchy and I was dropped off at my hotel, bone weary from our bouncing progress along the uneven roads. Time after time I had been slammed against the side of the jeep as it swerved to avoid bullock carts that, at best, had nothing more luminous than a storm lantern with a guttering flame swinging above the back axle; and my eyes were stinging from a combination of dust and the glare of oncoming headlights. A couple of days later, when I went to say farewell to Meenambal Thondaiman and Highness, and to return a book I'd borrowed, I reckoned that my departure from Kodai had been regulated by the Rajah's from his estate, delayed so that we could back up the royal Land-rover if it broke down again. Highness told me that he had returned to the palace only half an hour or so before I got in that night.

He was in his workshop, naturally, and he greeted me as before, cleaning a chair for me to sit down. He was, among other things, a very gentle man. "You didn't tell me you were a photographer, too," I said, after he had described the running repairs he had made and his uneventful journey home.

"Oh, yes," he replied, pleased and slightly embarrassed. "But not humans; only animals."

"I know. Why did you stop hunting them?"

A spasm of real pain crossed his face, and I wished I hadn't asked.

His eyes left mine and he looked out at the Land-rover, standing in the yard with its bonnet propped up, as though for the moment he could only face the inanimate.

"I used to be called by the villagers to track rogue elephants which damaged crops and were also dangerous. I did this many times, and I thought that shooting them was the best thing to be done. The villagers were my people." He said this very slowly, uttering each word distinctly, with a longer pause between each phrase.

"Always I had killed them with just one shot. But the last one I only wounded." He was struggling for the words now.

"As it stood there two other elephants came out of the trees. One of them pushed it and the other pulled it towards a nearby waterhole. And there they bathed its wound by squirting water from their trunks. They also took leaves from the trees and gave it these to eat." He made a hopeless little gesture with his hands.

"It was terrible, terrible. I had to put it out of its misery, but that was the last time I touched a gun. Thirty years ago."

He shook his head very slowly, as wretchedly sad as anyone I'd ever known. There was nothing I could tell him that would have helped.

He sat looking at his hands in silence until I got up. "I wouldn't have missed all this for anything," I said. "Thank you for being so kind."

He rose from his chair and gave me namasti with his palms together in front of his face. "God go with you," he said.

# *Pondicherry*

I saw the sea again, for the first time since leaving Cochin, when I was bowling along the Rue de la Marine in a cycle-rickshaw, trying to find somewhere to stay. The lightest of onshore breezes was enough to make the little man in the saddle stand up and tread harder on his pedals; and there, as we cleared a tennis court straddling the bottom of the street, were milky rollers coming in off the Bay of Bengal. I was exhilarated by this as much as if I had just crossed the subcontinent at its widest latitude instead of almost its narrowest.

We turned south along the Cours Chabrol, where one villa after another had an uninterrupted view of the ocean across a great width of promenade, and finally fetched up two blocks inland on the Rue Romain Rolland. There were many street names in Pondicherry to remind everyone of the French connection. Along that promenade there was also a statue of Clive's old adversary, Joseph François Dupleix, and a memorial:

> Aux Combattants
> Des Indes Françaises
> Morts Pour La Patrie
> 1914–1918

What had once been l'Hôtel de Ville, opposite a pleasant little public park, was now the local headquarters of the Union government,

which for more than a generation had administered the old colony
direct from New Delhi, so that it remained what it had been for
more than 300 years: a small peculiar which did not kowtow to the
provincial authorities in Madras. At the gate stood a sentry wearing
a smart red kepi, like every other policeman in town, but nowhere
else in Tamil Nadu or in the country at large. This was another
souvenir of a past which began in 1672, when the French bought a
village here from the Rajah of Bijapur, and did not end until 1954,
when they left India as gracefully as the British had already done
seven years earlier.* Pondicherry was obviously as Indian now as
anywhere else in the republic: but at the same time there was an
ambience, something about the pattern of the streets, something
that included the climate, the strong light, the bougainvillaea and
the other vivid flowers, as well as all the tangible souvenirs of
relationship, that would have made me feel even more at home here
if I had been French, especially a Frenchman from Montpellier,
Béziers or somewhere else in that coastal region curving round to
Spain.

The souvenir I became most familiar with was Le Grand Hôtel
d'Europe, which had been built in the nineteenth century as the
town house of a celebrated local avocat, Camille Guerre. It
subsequently passed into the hands of the Magry family, whose
ancestor had sailed here from Marseilles in the days when Paris
was confident that Governor Dupleix would outflank the acquisitive
British and lay the foundations of a French empire in India. Many
a young Englishman, also hungry for adventure and a fortune at
the end of it, was simultaneously shipping out of Blackwall aboard
some three-master from the fleet of East Indiamen, bound for a start
as clerk in the Honourable Company's enterprises at Madras or
Calcutta. Robert Clive was such a one, before he got his big break
when the French attacked Madras and the British besieged Pondicherry in 1746.

There was nothing particularly grand about the Hôtel d'Europe
any more, but for a week it provided me with decent shelter, endless

---

* The Portuguese colonisation of the subcontinent, which began long before either the
British or the French arrived, outlasted both of them. Lisbon did not give up its claims
to Goa and other enclaves until the Indian Army marched on them in 1961.

and sometimes unexpected entertainment and victuals that were balanced – often surprisingly – between the cuisines of the Rive Gauche and the Coromandel coast. I occupied quarters that were spartan, dusty and stuffy despite a fan working; and the mosquito net made things even more stifling. The net had several small tears in it, which someone had patched with Scotch tape.

The public room, on the other hand, was splendid. It had presumably been M Guerre's salon, where he would relax after a hard day in court or after dining more agreeably than was good for any European in that climate. Now it was both the lounge and the dining room, open to the garden along one side, plentifully supplied with luxuriant pot plants of its own, so that each area seemed to flow naturally into the other. It reminded me a little of a gently mocking number that Flanders and Swann used to sing: "We're frightfully House and Gardens at Number Seventeen . . ." The furniture was solid rather than elegant, unfailingly dusted and polished every day. A table was invariably covered in carefully arranged glossy magazines: *Approche*, *Classique Traveler*, the colour supplements from *Le Figaro*, *L'Express* and suchlike. There were posters of the Tour Eiffel, Arc de Triomphe, Place Furstemberg and other tourist attractions in and around Paris. But the most eyecatching things were displayed on special stands along the back wall. Two of these were bronzes of Indian temple figures: between them in white plaster was a bust of the French Britannia, Marianne. I had stayed in places somewhat like this elsewhere in India from time to time; but they had always been wilting bygones from the British period, carefully not letting go of an old nostalgia for Dorset and Tunbridge Wells.

Presiding over this establishment, however, was someone quite outside my experience. Raymond Magry was as lordly and attentive as any patron who yet hopes to achieve three rosettes in the *Guide Michelin*, and revealed the European side of his ancestry in every syllable he uttered, every gesture he made, though he had never in his life been to France. Somewhere up the line a Magry had gone native, and the result in this descendant was a certain eccentricity of dress in an otherwise extremely proper old gentleman. In the evenings he affected a pink pyjama suit, but spent much of the morning wrapped in a striped winding sheet, which might have been redundant curtain material and which was slung over one shoulder like a toga, in order to be tied in a great bow at the back. Once or twice I saw him awheel, shopping in town, thin brown legs clad in shorts, with a polo shirt above and a beanie advertising Perrier on his grey head.

Early each evening, M le patron emerged from his den in his pinks and unveiled two hi-fi speakers, which otherwise stood shrouded in more curtain material in a corner of the room. A record player was similarly revealed and, after setting it up, M Magry retired to the adjacent couch, crossed his legs, propped his elbows so that his splayed fingertips touched, composed his aquiline features into an expression of distant serenity, and scarcely moved a muscle until the music was done. Meanwhile, Felix, Stephan and Bapu, his Tamil handymen, watered the pot plants and some of the garden shrubs, set the tables for dinner, and moved busily back and forth from the kitchen, where women were preparing the meal. On my first evening I, too, was there when the concert began. Catching my eye as they came past, each servant grinned conspiratorially in turn, did every-thing but wink, as if to say, "You mustn't mind, we think he's a funny old bundle, too, but it's just one of his little ways."

That first night we had some piano music I didn't recognise and I called across the room to him when it finished to ask what it was.

"Couperin, M'sieu. Played by Nadia Boulanger." He cocked his head like an old blackbird and beamed at me. "You like?"

I asked whether he always played in the evening.

"Not al*ways* but al*ways* classical music. I also hear Pur*cell*. You know Pur*cell*?"

He played every night that I was there, and once just before lunch. Mostly we had French chamber music, but his tastes also ran to Schubert, to Monteverdi and, on one memorable evening, to Mahler.

The hotel was full that week and I had only managed to get in through the intercession of a young artist I had first met in Kerala. Jean-Louis's weakness for India was even greater than mine: he came every year, never failed to stay in Cochin and Pondicherry, wherever else he might go, and returned to Paris with notebooks full of sketches and other ideas which he then spent the rest of the year transforming into oils and watercolours. Besides Jean-Louis and myself, the Hôtel d'Europe housed two French couples in their forties and a Junoesque Grande Dame of about my own age, dressed and decorated in a manner that outdistanced by a long way the rest of us put together. Jean-Louis said she was at least the buyer for, quite possibly the owner of, one of the big Paris houses, who came every year to place large orders in the local arts and crafts workshops. She had been received effusively by our host the day before, where normally he was no more than courteously correct. He entered the dining room next morning with an encore in the same key, when she was in the middle of breakfast. She took one look at the spectacle advancing towards her in its winding sheet and dismissed it in four short words: "*C'est très chic, M'sieu!*"

That evening I was aware of a certain tension in the kitchen, long before dinner was served, because two of the men were missing, which meant that the three women had to help Bapu as well as cook. M Magry, however, did not allow any of this to disturb his routine. He ceremoniously unveiled the speakers, put Mahler's Fifth on the turntable, settled back on the chair and went into his aesthetic mode. Halfway through the second movement, when the score was moving steadily from *forte* to *fortissimo*, Mlle Magry – forty-ish, well built where her father was spare, but not so well built as her mother, who was vast – came into the room and switched on the fan above me, then opened a door nearby. It revealed an Indian film on TV, which if anything was being played *fortississimo* for the benefit of Mme Magry, who seemed to be propped on cushions within. The daughter put a chair under the fan so that she, too, could enjoy its benefit while watching the film, then shouted across the room "*Doucement*, Papa!" This elicited no more than a contemptuous wave, and Mahler's Fifth continued as before. So did the film; to produce sounds where I was sitting, halfway between them, that I can only describe as indescribable. At this point, one of the couples came down the stairs gaping with astonishment; but the evening's climactic entertainment had not yet begun.

At dinner, the only thing we lacked was an audience, watching from stalls in the garden. Just inside the footlights, stage left, were Jean-Louis and myself. Upstaging us a bit were one of the couples, the other pair having been allotted a table in a similar position at the other side of the room. Centre stage, and profoundly conscious of it, was the Grande Dame, entertaining a French resident of Pondicherry. Enter Bapu, from the back, bearing soup. He has set the tables perfectly, single-handed, but now his troubles start. By the time he has served three of the tables he realises that not much remains for the fourth and, flustered, he gives the last couple only two spoonsful of potage each, which leaves them looking a little hurt.

M Magry now sails in from his den, having composed himself anew after the earlier assault on his senses. He is again le grand patron, a role he performs so well. Tonight he claps his hands to gain our attention and announces that this evening there will be a spécialité, a mélange of couscous and fish, the couscous having been brought from Paris by special courier; at which he ogles the Grande Dame gratefully, while she pretends it has nothing to do with her. The mélange arrives and it is adequate, but only just. Next course is an excellently stuffed and spiced tomato, but there is only one per person and soon we have all finished; disconsolately, when we realise that we have just enjoyed the main dish of the evening.

At this point Bapu, who has shown increasing signs of strain, arrives with boiled rice and goes round the tables, sweating heavily, but there are few takers and no enthusiastic ones. There is either consternation or mild amusement at every table but one, where the Grande Dame carries on with her conversation, pretending not to have noticed the gaffe. M Magry is now losing a little of his own cool, torn between his desire to fulfil his customary role – enquiring solicitously after the welfare of each diner, drawing up a chair and conversing with the favoured ones – and his gradual realisation that unless he kicks ass fairly soon the evening is going to be a disaster. He doesn't want to make it too obvious that just out of our sight he's berating poor Bapu, who begins to look as if he doesn't know whether he's coming or going. News of a débâcle has spread to the kitchen, and the three women poke their heads round the doorway to see how we're all doing, which makes Magry even rattier and Bapu yet more distraught. I spot him in the anteroom to the kitchen, banging his fist on a chest of drawers, very confused indeed and mightily upset.

With only one more course left to redeem the situation, Bapu and the girls make a last great effort. He brings in a chocolate blancmange, grinning nervously at the assembled company. It is perfect and I nearly applaud, but restrain myself in case this is misconstrued. It looks so good that the first people to be served tell Bapu to give them one more spoonful each; which the poor dear innocent lad obligingly does. By the time he reaches Grande Dame and her guest, not much is left and there is still one more table to serve. Leaving nothing to chance, she seizes the spoon before Bapu can use it, and divides the lot between the two plates in front of her. Bapu stares at his empty dish in dismay, Magry gives up and retreats to his den, where he closes the door. The couple who have just missed out look as if they've seen nothing remotely like this since the last production of Feydeau at the Comédie Française . . .

I had come to Pondicherry in order to visit the Sri Aurobindo Ashram, and sought lodgings at l'Hôtel d'Europe because all the ashram's guest houses were full. The three that I tried, before giving up, conveyed this information curtly, and in one place the woman at reception didn't even open her mouth, but nodded at a notice on the counter: "We are sorry, Friend, we have no accommodation today." They didn't feel all that friendly to me, but rather as if they dwelt on an altogether higher plane than any travel-stained itinerant. It was no consolation to recall that they were treading in the steps of a master who handed down intimidating concepts like Supermind and Superman. Here, in Pondicherry, Aurobindo Ghosh had worked out his tortuous amalgamation of Hinduism and Occultism, Neo-Platonism and Gnosticism, Theosophy and many other creeds, settling down to an intense spiritual life with its basis in yoga after a previous existence as Cambridge graduate, teacher of English and anti-imperial revolutionary. He fled to the sanctuary of French India from his native Bengal in 1910 because the British, who had already jailed him once, were after him again, in the wake of various incidents that they identified as terrorism; Aurobindo's brother, who also struck spiritual attitudes, ran one of Calcutta's biggest backyard bomb factories. Eighty years later, a booklet published by the ashram to explain Aurobindo to the interested outsider, proudly likened the revolutionary activities of his youth to those pursued nowadays by the political wing of the IRA: "What he planned was very much the same as was developed afterwards in Ireland as the Sinn Fein movement."*

And now, Pondicherry was very nearly subordinate to the Sri Aurobindo community, which claimed ownership of some 400 buildings in the town. On every street of the old French quarter it was impossible to walk more than a few yards without coming across a guest house or an atelier or a shop or some other premises belonging to and more often than not making money for the ashram. The shops did not sell anything that could be described as junk, and there was a strong emphasis on the hand-crafted as well as on quality: I could well see why the Grande Dame made this a regular port of call when she descended from Paris on a bulk-buying spree. She would make a notable profit, too.

Just across the threshold of virtually every building, including the Sri Aurobindo Post Office, the Mother was awaiting the visitor, scrutinising everyone from her portrait on the wall. Half Turk, half Egyptian and six years younger than Aurobindo, she was named Mirra when she was born in Paris in 1878; but no one seems to have known her as anything but "the Mother" from the day in 1920 when she came to live permanently in the ashram, after two failed marriages, sojourns in Algeria and Japan, and various psychic experiences which led her to conclude that it was possible to unite man with God and manifest Him on earth. She had identified Aurobindo as the Master when she and her second husband met and worked with him briefly before the Great War. When she returned alone six years later it was not only as his disciple but as his organiser-in-chief, his mouthpiece and his interpreter. Aurobindo gradually withdrew to contemplate the evolution of Superman, unsullied and undistracted by anything over the ashram wall; or, increasingly, outside his meditation room. Simultaneously, veneration of the Mother grew, as she shouldered much of the Master's authority and began to make weighty pronouncements of her own. The day was to come in 1969 when she would confidently declare that "Since the beginning of this year a new consciousness is at work upon earth to prepare man for a new creation, the Superman. We are attending on the birth of a new world." Aurobindo had been dead for nineteen

* *Sri Aurobindo and His Ashram* (SAA Press, 6th ed, 1990) p 11.

years by then, but she lived for another four, until she was ninety-five.

If the iconography was anything to go by, she had become much more of a cult figure than Aurobindo himself. Pictures of him were not all that hard to come by if you knew which shops to try, but there were only two of them: one taken when he was relatively young, with dark hair, a beard just beginning to grey, and steady dark eyes; the other of the ancient seer, with white hair and beard that hadn't been cut for years, a face that was fleshier and less ascetic-looking than in his youth, and eyes that brooded between heavy lids and even heavier bags. The Mother, on the other hand, obviously liked being photographed for there were many versions of her, all artfully and self-consciously posed. She had enormous ears, fully visible because her hair was not only cut as short as any man's but brushed close to the skull: she went unisex long before the word was coined. It wasn't a pretty or even a handsome face, disqualified because its proportions were not good and a prominent feature was its jowls. But it didn't intend anyone to forget it easily. Its eyes conveyed two separate messages: "This is the gaze of ultimate wisdom" and "Look at me when I'm watching you!" There was something uncomfortably Orwellian about that face, lying in wait for all who stepped across those hundreds of doorsteps in Pondicherry. Jawaharlal Nehru never fell under its spell, though. After meeting the Mother at the ashram once, he told his daughter, "She produced no great impression of spirituality on me."

There were said to be nearly 3,000 permanent inhabitants of the community, and a floating population that at any time was probably at least as numerous, a large proportion of both being from the West, especially from France. At any hour of the day the traffic of Pondicherry included many foreigners – attractive young women buzzing about on motor scooters, sturdier matrons careering round corners with their legs firmly gripping Royal Enfield motorbikes, men of all ages pedalling sedately on the sit-up-and-beg model of the Hercules bicycle beside what was still known as Le Canal but was now nothing more than an open sewer. What all had in common, apart from being in hock to the Bengali who was reputed to be making a fortune in hire charges, was an earnestly spiritual countenance. These were Fabian faces whose owners, it seemed to

me, would at another time and in another context have been deeply
addicted to the Women's Page of the old *Manchester Guardian*.

The ashram itself, the focal point of all those thriving enterprises
scattered around the town, was situated in a splendidly elegant building that had been designed in the Classical colonial style by French
settlers maybe a hundred years before Aurobindo came to Pondicherry. It was surrounded by a high wall which meant that only the
upper floors were visible from the street, and entrance was gained
through a narrow gateway, with a custodian sitting just inside. The
first time I went there he was an amiable old Parsi from Bombay
who waved me in after I'd asked if I might see round, warning me
only to take off my shoes, please, and leave them on the racks just
inside the gate. There was sterner management lying in ambush,
however, when I walked up the path between flowerbeds and entered
the house itself. I hadn't taken five steps inside before a heavily built
man in Bengali clothes intercepted me and very sharply told me that
I had no business in there "without requisite document".

So where did I obtain that? "Office is not open now. You must
come again tomorrow to apply. Bringing recommendation from
guest house." I backed off into the garden, and there he left me
alone.

I stepped through more flowerbeds, cornered the building and
walked straight into the ashram's centrepiece. I now saw that here
was not one but maybe four old colonial houses which had been
run together round a large courtyard. In the middle of this, a full-
grown neem tree spread a great deal of shade across the ground,
and protected from the sun the remains of Sri Aurobindo and the
Mother. These lay inside a mottled marble samadhi, a massive grey
and white slab of a sarcophagus, on which the most intricate pattern
of flowers I had ever seen in India was arranged. The scent, and
that of incense burning there, filled the courtyard and drifted headily
into the garden beyond. Dozens of people sat or knelt at varying
distances from the shrine, their eyes never leaving it, and one or
two were at the samadhi itself, kneeling in postures of absolute
adoration such as I had witnessed nowhere else; not at the Church
of the Holy Sepulchre in Jerusalem, not at the perpetual flame where
Gandhi was cremated beside the Jumna in New Delhi. A European
girl approached and bowed double over the edge of the samadhi, till

her nose touched its marble top. She held this position for ten minutes; others who knelt and rested their heads on their arms along the top did likewise, often for longer. The motionless duration of these obeisances was as exceptional as the impression of total surrender, made in self-abnegation and awe. There were notices on the edge of the courtyard ordering Silence, but never can an admonition have been so unnecessary. People were scarcely breathing in there, amid the fragrance of flowers and the thin blue columns of sandalwood smoke, the stealthy comings and goings of fellow worshippers. Some of these added to the decoration of the marble top, buying flower heads from a woman who sat quietly against the nearest wall with a basketful, others arrived off the street holding a bloom reverently in cupped hands, like Christian priests approaching the altar with the unconsumed Host, and some came more naturally with a single rose or carnation still on its stem. I sat in the courtyard many times that week and always the genuflections, the stillness, the submissive atmosphere were exactly the same. It was like being at a lying-in-state; but one of those cadavers had been entombed for forty-two years, the other for nineteen. I could see why the Mother might have chosen this form of disposal, given her background and her desire to follow the Master in all things. But why had Aurobindo turned his back on cremation before her, when it was the traditional end for someone with his pedigree, even after his early exposure to Irish nuns in Darjeeling and Congregationalists in Manchester? Had he secretly hankered all his life, even in the years of his seclusion, for masses of people to humble themselves before him in this way when he was dead? Everything he had written or said in public suggested that he was loftily above such vanity; but now I was not so sure.

Next day I returned immediately after breakfast, in order to join a guided tour of the whole Auro enterprise in Pondicherry. This time I was challenged at the gate by an old man who asked "What exactly is it that you want?" and waved me crossly in the direction of another man, sitting on the verandah by the front door. He told me to sit and wait over there, on that chair, which I meekly did; to be joined ten minutes later by a German couple who also looked a bit miffed at the peremptory tone of these directions. Ten more minutes passed, when a dapper and officious man, wearing a badge identifying him as Mitra N, appeared in some agitation to say that there would be no tour today. It had been cancelled because of "difficulties", but he refused to say what these were. "You'll have to leave," he said, and the Germans did, muttering fractiously. I stood still, stammering that I'd really come to collect the precious laissez-passer urged on me the day before. Mr Mitra waved this notion aside, fussily, as if to say that he'd be in hot water any minute if anyone saw us talking together like this. I still stood my ground, feigning incomprehension.

And then the insurmountable obstacle was suddenly removed, as though by a magic wand. Mr Mitra stopped flapping his hands like a wet hen, seized my arm and propelled me into the Reception office, where half a dozen people were absorbed in paperwork and twice as many were waiting for attention. I was thrust ahead of them and in five minutes I had the precious piece of paper. Then my good fairy told off a couple of young men to take me to another office where it could be countersigned; when that had been done he conducted me himself (and jumped me past another queue) into a long and narrow room, full of people squatting before an empty chaise-longue, which was surrounded by flowers. "Meditation Hall," he whispered and gave me a final shove towards the one empty space on the floor. Left alone among all those rapt contemplatives, I surreptitiously examined the laissez-passer. Its hand-made grey leaves had indeed been signed and countersigned, my details affixed, including the name of my hotel and how long I was staying there. I felt as though I'd just cleared security in some multinational corporation or a hush-hush agency of government. There were three stern injunctions about the pass's validity, including the note that it did not cover any servants I might have in train. I turned its pages and looked at the back. This bore what I supposed could be thought of as a motto:

The Ashram is the cradle of a new world, of the creation of tomorrow.
                                                                    The Mother

Armed with this credential, I could now enter any part of the Sri Aurobindo township except the children's playground, "unless suitably endorsed by P.E.D." (whoever he, she or it might be). My first foray into the esoteric was not a success, however. The ashram noticeboard announced that Professor Manoj Das was to give an evening homily in the school building down the street, entitled "Hours of the Unexpected (Reflections on Aspects of the World Today)", and this seemed a good opportunity to catch up with contemporary thinking in the Auro world. By the time he began in the floodlit garden of the school, addressing us from a table and chair set up beneath a tree, scores of people sat around him in the lotus position, on tarpaulins that had been considerately spread beforehand so that we shouldn't get our bottoms damp. Yet more had entered, so that when the microphone was switched on and the professor's mellifluous voice began to caress the night, it was standing room only on every side. For forty minutes I followed him attentively, but with a growing sense of desperation: for by then he had scarcely finished reviewing the Bandung Conference of 1955 and was only just lining up his major theme, which was that the upheavals of the past year or two in Eastern Europe and the Soviet Union were simply an evolutionary change in the fortunes of mankind. Everyone but me appeared to be riveted by these disclosures; at least, I noticed no one else fidgeting.

It was there that I was first struck with a depressing thought. Not one of M Magry's staff at L'Hôtel d'Europe would have understood a word of what was being said, even if their second language had been English instead of French. For all its large claims to be introducing mankind to a new and nobler vision of humanity, the Sri Aurobindo movement was elitist, steadfastly rooted in and nourished by an educated Indo-Western middle class, totally inaccessible to Tamil dhobeywallahs or men who pulled rickshaws around Calcutta. Two other things I had begun to notice, which the rest of that week merely confirmed. All public discourse was in English, not French, almost certainly because the leadership of the movement was once again firmly in Bengali hands; but this was odd, given that the ashram had been in Pondicherry for almost the whole of the twentieth century. A resentful Tamil might have described it as Bengali colonialism. My other realisation was that although the local beggars blockaded a Hindu temple and a Catholic cathedral in other parts of the town, and were presumably sustained by them, no beggar was to be seen within half a mile of the Sri Aurobindo ashram. It was not, perhaps, a particularly charitable institution.

The flatulent professor's discourse was the low point in that week. By morning things had taken a great turn for the better. It was the Golden Day, not because it was February 29 and Leap Year, but because of yet another Mosaic pronouncement by the Mother. On this day in 1956 she informed her disciples that the Supermind had at last descended with Supra-Mental light, force and consciousness. The devotee who told me this added that, yes, this did mean Aurobindo had manifested himself again on earth, that he was beamed down right into the courtyard of the ashram: where else? The Mother later enlarged on this proposition:

The Supra-mental substance is now almost everywhere spread in earth's atmosphere, preparing for the emergence of intermediaries and Supermen. As the beginnings of the Supra-mental life, which is next to be realised in the evolution of the universe, are developing, not perhaps in an apparent but a sure manner, it appears more and more evident that the most difficult approach to this Supra-mental life is intellectual activity.*

To celebrate the apocalyptic descent, the ashram had devised an anniversary of special happenings, culminating in an evening event at the Playground, which was a narrow expanse of tarmac hemmed in by high walls with galleries on two levels, one block over from the main buildings. A programme of Consecration had been advertised on the ashram noticeboard all week, though I was less than clear about the form of the demonstration after looking at the timetable:

1 An Exceptional Hour. 2 Bride of the Fire & Hymns to Agni. 3 The Sun-Eyed Children. 4 We, the Mother's Children. 5 Mass Exercise 1992. 6 Offering. 7 Ups and Downs. 8 Formations. 9 Effort. 10 Peace. 11 Aspiration. 12 A Joyous Offering. 13 Surrender. 14 We Implore Thee.

An hour before the appointed starting time the streets were as full of intending spectators as if they were bound for a big football match. Participants, too, were there in strength, preparing for their moment of consecrating activity, whatever that might be. Middle-aged men in running gear trotted up and down the road, loosening up bodies that already appeared in good shape. Small boys and girls in green or red shorts drifted over from the ashram in orderly squads, very conscious of being spick and span. Women who would have

---

* *Guru: the Search for Enlightenment,* by John Mitchiner (Viking, 1992) p 96.

been at least moderately attractive in sari or shalwar kameez appeared in baggy white shorts, with their hair tucked into white muslin scarves, which made them look ludicrously like munition workers in the Second World War. All these performers had disappeared and a gorgeous peach and apricot sunset was fading, when the shuffling queue of spectators came to a standstill, and word came down the line that the stewards had called a halt until more room could be found within. At that moment, a well-drilled chant was heard over the wall – it sounded disturbingly like an Indian version of "Sieg Heil! Sieg Heil!" – followed by a military band striking up the old freedom fighters' tune, "Bande Mataram".

By the time I got inside, the Playground contained more bodies than it could decently hold. There was no elbow room on the tarmac, where we surrounded the performers, the galleries were crammed with spectators, and there were even people crowded across the rooflines, craning their necks to see what was happening far below. My first view was of little girls doing convolutions with hooplahs to the accompaniment of Eine Kleine Nachtmusik, at a different tempo from Mozart's, jazzed up by a synthesiser. Then strapping teenage boys formed human pyramids and other gymnastic patterns to an authentic version of the Emperor Concerto, punctuated by blasts on their coach's whistle to signal the next evolution in the set. Next came the munition workers and their eurhythmics, while a female voice intoned solemnities about the pursuit of Truth. These were succeeded by those grey-haired yet supple men who contorted themselves marvellously in the improbable postures of hathi yoga, their coach announcing each fresh torsion on the Tannoy with the precision of an Army drill sergeant. Any one of these turns might have been Ups and Downs, it seemed to me afterwards, though I hadn't seen anything that suggested A Joyous Offering. It was correct, emotionless, disciplined and old-fashioned; an unacknowledged throwback to the Sokol movement of the young Czechoslovakia, through which Tomas Masaryk's people dedicated themselves to moral and physical improvement. The crowd clapped everything, but respectfully, encouragingly, completely under control. Nobody was amused when one of the human pyramids buckled comically under the strain, so that the boys had to hurry to catch up with Beethoven. As I struggled out into the night I wondered why joy was conspicuously missing from everything associated with Sri Aurobindo and the Mother. The atmosphere that suffused their ashram was as stifling as a Sabbath dominated by the Wee Frees in the offshore islands of Scotland. Here in Pondicherry was another cult which made no distinction between shades of potential or actual vice, and simply inscribed Thou Shalt Not on the wall: "no smoking, drinking or drug-taking, no sex and no politics. These prohibitions, the only regulations the Ashram imposes on its members, are meant to exclude activities contrary to the right practice of yoga by persons who have consecrated their lives to it."*

Joy certainly had been nowhere in evidence that morning, when the highlight of the entire celebration occurred. There was one part of the ashram that no laissez-passer could get anyone into normally, and that was the rooms occupied by Aurobindo and the Mother on the far side of the courtyard. But every fourth year, when February 29 arrived again, these hallowed quarters were opened for the day so that the faithful could touch the hem and be refortified in their beliefs. This, above all, was the reason why Pondicherry was bursting at the seams that week, with all the ashram's guest houses booked up long before. People had come from all over the world in order to be here on the bissextile, the seminal, the Golden Day.

When I reached the ashram – as soon as I'd finished M Magry's coffee and roll – the streets around it were already thronged with people; and everyone but me seemed to be wearing new clothes. Young men were guarding the gate this day, and evidently expected a full house: "Will you please leave your shoes in the school across the road?" said one, who admitted me as soon as I'd hobbled back. I made my way to the courtyard, and it was already almost full of people sitting upright, row after row of them surrounding the samadhi. Some of them had come as early as 4.30 a.m. when the gates were opened. They had made the pilgrimage, and now were waiting for the mass Meditation that wouldn't start for another two hours. There wasn't a sound from perhaps 200 of these zealots; not a sound and not a movement once each had found a small space and taken possession of it. In India I had never thought to see such prolonged stillness in so many human beings. I paused, then saw that a queue

* *Sri Aurobindo and His Ashram* (op cit) p 40.

wound its way along a verandah at the courtyard's edge, and joined it at what seemed to be its end, others coming through a nearby door just afterwards and adding themselves behind me. We shuffled slowly round two sides of that pensive congregation and were approaching some stairs when I noticed three young men collecting tickets from everyone in front. When my turn came I produced my pass. It was not enough: the lad wanted a numbered ticket that I should have obtained when I joined the queue outside in the street.

"But no one told me I had to queue in the street."

"Without ticket no one can proceed further," he explained, courteously but firmly. Orders were obviously orders today.

Exposed as a queue-jumper, confused and embarrassed, I clasped my head in frustration and pulled a face. "Oh, India!" I groaned. "What do you suppose I do now?"

He couldn't have been more than twenty-one. His head wobbled just a fraction and a twinkle came into his eye. "I think you should continue in the queue," he said, and reinstated me two places behind where I'd originally been.

More invigilators stood at the foot of the stairs which rose up the outside of the Mother's quarters, but slowly we were allowed to climb the pale blue steps without further impediment. At the top was a corridor and at the end of that was the Room. A green light coming through tinted windows softened everything inside, so that I was first conscious of bowls of flowers everywhere, and their powerful scent. Then I realised that a way across the room had been carefully roped, and that more invigilators were there to ensure that no one put so much as a toenail beyond the ropes. It was uncannily like going through Lenin's mausoleum in Moscow, except that here there was no mummified corpse, nor did the guards have guns. There was, instead, a remarkably dull collection of bric-à-brac: spectacles and scissors and dumb waiters, and cups and saucers, and bowls that might have held biscuits or fruit. There was a small cuddly elephant, several silk firescreens, a number of stone or bronze Hindu figurines and lots of gewgaws carved from ivory. There were even more ivory pieces down another flight of stairs, in the room that had belonged to Aurobindo, together with many glass-fronted cabinets full of household things and files.

They shared an obsession with Time, those two. I lost count of the clocks in both chambers; not grandfather clocks or carriage clocks, not one timepiece that had any value at all beyond its capacity to keep track of minutes and hours; just tinny alarm clocks and other objects that might have come from Woolworth or Uniprix. Notable, too, was the fact that a lot of wild cats had been bumped off to decorate Aurobindo's living quarters. Tigerskins and leopard skins were draped over many pieces of furniture, usually where the Master sat or reclined or rested his feet; on the stool, the couch, the heavy upholstered chair. In the Mother's abode, yellow silk was the preference. As we shuffled along, mutely, people surreptitiously touched the furniture and its coverings, and one man prostrated himself before a couch and its tigerskin, which stood between him and a full-length painting of Aurobindo. A girl was waiting outside that room with a basket full of petals, handing a few to everyone; and everyone but me munched these as they continued downstairs to the ground floor, past the notice which said "Cling to the Truth". At the bottom more custodians awaited us, sitting at a table full of small packets and leaflets. Every pilgrim was handed one of each by an elderly man with a face that said pure bhadralok.* He looked as keenly at everyone passing him as any Customs officer tipped off about a smuggler.

I lingered for a while beside the courtyard, leaning against a pillar on the verandah and marvelling anew at the intensity of the people sitting there. Their number had swollen by half as many again and it seemed likely that yet more would be added to them before the Meditation began, for there was still no end to the queue silently wending its way round to the stairs. I tried to focus on the personalities of the deified couple whose bones lay inside that marble cube, under the smothering of flowers and the spiralling smoke of incense, but I could not concentrate in that supercharged atmosphere and picked my way along its fringes until I reached the herbaceous borders again and finally regained the street. I collected my shoes from the school, then waited against its wall just as altercation broke out at the ashram's entrance. Somebody had wisely concluded that

* The bhadralok (literally "respectable people/gentle men" in Bengali) were and remain the educated elite in and around Calcutta, very conscious of their status and quality. Aurobindo Ghosh was typical bhadralok, and so were/are many of his followers.

the place was full enough, and for safety's sake had decided to close the gates. This wasn't popular with the scores who were still trying to get in: there was much pushing and shoving, with many strident voices raised in anger, uttering sentiments that were far from sublime. It was comforting to know that human nature had not yet been perfected here, where there seemed to be so much certainty, so much rectitude, so little self-doubt.

I was still clutching my gifts and now I looked at them. One, in a saffron paper sheath, was a little transparent plastic box with pink and white plastic flowers adorning a small ikon of the Mother. The photograph must have been taken soon after she first came to the ashram for her jowls had not yet developed, she wore a little lace cap, she looked very Levantine, with a coy and toothy smile. It was a great piece of kitsch and a fine souvenir. The other memento was simply a folded leaf of paper bearing the date in gold and, inside, a rather good photograph of Aurobindo as the ancient seer, with those heavy brooding eyes. Opposite was a quotation from a book of his:

> When superman is born as Nature's king
> His presence shall transfigure Matter's world:
> He shall light up Truth's fire in Nature's night,
> He shall lay upon the earth Truth's greater law;
> Man too shall turn towards the Spirit's call.*

I left Pondicherry and went to Auroville, which had been conceived by the Mother in one of her grandly oracular moods. As well as being its founder she was the author of its charter, whose first sentence declared that "Auroville belongs to nobody in particular. Auroville belongs to humanity as a whole . . ." She amplified this a couple of years later by announcing that "Auroville is for those who want to live a life essentially divine but who renounce all religions whether they be ancient, modern, new or future . . . The whole earth must prepare itself for the advent of the new species, and Auroville wants to work consciously to hasten this advent." This was to be yet another of humankind's fresh starts, full of hope and high ideals, in virgin land set deliberately apart from any existing

---

* *Savitri*, Book XI, Canto I p 709.

community so as to avoid the contaminations of the past. This particular fresh start so gripped a universal imagination that not only did the President of India attend its ground-breaking ceremony in 1968 but young people from 125 other countries and all the Indian states also turned up, bringing little pots of their native soils, which were symbolically amalgamated where the New Jerusalem began. Alas for at least one of the ideals – "Auroville wants to be the bridge between the past and the future . . ."* – but friction developed between the new settlement and its source in Pondicherry almost as soon as the Mother was dead. By all accounts the rift had widened and become more bitter since, because the leaders of the Sri Aurobindo Ashram saw Auroville as their protégé and wished to exert control over it from their comfortable circumstances in the town; while the settlers, toiling in considerable hardship to create something out of nothing just up the coast, insisted on their independence; they had left the ashram, after all, because they wanted to pioneer one of the Mother's later visions, something she had thought up herself without the assistance of the Master, something that had grown out of, and away from, the Sri Aurobindo community.

The rancour became violent enough for the local police to intervene on a couple of occasions in the seventies, the plight of the settlers severe enough for the governments of the United States, France and Germany to offer Auroville humanitarian aid when its people were in some danger of starving. Eventually, in 1988, the Indian government came up with a solution that had at least restored peace in this corner of Tamil Nadu. It would, in effect, nationalise Auroville after enacting special legislation, with a committee of nine eminent persons to keep an eye on things and act as a link between the settlement and New Delhi. Under this regime more than 700 people were said to be getting on their feet at last out there. About one-third of them were Indians, but the others came from thirty countries besides.

The road north from Pondy was as congested and clamorous at first as the outskirts of any Indian town. But, once the buildings fell away, the traffic in bullock carts and trucks and cycles and other conveyances thinned considerably, so that my auto-rickshaw wasn't

---

* *The Charter of Auroville*, Article 3.

swerving perpetually to avoid obstacles; the biggest threat to both safety and sanity was now the long-distance buses which hurtled up and down the tarmac with their horns blaring almost nonstop. Otherwise it would have been a pleasant ride, with trees on either side and an occasional glimpse of the ocean half a mile away to the right. We puttered through villages every mile or so and paused in one of them so that I could examine the most elaborate ayyanars I'd ever seen.

These were two white horses, slightly larger than life, set on pedestals in a clearing just off the road. One carried a rider flourishing a baton, the other had two small figures holding its bridle on either side. Not only were the size and the embellishments exceptional in my experience, but the decoration was uniquely and vividly detailed. The rider was bronzed, in yellow pants, with turquoise brooches in his long black hair, golden sandals and silver toenails. The insides of the horses' ears and nostrils were pink, as were their mouths, apart from their teeth. They were stallions, each with its penis erect and swollen purple at the extremely human-looking end; but I wasn't sure that horses were quite built like that. The harnesses and the saddles came in dapples of saffron and viridian, scarlet and ultramarine. Apart from anything else, it was all a remarkable testimony to the subtle variety of vegetable dyes. A garland of real flowers lay between one pair of jet black hooves, to remind me of the mystical properties attributed by the villagers to these beasts, and the homage that would be ritually paid them every day. But they still looked to my Western eye as if they might have been borrowed from some fairground that prided itself on doing things on the ample and colourful old scale. No showman from my culture, though, would have dared to install stallions in such upstandingly lusty health on his merry-go-rounds: each horse would have been a gelding or a mare.

Shortly after this we turned inland off the road and came across more ayyanars, standing sentinel outside another village which straggled along a dirt track among palms. These were more conventional in size and decoration, a row of four horses which scarcely reached my waist and had been given only token daubs of paint. They were within ten yards of a shrine which was well painted and in good repair. The horses and the solitary rider had been damaged, however: he had lost his arms, one of the horses its head, while another had its terracotta flank stove in. Also beheaded and truncated was a small human figure perched on a clay base at the foot of a palm. What did all these mutilations mean? And why were there so many broken clay vessels, the sort used for carrying water, scattered around these ayyanars? Had the crops perhaps failed, the well dried up, or some other misfortune befallen villagers who had trusted their roadside idols to protect them from all harm? Was this an indication of human displeasure in the gods, rather than the more customary other way round?

We left a trail of choking red dust in the air as we bounced on along the heavily rutted dirt, through a landscape that was full of young trees. Other tracks began to curve off in different directions, and nearly always there was a hand-painted sign at the junctions: La Ferme, Aspiration, New Creation, Acceptance, Gratitude, Recueillement and others. These were some of the communities, over sixty of them all told, that together constituted the settlement of Auroville. I had been warned that it was not at all like any other town I might have visited anywhere else on earth, that its relatively small parts were scattered over more than a dozen square miles, each of them in some degree of isolation from the neighbours. All I could see, as my auto-rickshaw bucked and swayed along the dirt track that morning, was the occasional end of low buildings which looked as if they were made of wood, or brick or maybe concrete breeze blocks, colour-washed in whites and pinks. One of the places inhabited by some French settlers was supposed to consist of treehouses. By chance, La Boutique d'Auroville down in Pondy had booked me into easily the most stylish little commune of the lot.

My first sight of Samasti was of pink pantiled roofs rising from dazzlingly white walls, set close together and high enough off the ground to be visible above the treetops half a mile away. When we had crossed a cattle grid and I had dismounted, I found myself walking into something distinctly modern and well designed, but strangely oriental in a deeply traditional way. All the tiled eaves were very wide, well away from the walls, in mood not far from the tip-tilted Chinese style I had become acquainted with in Kerala. Each building had two storeys and a small square tower with glass sides rising higher than anything else. The buildings faced each other around a courtyard which had saplings in the middle and water channelled around each wall. My room was austerely immaculate, with simply designed modern furniture and fresh flowers in a hand-thrown pot. It felt Japanese, but what gave an impression of paperscreen walls were in fact frosted glass louvres that could be adjusted to let as much or as little air in as one wished. Someone who knew what he was doing had also installed wire screens with a tiny mesh, which excluded anything at all that might try to fly in.

"I like it," I said, when I was sitting at lunch with four of the inhabitants and another visitor. Ila and Paolo, who were Brazilian, lived in the house next door; Jerome from the Netherlands had a room in the guest house, but only until his own place was finished, as he hoped it would be in a month or two more; Olga had recently arrived from Odessa and appeared to be chief cook and bottle-washer; Ruth was German but had been investigating Auroville on holiday from her home at the Findhorn Community in Scotland.

"I like it but why does it feel so much as if it had been designed by someone from the Far East? *Did* it have a Japanese architect?"

The residents chortled and shook their heads. "No," said Paolo. "We decided among ourselves how we wanted things to look – the houses facing each other and with not much space between, like traditional villages, but not the way of Auroville so far, where there are usually wide gaps between all the houses." He stretched his arms out to emphasise the point. "Here we wanted to put our faith in community, to make a thing of being neighbours and friends, sharing each other's lives to a great extent. We think that's important."

"A lot of the things you recognise as oriental," added Jerome, "are really very practical considerations." He nodded at the eaves jutting out over our heads, where we sat eating on the verandah. "That's so the monsoon rains will be carried well clear of the walls; and that's because they're made of compressed clay instead of fired brick. It's an experiment to save on energy. But we've been doing tests on them in water and so far they've stood up very well." He pointed to the water channels running round the walls. "Sure they're pretty, but we put them in to stop snakes and scorpions and ants getting into the rooms." He was a tall, athletic blond in his thirties, very serious most of the time, with a bony face that broke unexpectedly into wide grins.

His own house was rising nearby, almost ready to be roofed, with bamboo scaffolding attached to the walls and Tamil workmen perched on it with buckets of cement and trowels in their hands. Jerome was a physiotherapist by training, but he spent much of his time building his own home, too, when he wasn't required for other projects around Auroville. He had been coming for years for a few weeks at a time before he decided to throw in his lot with the settlers. They had vetted him and accepted him and now he wanted to put down his roots here permanently. The house was more than a token of his commitment: it represented everything he had saved in his life. It was his and only his for as long as he lived in it, and he could leave it to any descendants he might have. But if he or his family moved away from the community they could not take that wealth with them in any shape or form: the house would belong to the settlement. That was the rule of Auroville.

Ila lent me her bike and I began to explore. Two wheels was by far the most common form of transport here, the most obvious similarity with Pondicherry being the great number of people careering round the district on cycles, scooters and motorbikes, mostly on red dirt tracks, always winding through trees. All but a few of these had been planted by the settlers, who had come to this area when it was effectively desert clad in nothing better than low scrub. The local villagers were small farmers and labourers of the inferior Gounder caste, or they were even lowlier Harijans. As recently as 1984, the Collector of South Arcot District had condemned the whole area round Auroville as "backward and in need of development".

The settlers were doing something to help. The extraordinary plantation policy at the outset had been a start, to make rainfall more likely in years when the monsoon hung in the balance. The Tamils working on Jerome's house were among many who had been given jobs in Auroville, whose enterprises already ranged from the production of computer software and the manufacture of textiles for the export market, to farming and making those low-tech, rainproof, unbaked bricks. There was also a school for Tamil children, which had been started by and was in the care of a retired policeman from Essex. Jerome and the others had urged me to see it as an example of Auroville's relationship with its neighbourhood; but I decided afterwards that, as much as anything, they thought it would probably do Roy good to meet a compatriot nearer his own age. I had the impression that not many of the settlers were over forty.

He was tall and well built and he looked fitter, less stiff when he moved than most retired men; had I not been told of his previous existence I would have guessed that somewhere down the line he had been a senior Army NCO. His manner suggested that he was accustomed to giving and to receiving commands; and he greeted me warmly with one of those handshakes that makes a point of conveying its owner's steadfast character. He showed me the open-air classrooms and their occupants with great pride, telling me that they were lucky to have a couple of Australian girls teaching at the moment. At a break in proceedings he grabbed a small boy who was running across the compound and pretended to wrestle with him, so that the kid giggled in an arm-lock. "This is Suresh," he said, "He's the boss round here." He let Suresh go and as the child ran happily away, Roy looked sadly after him. "You don't really know what underprivileged means until you come out here," he said. "But we're trying to open a window for them, so that they can see better things."

Auroville was a window for Roy, too. In our first few minutes together he told me how his wife had died three years before and his daughters, who knew India, had suggested he take a trip to get over things. He had been pottering down the tourist route from Bombay when he heard of Auroville, had come here out of simple curiosity and had returned to stay. He said, a bit too emphatically and more than once, that it had already taught him how we in the West are too tied to possessions. "I've still got my house in Chelmsford packed to the rafters with things I don't really need." His voice betrayed that for the gesture it was; then cracked as he added, "But I miss it quite badly sometimes." He took me to see the solitary room over the school that was his dwelling now. It was almost as bare as Bede Griffiths's hut at Shantivanam, but there were no religious symbols here. On the walls were four prints of the same scene, painted at the different seasons of the year. They pictured the edge of some town in southern England, where it ran out into the countryside. Roy pointed to one of the semi-detached houses facing a field of grazing cows. "The kids think that's my house," he said.

He was very proud of his relationship with those Tamil children and what he was doing for them as the school superintendent. He had found a niche at Auroville and it was obviously his for the rest of his life if he wanted it: he was the sort of person around whom legends grow, to linger in the place they've known long after they have gone. I had been told that it was only Roy who kept the school going, because the teachers tended to be transients. It was also true, I suspected, that the school was the only thing which kept Roy going. He was grieving still, painfully; Suresh and the other children gave him something of the human warmth that had lately gone out of his life.

That same day I met Barbara at one of the other settlements, where I had been invited for lunch. She was a stringy, lantern-jawed woman with grey beginning to show in her girlishly long brown hair, who had come from New York twenty years ago and had never returned to the States even for a short visit. She went so far back in the community that she could even remember Auroville's creator. "The Mother was a tiny thing of five foot two, and Aurobindo was only two inches taller," she said, and laughed. "They were both shrimps. But her voice was very old and quavery. Strangest thing was her eyes. Nobody could agree what colour they were. Some people thought they were green, others blue, some swore they were brown."

She told a good story about the Mother. I had already heard of Auroson, so-called because he was the first child to be born to settlers at Auroville. Not quite true, according to Barbara. "His parents had a child here before him but it was drowned in a tub of water when it was eighteen months old. They were so distressed they went down to see the Mother and said 'What shall we do?' She just smiled at them and said, 'I think you know what to do.' Auroson was the result."

"Is he still here?"

"Not at the moment. He's pretty mixed up for a twenty-one-year-old. Doesn't really know where he belongs. His Swedish mother and his German father split up and she lives in the States. So he keeps going over there to see her, then coming back here to be with Dad."

Auroville, I had by then discovered, did not wholly share the utterly uncritical devotion to the Mother and Aurobindo that hung over so much of Pondicherry like a miasma. I had a feeling that the bereaved parents who rushed to consult the oracle in their distress in the early seventies would have been much less likely to do so today. There was a great deal of impatience out here with some of the old-timers in the settlement who, whenever a decision had to be made about even the most trifling things, tended to begin with "Mother said we must . . ." In many ways Auroville reminded me of a kibbutz near Haifa I had visited a long time ago, when my sister was living there. It had the same dogged devotion to an ideal, the same pioneering energy, the same tough resilience, the same readiness to graft, the same attachment to a long view. It, too, was a place where a people who had set themselves apart were making a desert green. And at Ein Hahoresh, as I recalled, there had been those who constantly harked back to Weizmann and Herzog and the other founding fathers of the state of Israel, as well as to the prophetic figures of the Old Testament. They had not always seen eye to eye with the young pioneers who would do whatever might be necessary, without reference to their begetters, to make a secure living in a precarious land.

This contrast with the pervading mood of the ashram did not mean that Auroville was without a spiritual dimension: only that it did not go in for ostentatious pieties. I went one day to the building complex which housed, among other things, the Auroville library. Next to it was a room devoted to Indian culture and beyond that another, this one dedicated to Tibet and its distinctive form of Buddhism. For an hour I had the place to myself, probably because every settler had a job to do during working hours. On a low platform, recessed into a corner, was one of the loveliest things I had ever seen: a complicated mandala made of coloured sand and other mineral particles, which looked as firm and delicate as icing sugar. Concentric circles enclosed a number of rectangles, each of which led to a smaller one within, a maze which finally ended in a tiny square containing a lotus flower. The composition not only glowed with colour, especially variations of red, but was richly embellished with abstract designs, including calligraphy, and also with tiny representations of animals, humans and other figurative shapes. Five Tibetan monks had arrived one day and it had taken them several weeks to create this wonderful wheel of time on the floor, in a remarkable feat of collective memory for the intricate pattern, which had been handed down from generation to generation in their parent monastery, something that would worthily introduce initiates to the study of the tantra, to be consecrated on completion with the sound of bells and chants. That night I mentioned my discovery at supper in Samasti with great enthusiasm.

"The monks are returning next week to sweep it away," said Jerome calmly.

"But why?" I asked, appalled at the wilful destruction of something so beautiful.

"To emphasise the impermanence of *everything*."

I didn't understand that at all. Nor did I think it acceptable.

The spiritual dimension to everything that happened in Auroville was also expressed in its most astonishing building project. At the geographical core of the community grew a large banyan tree which must have been there for most of the twentieth century, with five subsidiary trunks already challenging the main one for size, and five more dropshoots as thick as sturdy saplings. Surrounding the tree was a great circle of low stone henges which acted as both a fence and as something that people might sit on in the banyan's ample shade. This was a soothing place, from which they could contemplate the shallow amphitheatre nearby, where those token soil samples from the nations of the world were mingled in a stone urn. They could also ponder the significance of the huge construction that workmen were crawling over in the next field. After dusk, when it glowed from within as work there continued under arc lights, this strange object looked as if it might have descended from outer space with ET aboard. A sea fret rolling inland one day made it even spookier, as if it were waiting for the mist to clear before it took off again.

It was the Matrimandir, which is a Sanskrit word meaning "dwelling place of the mother", and the Mother had conceived this as "the living symbol of Auroville's aspiration for the Divine". She had not, oddly enough, chosen to be present when the first sod was ceremonially cut on the site in 1971, a couple of years before she died, preferring to bless the endeavour from the established sanctity of the ashram eight miles away. This was not totally unpredictable, however: she had a great deal in common with the Mother Superior of an enclosed convent, who has retreated from the distractions of the world but is more than willing to have the world come to her for enlightenment.

At first sight the Matrimandir could have been mistaken for one of Buckminster Fuller's more ambitious geodesic domes, though it had been designed by the Frenchman Roger Anger and the Italian Paolo Tomassi "through consultations with Mother". The external effect of a huge steel mesh enclosing a sphere concealed a more complicated inspiration in this remarkable structure. It was, almost, a sphere within a sphere within a sphere, and although it was far from complete I did not doubt that when it was finished it would be applauded as one of the great and original buildings of the modern world: a tour de force which had largely been wrought by the settlers themselves. Computers had been used to plan the engineering at a research centre in Madras, and experts had been recruited to perform the really crucial tasks on site. But the skilled and the unskilled labour had been performed by the people of Auroville and by Tamils from the nearest villages. Every time I passed it, men in hard hats were up on the scaffolding with monkey wrenches in their hands, while others were driving around the base, shifting earth or concrete in dumper trucks. A derrick was perched on top of this tantalising globe, its boom traversing the sky as it lifted girders and other tackle from far below.

They had completed the heart of Matrimandir not long before I arrived, and it was truly a thing to wonder at.

A ramp led up from the excavations around the base, through a cavity in the great mesh, which was the first of the spheres. It then continued upward in curves, much like the ramp in the Guggenheim Museum. Eventually, high above the ground one arrived on the threshold of the Meditation Chamber, which felt like a sphere inside but was in fact twelve-sided under a conical roof. No one had told me what to expect when I first entered it, only that I must take my shoes off before going through the doors. What awaited me was entrancing and I stood still for a minute or more, not daring to move, lest I break the spell. The wall curved away roundly on either side, its marble surface unblemished and immaculately white. There was an inner circle of twelve pillars, white and gleaming, which stood freely, not quite touching anything above. In the centre of the white marble floor, poised upon four up-ended and golden Stars of David, was the innermost sphere of the Matrimandir. This was a crystal, maybe three feet in diameter: to it and from it flowed all the light in the chamber. Sunlight was pouring through a vent in the concave roof directly above, and this was radiated everywhere by that sensational, translucent ball; after sunset, artificial light produced a modified but still hypnotic effulgence. Darkness was never allowed to intrude for one moment in there. It was intended that the settlers of Auroville should meditate at any hour of the day or night.

I sat with my back to one of the pillars, as I was to do several times that week, conscious of a rare sense of mystery that was almost physical. There was something of abracadabra in the crystal, which absorbed the brilliant and powerful shaft from the sun so that it swirled smokily within the orb itself, but was then transmuted again to glow even more softly upon the walls, across the chamber and around my head. The stillness and the peace in that radiance brought me close to trance, as I tried to empty my mind so that I might dwell in clarity on the purpose of all this. The muffled hammering of workmen outside broke my concentration, but even so I began to see why Ruud Lohman gave the last few years of his life to creating this ideal, from a vision that had eluded him until he came to the community. He was a Dutch Franciscan, a theologian who had abandoned his orders and left his friary to be part of this for a while, till he became another of Auroville's untimely dead. During the earliest excavations on the site, he wrote the following:

A part of the person may feel lost in this great world: coming from the other end of the globe and now sitting on the edge of a deep hole in the middle of nowhere, somewhere in south India. Another, more subtle part of the person knows it has been chosen to live and work at the very centre of the new world that is being born – hidden still and almost invisible, but with a sure force and a definite direction. Matrimandir is nowhere, in a sense; far from everything and everywhere. But we know it for sure to be in the very heart of everything, in the centre of a cosmic play of forces redirecting the universe towards the divine spirit which, almost palpably, seeks to manifest here and now.*

* *A House for the Third Millennium*, by Ruud Lohman (Pondicherry, 1986) p 1.

Every time I returned to the Meditation Chamber that week I found it increasingly difficult to drag myself away from its sublimely calming atmosphere; and I could well see why it was that whenever I passed the Matrimandir, members of the community unconnected with its construction had dropped by in their twos and threes to see what progress was being made. It mattered to them all tremendously, and they looked up at its complicated tectonics not only with a simple and concentrated desire to see it finished but with something close to adoration in their gaze. People similarly enthralled in medieval Europe would have watched their cathedrals rising towards, it was supposed, Almighty God and the whole company of saints.

I left Auroville much less pessimistic and far less sceptical than I had come. It seemed to me that here, instead of being solemnly fixated and deflected by the remains and possessions of their idols, people had focused themselves more surely and more happily on pure spirit. They had not turned away from laughter and other manifestations of sheer joy. Except in M Magry's establishment, I had been missing these badly ever since reaching Pondicherry.

# Madras

I had been looking forward to seeing Madras again. I came to it for the first time several years after I was already well acquainted with Delhi, Calcutta and Bombay, but India's fourth city had grown on me with each succeeding visit. Its principal thoroughfares were much wider and less congested with traffic than any in the other three, apart from the radial system that Lutyens grafted on to the capital between the wars, and this helped to give Madras a uniquely open feeling. The fact that one of the most important, Beach Road, ran broad and straight for miles – at least it felt like miles if you walked along it beside the endless sands – between great public buildings and the Bay of Bengal, heightened the impression that for room to spare the Madrassis had no competitors. The only other seaside metropolis, Bombay, was unpleasantly claustrophobic by compari-son, its centre increasingly dominated by high-rise offices, hotels and apartment blocks. Madras had not yet surrendered to the commercial pressure for more and more skyscrapers, for it rarely attempted to climb more than half a dozen floors off the ground. This, too, helped to make it an uncommonly agreeable place.

It had many other things going for it, too. In the suburb of Mylapore was the Sri Kapaleeswarar Temple, which I had thought the most enchanting in all India until I visited Madurai, its superior perhaps only in size and population; and still, to this day, nowhere but in Sri Kapaleeswarar have I seen a man stand for three hours on one leg in front of a shrine, the rest of his body arranged in a yogic contortion that bore some resemblance to a reef knot. Almost across the street was the Portuguese cathedral where Doubting Thomas was originally buried at the close of his long mission to India, whose beginning I had encountered on the coast above Cochin and which ended in martyrdom alongside the road which now leads to Madras International Airport.

Elsewhere in the city, not far from the still dazzlingly white bastions of the old Fort St George, was St Mary's Church, Anglican colonialism at its coolest, with fans whirring overhead and cane-bottomed pews underneath, where both Robert Clive and Elihu Yale were married; and where a military (and unrelated) Moorhouse has been remembered on the south aisle this past 200 years after – if the sculptor got it right – expiring gloriously in battle just outside Bangalore. All Madras's religious strands, and then some, were entwined in an extensive parkland which came down to the mudflats of an estuary and the oceanic shore, where Madame Blavatsky and Colonel Olcott established their Theosophical headquarters, in whose Great Hall today Zarathustra and Buddha, Christ and Krishna, Moses and Nanak, Confucius and Orpheus and many more sages from the beginning of time are equally honoured in bas relief. With due sensitivity to the proscriptions of Islam there is no representation of Mohammed, but a verse from the Koran is embossed instead.

This was a cultured city with a fine appreciation of all arts, and a particular regard for literature. Its English daily, *The Hindu*, was one of India's outstanding newspapers partly because it possessed the sort of imagination that would employ R. K. Narayan as a Sunday essayist for thirty years. None of this community's three great rivals could boast a guidebook remotely as readable and scholarly as Mr Muthiah's *Madras Discovered*, and it was almost inevitable that when India at last launched a decent national journal devoted to book-reviewing and the craft of writing it would be edited and published in Madras. I envied these Tamils their access to the Adyar Library, in which the Theosophists housed one of the world's greatest collections of Orientalia, and I had long since conceded that not even Delhi had as many good bookshops as were to be found here. Among these was the seriously engaged Giggles, which traded in the Connemara Hotel within earshot of a dark little old man in a bow tie, who entertained the hotel's coffee shop guests on the grand piano each day to a mixture of golden oldies and an occasional performance, slowly and pensively, of "There is a Green Hill Far Away".

Madras had changed but little since my last visit, it seemed. I encountered the most startling innovation the moment I arrived. Instead of the exhausting hassle normally inseparable from booking a passage by train in India, which involves painstakingly handwritten entries in ledgers and duplication on multiple chits before a ticket can be released, the Central Station's system of reservation here had become computerised, in a specially air-locked and air-conditioned section so as to keep the dust out of the disc drives and the micro-chips. More than that, the main booking hall now brandished, like trophies from some inter-state railway communications tournament, the gaudiest video displays I'd ever seen outside English amusement arcades; but these screens shimmered in five carefully tabulated colours, and were useful. At a glance the traveller could tell whether any and how many seats were still available on every long-distance train leaving Madras Central in the coming week and beyond. I couldn't recall seeing such information so conveniently dispensed anywhere before, not even in North America. On the other hand, few cities outside New York in the Western world would have allowed Mount Road to deteriorate so badly in the couple of years since I was last here. For most of its length it was as accommodating as I had previously known it, wide enough for six lines of traffic at a pinch, with its sidewalks in good repair. But as it ran downhill past Spencer's famous old emporium towards one of Madras's biggest junctions its pavements seemed to have fallen apart into jumbled heaps of smashed flagstones, with piles of sand and granite chips everywhere for the pedestrians to fall over. It looked as if the money had run out in some demoralised highways department. And the traffic was surely heavier than ever I had known it, so that the footsloggers were dangerously intimidated on either side, by vehicles which belched dark fumes as they lunged past, and by an unavoidable obstacle course.

My auto-rickshaw came to a standstill in the thick of a traffic jam en route to Beach Road. As we stopped, a motorcade flashed by a roundabout some distance ahead, and my driver turned to me with a wobble of the head, an explanatory one this time. "CM," he said, and he made it sound like an apology. I hadn't been quick enough to get a glimpse of Tamil Nadu's Chief Minister in the flesh, though it was hard to avoid her glance in Madras that week. She had lately taken the cult of personality in Indian politics to a more brazen level than I had hitherto come across, with monstrous cut-out replicas of herself, four or five times larger than life, attached to high scaffoldings across the city. In one, Jayalalitha had chosen to represent herself in academic robes, but usually she was pictured in various colour combinations of sari and the sort of poncho that a fashionable potter might have affected at exhibitions of her work. The one pose I never noticed was the Chief Minister portraying a buxom movie starlet, which is what she was before spotting larger prospects in politics.

There was nothing exceptional in an actor moving from one stage to the other in this country, though people in Kerala tended to be stuffy about Tamil Nadu's weakness for repeatedly electing old matinee idols, which confirmed their opinion that their neighbours were not only a bit grubby but decidedly immature as well. It could reasonably be argued, however, that the two forms of show business were always bound to be especially close down here ever since Madras overtook Bombay as the nation's movie capital, making two-thirds of the 900 films churned out by Indian studios every year. More relevantly, for far longer than there had been an Indian film industry, there had been a powerful tradition of making political propaganda of one sort and another here by means of dance and theatre troupes touring the Tamil villages; this was merely, in due course, transferred to celluloid, with a new generation of performers, scriptwriters, directors and technicians involving themselves equally in entertainment and something much more serious. They were soon playing both roles to the most passionate filmgoers of all in a nation which is probably more besotted with the big screen than anywhere else on earth. A cinema is the only place where the poor can enjoy air-conditioning in this sweltering land; and that, too, has always helped pull them in.

The remarkable fact about Jayalalitha Jayaraman, therefore, was not that she had decided to switch careers but the manner in which she had made it to the top in state politics. This would never have happened had it not been for her relationship with one of the biggest hams ever to posture before a cine-camera. Marudar Gopalan Rama-chandran, who has never been known, alive or dead, by his fans as anything but MGR, was equipped only to play the crummiest swashbuckling roles, of which repeated performances as Robin Hood were typical. He became, as a result, one of the great popular heroes of his time, throughout the republic and wherever Indians living abroad also watched his films. He was also the first Indian movie star to become a major politician, his success in the second role owing almost everything to his established popularity in the first; so that when, as Chief Minister of Tamil Nadu, he was at death's door in a New York hospital in 1984, thirty people back home in India committed suicide in separate deals they made with the gods, offering themselves in exchange for MGR's life. Human sacrifice, with some help from American surgery, evidently worked on this occasion for MGR. He lived to rule on for three more years, though a stroke had rendered him speechless and, one would have thought, not even fit for a seat in a state assembly let alone its highest office. There was nothing that New Delhi could do about this, however: between his discharge from the Brooklyn Hospital and his return to Madras, the Tamils voted him and his party back into power for the third time in eight years with an enormous majority in a democratic election. But on Christmas Eve 1987 MGR was at last no more, at an unacknowledged age well over seventy. Responsible observers reckoned that his funeral was the biggest India had ever seen, includ-ing the mass mourning that attended the cremations of Mahatma Gandhi and, much later, his namesake Indira.

Jayalalitha was well on her way by then. She had been one of MGR's leading ladies, both on and off the screen, since playing opposite him in her very first film in 1965. Brahmin daughter of an actress, convent-educated and originally aiming for medicine, she got into movies because the old lecher spotted her dancing while she was still at school. By the time she had appeared in twenty-five films with MGR, he had persuaded her to leave acting and dis-pensed with his third wife. He was by then the coming man in Tamil politics and he took Jayalalitha with him to the top, orchestrating her entry into parliament in much the same way that he had earlier promoted her debut in the film studio. She became his party's greatest electoral asset after MGR himself, not only a rousing figure on the hustings but its highly efficient Propaganda Secretary. She was also extremely ambitious. In all the bitter disputes for position after the muted Chief Minister's death, she was always the one most likely to emerge triumphant. She was in her prime at forty, and she had been trained by a consummate manipulator.

Some of the political dramas Jayalalitha appeared in were outrageous by any standards, even if this was India. She was locked out of the room where MGR's body reposed on the day of his death, but at the lying-in-state she made herself visible to television viewers for hours on end, ostentatiously griefstricken by his side. At one point she was holding MGR's head while his widow, a quarter of a century her senior, hung on to his hand. When the body was placed on a gun carriage for procession through the streets of Madras Jayalalitha pushed her way aboard but was promptly hauled off again by members of the Ramachandran family and had to be escorted to safety by police.

MGR's party had split into two factions behind the principal women in his life, and it was Janiki Ramachandran who was invited by the Governor of Tamil Nadu to succeed her husband as Chief Minister. Her administration lasted just three weeks, after street violence between rival supporters culminated in a pitched battle on the floor of the state assembly, whose elected members fought each other with paperweights, microphones and anything else that could be used as a weapon. Inevitably, the division between the rivals meant that, when the ensuing elections were held, a third party formed the next Tamil government; but Jayalalitha, not Janiki, had become Leader of the Opposition, and the party reunited under her, largely as a result of the widow's magnanimity. This did nothing to improve behaviour in the assembly, however, where another fracas occurred, again revolving round Jayalalitha, who had her sari torn when a government Minister grabbed it and pulled hard.

And now she was Chief Minister herself, having won the state election which was called in the aftermath of Rajiv Gandhi's assassination in May 1991. She actually wielded more power than MGR or any of her other predecessors had exercised, with no fewer than nineteen portfolios in her own hands, including important ones like industry and the office which controlled religious and charitable endowments. More than ever she upstaged everyone else in Tamil Nadu, and once again she made news she could have done without, this time when she was involved in a catastrophe, a very Indian kind of tragedy.

As I left Kerala and began to travel through Tamil Nadu, I became aware that an important Hindu festival was shortly to be held at Kumbakonam, to the east of Tiruchy. Day after day the newspapers carried full-page advertisements placed by the state government, all picturing Jayalalitha prominently and all exhorting pilgrims to be at the Mahamakham tank in Kumbakonam on February 18. The headline was: "Come, have a holy dip on the auspicious day – only once in twelve years." The text then explained that, according to legend, all the sacred rivers of India flowed that day into the tank, where the seeds of creation had once been deposited in nectar. On the day, some four million people obediently turned up. Among them was Jayalalitha, clearly intent on wringing as much publicity out of the occasion as she could. Not only were the huge replicas of her posted high above the crowds on all four inner walls of the tank, but she had let it be known that this was coincidentally her birthday, and that she, too, would be taking a holy dip. She arrived by helicopter, which flew over the crowds five times before landing. A corner of the tank's bathing ghats had been reserved for the Chief Minister, and there, after performing puja, she was sprinkled with water from each of the sacred springs in turn. The crowds standing knee-deep in the tank pressed closer, in order to do what they had been implicitly invited to do: see the Chief Minister saying her prayers, identifying with the humble electorate. It was said afterwards that the police had been too preoccupied with the politician's personal security to control the crowd properly, that the crowd in consequence came too close for comfort, and that the police turned on them and made a lathi charge, which provoked a stampede of frightened people trying to get out of the way of those brutal, swinging bamboo staves. When it was over, forty-eight pilgrims had been trampled to death, though the police carried on as though nothing untoward had happened until the Chief Minister was on her way back to Madras; someone in authority had decided that she must not be troubled with sordid detail until her official engagement was over and done with. I read all this one morning over breakfast in Madurai.

The puzzling thing was not how soon the tragedy was forgotten, as it was within a few days, except by the bereaved; that is normal in India, where tragedy is almost commonplace. Much stranger was the popularity which Jayalalitha enjoyed both before and after the disaster. Quite aside from her political skills, this was obviously due in part to all her old associations with the film world, including MGR himself. It doubtless owed something to the Hindu susceptibility to the Shakti, the Divine Goddess, the Mother, Ma, an admiration of and submission to female energy that also did something for the repeated re-election of Indira Gandhi. But even so, Jayalalitha was a Brahmin, in that part of India where the Brahmins are more wholeheartedly detested by a larger proportion of the population than in any other state. Her party, and every other party which had ruled Tamil Nadu since 1967, employed the word "Dravida" in its title to emphasise its identity with Tamil pride in a distinctive culture and past. Long before MGR went in for politics, there had periodically been talk of a Dravida Nadu, a separate federation of the four states which constitute South India – Tamil Nadu, Kerala, Karnataka, Andhra Pradesh. Always the talk was loudest in Madras and its hinterland. And always it harked back to an ancient time when the Dravidian people were driven down the subcontinent, ejected from their ancestral lands by Aryan invaders from somewhere to the north.* The Brahmins were descended from those Aryans. They could be – and were by some Tamils – seen as the natural, historical and racial enemies of the darker and generally smaller Dravidians. Rajiv Gandhi was also a Brahmin, with family origins up in Kashmir; moreover, he was a Brahmin who had assisted the government of Sri Lanka in its long struggle to put down the Tamil rebellion in the north of that island. That is why the Tamil Tigers killed him in the village of Sriparumbudur, not far from Madras, when he was addressing an election meeting. His head and torso were bisected vertically by the explosion when the innocent-looking young woman knelt before him and detonated the bomb; a mutilation so hideous that one local journalist who came from the back of the audience

---

* One theory, no more than speculative, is that the Dravidians were the original inhabitants of the Indus Valley, in what is now Pakistan, whose civilisation came to an end abruptly circa 1500 BC, possibly as a result of Aryan invasion. (See *To the Frontier*, by Geoffrey Moorhouse (Hodder & Stoughton, London, 1987) Chapter Two.)

for a closer look at the result of that day's terrorism vomited uncontrollably for a long time afterwards.

The roots of all the self-consciously Tamil political parties lay in the Dravida Kazhagam (Dravidian Organisation), and one day I went in search of its headquarters. This was not a straightforward exercise, because it had been keeping its head down since the Gandhi assassination, and people I canvassed seemed reluctant to give it away. Not, they all hastened to assure me, that the DK had been responsible for the killing; but it had been known to give moral support to the Tamil Tigers in their struggle for autonomy in Sri Lanka and therefore was deeply mistrusted by the New Delhi authorities. If it came to that, all Tamils had been potential suspects in the weeks immediately following that terrible Tuesday; and for a couple of days after the murder Madras had been deserted, its population hiding behind closed doors lest there should be some form of reprisal against anyone caught on the open streets.

I eventually tracked down the DK near the main road which, when it had shaken itself free from the city, would take the traveller directly to Sriparumbudur. I walked down an alley and under an arch into what looked like a cross between a campus and a parade ground: it had been the Madras tramcar depot until the trams were abandoned forty years ago. There were white buildings on either side of the open ground, a statue in the middle of this and small groups of young people loitering in the shade on the perimeter or under some trees. Every male was dressed uniformly in black shirt and white trousers; many of the females wore the black shirt with a white skirt. They took not the slightest notice of me as I sauntered in and made for the statue, which could have been made of stone or metal or even wood for all that I could tell: both it and the plinth beneath were painted an unrelieved black. The figure was of an elderly man with a high forehead and huge bushy eyebrows, and with spectacles straddling a very large nose. His hair and his beard had been reproduced much more tidily than they were in real life, judging by photographs I had seen.

He had been born E. V. Ramaswami Naicker, but for most of his life he was known as Periyar – the Elder; which he was for many years, not dying until he was ninety-four. Coming from a wealthy Hindu family, in his youth he had been a member of Congress, the chief agent of Indian national aspirations during the British time, but he subsequently left in order to start something he called the Self-Respect Movement. This was a rationalist, agnostic crusade which embraced among other things the emancipation of women, though its chief target was the caste system. In 1937 both its founder and its adherents transferred their allegiance to the Justice Party, which had started life during the First World War as the South Indian Liberal Federation. This had been formed in the old Madras Presidency of British India by a local elite which included minor princes, landlords and businessmen with one characteristic in common: not one was a Brahmin. Under the British, the Brahmins tended to monopolise the best government jobs available to Indians, for the simple reason that they were, on the whole, the most broadly educated Indians, equally at home in English and in one or more of the native tongues. For the same reason, the Brahmins also provided the intellectual leadership of Congress, which was bent on removing the British from the subcontinent. Given a choice between the British and the Brahmins, however, the Justice Party and their new supporters preferred the imperialists every time, which alienated them from most Indians outside the South. One of their most vehement campaigns was against any attempt to impose Hindi as an official language throughout the country when the British left. Hindi is based on Sanskrit, as the Dravidian tongues are not.* All Brahmins have some familiarity with Sanskrit because it is the language in which the scriptures of the Hindus were set down; and an acquaintance with scripture is what has always hallmarked the Brahmin pre-eminence among Hindus.

On the plinth of Periyar's statue were two different inscriptions, each rendered in both English and Tamil, which between them spelt out starkly the essence of his philosophy. One was attributed, a little vaguely, to "UNESCO 27-6-1970" and said:

Periyar the Prophet of the New Age. The Socrates of South Asia. Father

---

* The Dravidian languages – Tamil, Malayalam, Telegu, Kannada and Sinhala – come in variants of the rotund Grantha script; the Sanskritic derivants of North India are written in different forms of the more linear Devanagari script. Scholars still debate which of these scripts is derived from the yet undeciphered writing of the Indus Valley civilisation. (See *Archaeology and Language*, by Colin Renfrew, (Cape, London, 1987), pp 183–9.)

of the Social Reform Movement and arch enemy of ignorance, superstitions, meaningless customs and baseless manners.

The other quotation, even more vigorous and absolutely unequivocal, was from Periyar himself:

There is no God. There is no God. There is no God at all. He who invented God is a fool. He who propagates God is a scoundrel. He who worships God is a barbarian.

I wandered over to a nearby kiosk after digesting this, to see if I could obtain something that might amplify these assertions persuasively; but the kiosk was firmly shut, though its windows were stocked with a number of pamphlets whose covers had begun to fade in the strong light. None of the young people in the compound seemed at all concerned about my intrusion, resuming their conversations after casually glancing my way. They were pretty laid back, I thought, for members of an organisation that was supposed to be on edge with anxiety about the government's next move: it was only nine months since the assassination, after all, and those responsible had not yet been found, apart from the wretched girl who carried the bomb and had blown herself to bits. An open doorway in one of the perimeter buildings beckoned and I walked across, asked whether anyone was selling books today, but was directed next door.

Inside, in what might have been a warehouse with a few shelves, some rickety desks and chairs added, many young men in black shirts were industriously filling in forms and making entries in ledgers: always, in India still, those heavily bound, double-entry, painstakingly filled ledgers that were the definition of accurate book-keeping, the foundation of profitable commerce and the basis of successful government throughout the world until parts of it discovered the computer and the printout. I had noted some promising titles through the kiosk window and I now asked one of the clerks if any of them were in stock. While he was gone to see what he could find, I glanced along the row of bent heads and saw a much older fellow, bald with white back and sides, steadily making entries like everybody else. A small notice on the wall behind suggested that he was Professor G. Ayyaswami (Ohio USA). I asked if we might talk.

"Of course," he said, scarcely looking up from his work. "I shall be entirely at your disposal in a minute." His mouth resumed its amiable pout. He scribbled a few more English words on a sheet of paper, then straightened up and began to put his materials into a small briefcase: a gent's handbag, really, but larger than most. His eyes, behind horn-rims, brooded owlishly. "We shall go to upper room," he announced, "for greater ease of communication. There are too many interruptions here."

On the way, he put his head round a door and spoke to someone inside. The upper room was bare and empty apart from half a dozen plastic chairs in a stack. Noisily we dragged three across the concrete floor and put them under the window. The door opened to admit another man in his sixties, sharper-featured than the professor, and the colour of mahogany rather than dark oak. He wore a baggy cap in red leather with the word BRILLINT (sic) painted in white just above the peak. "Balram," he said as he shook my hand.

"Mr Balram is chartered engineer," said the professor. "I am traffic expert, formerly with state transport undertaking. But now our lives are entwined in the service of DK."

"We both hail from Coimbatore," said Mr Balram. "It is the Manchester of India," he added solemnly, as though he were announcing an important credential. I remembered someone once telling me, in much the same tone, that Faisalabad was the Manchester of Pakistan. Did they not realise that the comparison was now meaningless, that the Lancashire cotton industry went to the wall a generation ago, finally defeated by the cheap labour of the subcontinent?

I asked about the bifurcation in Dravidian politics that had led to the formation of the Dravida Munnetra Kazhagam.* This was the party that ended the Congress hegemony in Tamil Nadu in 1967, the party that MGR left five years later in order to form his own splinter group, which eventually controlled the state assembly. The DMK subsequently regained power in Tamil Nadu but lost it to Jayalalitha in 1991, because it was discredited by its implicit support for the Tamil Tigers.

"DMK separated from DK in 1949," said Professor Ayyaswami, "because we never saw ourselves as anything but force for agitation.

* Dravidian Progressive Organisation.

DK in consequence became the social arm, DMK the political arm of the same movement –"

"We have got a name, we have a reputation," Mr Balram interjected sharply. "We are the Dravidians who came south from the Indus Valley." His red leather cap wobbled defiantly.

"And so," continued the professor, "we were a double-barrelled gun. Our aim was the same."

Maybe so; but this brief synopsis glided over certain details I was already aware of. The break of 1949 had something to do with the fact that in that year Periyar, at the age of seventy, married a woman forty years his junior; a union that was strongly condemned by C. N. Annadurai, the film scriptwriter who had been the old man's protégé since the days of the Justice Party, and became his number two in the DK. But Annadurai had already begun to feel at odds with Periyar's autocratic style of leadership, and with his unwavering preference for the British times: the Elder would invariably speak of India's Independence Day as one of mourning for Tamils. The 1949 marriage was simply the final crack in a breach that had probably become inevitable. So Annadurai walked out of the DK and set up the new party, which soon called for a Dravida Union within the existing constitution. Its effect would have been to make India a federation rather than a centralised republic. It was Annadurai and the young DMK that ended the teaching of Hindi in Tamil schools, which henceforth offered only the local tongue, with English as a compulsory supplement.

"Do you still want complete autonomy, Dravida Nadu, in the DK?" I asked.

"We have modified our terminology," said the professor, with a modified wobble. "When Chinese invaded thirty years ago unity was imperative for national survival. The separation issue has never been revived. Autonomy is now our aim –"

"What's the difference?" barked Mr Balram.

"A greater say for the states in running their own business, leaving only defence and foreign affairs, currency and communications in the hands of the centre." The professor glared at me benignly through his horn-rims. He sat almost primly on the plastic chair, hands folded over the little briefcase.

"And where do you stand in relation to the Tamil Tigers?"

The professor's pout became even more amiable, almost a full-fledged smile. He spoke as one who was choosing his words very carefully.

"We have been inclined to extend moral support to the Tigers. But because the Tigers were alleged to be involved in some murders, they are not now having the moral support that was originally extended . . ."

Mr Balram nodded emphatically.

". . . All the same, non-Tigers in Sri Lanka are being harassed and we think that is not fair. We want action against the real culprits without using it all as a stick to beat all Tamils with."

Professor Ayyaswami sounded like someone utterly dedicated to fairness in all things. I liked him, especially as he said "harassed" with emphasis on the first vowel, and not in the jarring manner that has shoved its way across the Atlantic in tellyspeech.

"Have you had trouble from the authorities since the assassination?"

Mr Balram looked at the floor and cleared his throat. The professor regarded me as gravely as an owl interrupted on a mouse hunt. His pout was for the first time not especially amiable; just a pout.

"Our General Secretary was in US having bypass operation when the assassination occurred, and he rose from his sickbed to issue unequivocal condemnation. Nevertheless many DK people were arrested, though the ones in Madras were fairly soon released . . ."

"Very smart lawyer working for them here," said Mr Balram.

". . . but elsewhere the known Dravidian zealots were not so lucky."

I asked them about the size and extent of their organisation. There were a couple of hundred people working in the old tram depot, where they published two journals in Tamil and two in English, ran a free clinic, free legal aid, and a marriage bureau which specialised in the remarriage of widows, inter-caste marriages and marriages without payment of dowry – all unheard of in orthodox Hindu circles. There was a similar set-up in Tiruchirappalli, where DK ran an orphanage, an old folks' home, a pharmacy and several schools; and in Thanjavur, where they claimed to have established the only women's engineering college at degree level in the whole world.

"We also have our Intellectual Forum here –"

"Think tank! Think tank!" snapped the irrepressible Mr Balram.

"– of which I am honorary secretary and Mr Justice Venugopal is the president. We meet on the first Saturday every month at five o'clock precisely and we finish at not one minute after seven p.m." For the first time Professor Ayyaswami removed a hand from his lap, and wagged a finger to point up the exactness of their timekeeping. "We discuss only non-political topics such as those to do with development and we submit our conclusions to the government." The pout had become a smile again. "We don't have an axe to grind and we speak only English."

I expressed surprise. "It is the international and the scientific language –" said the professor.

"A gateway to opportunity," said Mr Balram, only just managing to get his piece in this time.

"– and we've had contact with English for 300 years. We don't want to lose it."

They took me downstairs again and out into the yard. Someone had draped Periyar's statue with a long garland of purple flowers since my arrival. It matched the purple disc in the middle of the black DK flag. There were dozens of these flags in miniature, fluttering from wires which converged on a pole behind the statue from all corners of the compound. Some kind of celebration was evidently imminent. At the far end of the compound, wreaths had been placed against another black plinth; and above this rose a carved hand upholding a torch, twice the height of a man, all painted black. Periyar and his wife, I was told, were buried on either side of that torch.

Young people were still lingering quietly in their black and white uniforms in the shade. But another group had appeared, young men dressed in khaki, with black anklets above black boots and black berets on their heads.

"They are our security force for this place," the professor explained. "It is, alas, necessary in these times."

The guards were drawn up in drill formation and I was startled by the salute they gave to the man in charge. The right arm was raised and held out stiffly, not at an angle like the old Nazi salute, but levelly. It was, all the same, sufficiently close for all the old memories to stir uneasily again; just as they had done in Cochin when I mistook the Vedic swastikas on the balcony for the symbol that meant evil, not sanctuary, to the Jews. But no swastika would have been acceptable here. Both versions were associated with domination by detested Aryans.

An uncomfortable thought crossed my mind, as I watched those virile young men being drilled for the greater security of the Dravida Kazhagam; even, perhaps, for the greater prosperity of all Dravidians. Surely not for Lebensraum?

"Why is black the predominant colour round here?" I gestured at the flags, the uniforms, the monuments. "Is it because Dravidians tend to be darker than most people in India?"

Professor Ayyaswami looked more owlish than ever. "No," he said, "it is not that at all. Black is the colour of suppression, of the people who are oppressed." I waited for some confirming or amplifying sound from Mr Balram, but he was silent now.

# Brindavan

I sought one other encounter before leaving India again: I wanted to find, and if possible talk to, the subcontinent's most celebrated living guru. Now that the largely discredited Rajneesh was no more, the name mentioned more often and more fervently than any other was that of Sathya Sai Baba, whose fame was such that a fish restaurant in Boston was said to have his portrait hanging prominently in its dining hall. There were several reasons for his celebrity, not least the fact that he was widely believed to possess miraculous powers. There was a rumour that he had once raised someone from the dead, though his stock-in-trade was a variety of manifestations that sceptics might dismiss as brilliant legerdemain. Most commonly, he materialised vibhuti, the sacred ash which devout Hindus apply to their bodies in imitation of Lord Shiva. Other objects he conjured out of thin air included gold rings and similar trinkets. An elderly Australian admirer described the most remarkable of such happenings that I had heard of. Sai Baba, in this eyewitness account, was holding a public audience attended by a considerable crowd. "First he sang a sacred song in his sweet celestial voice that touches the heart. Then he began his discourse, speaking as always on such occasions in the Telegu tongue. The thirty thousand or so people were as one, expectant and utterly silent, except when Baba told a funny story or made a joke. Then a ripple of laughter would pass over the star-lit field of faces."* Sai Baba had been speaking for half an hour when his voice broke and he appeared to be distressed, as if in pain. The crowd began to sing bhajans to comfort him, and after twenty minutes of writhing and smiling, and more unavailing attempts to sing, the miracle was performed. "I saw a flash of green light shoot from his mouth and with it an object which he caught in his hand, cupped below. Immediately he held the object high between his thumb and forefinger so that all could see it. A breath of profound joy passed through the crowd. It was a beautiful green lingam and certainly much bigger than any ordinary man could bring up through his throat. Sai Baba placed it on the top of a large torch so that the light shone through its glowing emerald-like translucency. Then, leaving it there, he retired from the scene."

This charismatic figure had first seized attention at the age of thirteen, when he was bitten by a scorpion and went into a catatonic trance, broken by his occasional singing and recitations of poetry. After some weeks he startled his peasant parents with the announcement that he was no longer their Sathya Narayan Raju, the name they had known him by since his birth in 1926, but a reincarnation of Sathya Sai Baba of Shirdi, a holy man who had announced just before his death in 1918 that he would reappear on earth eight years later. The precocious youth who now assumed the old sage's mantle said that he had come to ward off all troubles in his home village, in return for which the peasants must keep their houses clean and worship him every Thursday. And worship him they did; more ardently than ever when, a few months later, he told his family that he no longer belonged to them, that his devotees in a wider world were calling him, that he had his work to do and must abandon them in order to do it. Some time later the word went round that the second Sathya Sai Baba was also an avatar of Lord Vishnu himself. Reincarnation, or hubris, could go no higher than that. But this extraordinary man was taken seriously in some quite level-headed quarters. The American owner of the Hard Rock chain of eateries had sold out in order to finance the guru's activities. Bede Griffiths had some reservations about Sai Baba's public mannerisms but did not doubt that he was an authentically holy man in the

* *Sai Baba, Man of Miracles*, by Howard Murphet (Macmillan India, 1971) p 46.

great Indian tradition. He did not dismiss as poppycock the story about a corpse being revived.

Locating Sathya Sai Baba was not as straightforward as it might have been, for he generally divided his time between two ashrams a long way apart and was liable to change his plans on a whim, travelling from one to the other unexpectedly. His original settlement was alongside his home village of Puttaparthi in the hill country of southern Andhra Pradesh, and by all accounts it had long since dominated the little farming community with its extravagant facilities: these included schools, a museum, a planetarium and a Super Speciality Surgical Institute in which cardiovascular bypass operations were performed on poverty-stricken Indians, who were thereby acquainted with the truly miraculous. Nearly a hundred miles away, just beyond the edge of Bangalore, was Sai Baba's alternative base in the suburb of Whitefield, which sounded as if it might be just as opulent.

I decided to make for Puttaparthi after discovering that a coachload of pilgrims would be leaving Madras for Andhra Pradesh before dawn one morning. They were not bound for Sai Baba's ashram, but were going to pay homage at the shrine of Lord Venkateswara on the holy hillside of Tirumala.* This lay in approximately the right direction, though I would need to make further arrangements in order to reach my own objective, which lay some distance beyond, to the north-west. The excursion, however, would meanwhile enable me to visit one of the most celebrated temples in India. In the nineteenth century the Abbé Dubois, who was not easily shocked, had taken a withering view of it as a place where young women were habitually seduced by the guardian priests, on the pretext of submitting themselves to the wishes of the god Himself. Nowadays its reputation was unsullied by any such shenanigans: it was said to be the shrine where petitions were more often answered favourably by the incumbent deity than anywhere else; and, in consequence, its income was reckoned to be by far the largest of any temple in the land. To cap all this, Tirumala was exceptional in permitting non-Hindus to enter the innermost sanctum of the shrine.

* Venkateswara is a local name for Vishnu.

This I gleaned from the young man sitting beside me in the bus, though it was hard work extracting the information from him as we roared out of the city just as light was beginning to edge the eastern sky. He had journeyed halfway down the subcontinent, from Jaipur, in order to make this pilgrimage and he appeared to have taken a vow of silence until it was over. After our first halting exchanges, he delved in his satchel and for the rest of the journey studied a Sanskrit text with an intensity that brooked no interruption from me. Other passengers were less rapt in privacy or scripture, babbling amiably to each other, fondling children, exchanging excitement at the prospect ahead. When we stopped for a tea break in the middle of the morning I discovered that among my fellow travellers that day was an old lady who had flown from Middlesex in order to make the pilgrimage with her sister-in-law. I had wondered how anyone on that bus could have acquired a Marks & Spencer plastic shopping bag.

It took five hours to reach the town of Tirupathi, which lay in an arid bowl amidst the hills. There followed an alarming ride with the trajectory of a rogue rocket as we careered upwards through a long succession of hairpin bends, an increasingly awful prospect of death and destruction awaiting us if the driver miscalculated by six inches and put us over the edge of the road. Twice I spotted the wreckage of trucks which had fetched up far below after shatteringly precipitous descents that their occupants could not possibly have survived. In even greater peril than bus passengers, perhaps, were the pedestrians we passed on the way, people labouring stolidly upwards with bundles of their possessions on their heads. Pilgrims all on their way to Tirumala, they were increasing their virtue in the eyes of the Lord by reaching His shrine the hard way, a penitential exercise made hazardous in this case by the constant flow of traffic, which threatened to squash every one of them against the rock face or knock them straight into the deepening abyss.

As we thundered up the last slope we reached a plateau overlooked by even higher hills of scrub and there we disembarked. Distantly, a white gopuram topped by golden finials signified the temple, but there was a small township to negotiate first, as well as hordes of people, half of whom were hoping to sell the usual religious bric-à-brac to the other half. The commerce here, however, was on a scale and of a variety that I had not encountered before, not even in Madurai. There were notices canvassing direct flights between a local airstrip and Hyderabad, Pune, Baroda, Ahmedabad, Bombay and Madras. In four different languages the temple authorities announced their Ear Boring Office, also their stall which supplied Fast Foods and, most prominently of all, pointed the Way to Free Meals Hall. A great deal of charity was obviously provided from the colossal income that was reputed to accumulate here. There were standard hotels in abundance, but there were also many choultrys where poor pilgrims could stay for next to nothing.

The largest building in sight, an unlovely concrete block several storeys high, contributed substantially to the temple's income. A long and trilingual banner hanging from one of its balconies proclaimed its function: Place of Surrendering Human Hair to Lord Venkateswara Swami. People were queueing to enter: shaggy men with unkempt growths on head and jaws, beautiful women whose long black tresses glowed with health and an electric blue sheen, sinewy old crones with lifeless grey hanks that hung dully down their backs, children whose dark mops had only just reached maturity, young fellows whose virility had been self-consciously displayed for years in fashionable styles and cuts which imitated their cinema and other pop idols. Awaiting them on the balconies and in rooms within were the barbers who would remove every last follicle in the Lord's name. It wasn't at all clear to me what virtue the pilgrim gained by being scalped: but I imagined that enough hair was surrendered at Tirumala in a week to keep the international wig industry going for months. Patiently the hirsute pilgrims shuffled forward to submit themselves to the scissors and the cut-throat razor, and happily they emerged some time later with heads that glowed like mushrooms in their pallor and their nakedness, with a smooth matt surface that I wanted to feel, so that I could trace with my fingers its unsuspected little contours, concavities and nodes. A phrenologist would have been in ecstasy at the spectacle, though some of the newly shaven had smothered their baldness in turmeric paste, which made them look as if they were being treated with pungent medication for a skin disorder. By no means all the pilgrims that day had surrendered themselves to sacramental depilation: but so many of them had that, striding on towards the temple, surrounded by hundreds of these zealots, was strangely like walking through a film set with a tremendous cast of extras playing cranial sci-fi aliens.

The temple lay beyond a great triumphal arch across the pedestrian thoroughfare, and an unusually wide flight of steps leading down to its entrance. It was at the top of the steps that I saw the cage and paused, unprepared for what I seemed to have let myself in for. People were moving forward in a tightly packed column through the bronze temple doors, but they had only just emerged into the open after being crammed inside a narrow tunnel of steel mesh, which wound round the building to a beginning somewhere out of sight. So far as I could see, there was no opening of any sort in the cage, no way of escaping from it if you were taken ill, no way of getting past the people in front of or behind you in order to find space or air: the heavy mesh completely enclosed everyone, and I had never seen human beings so tightly and inhumanly compacted. It looked much, much worse than the plight of battery hens, and that was loathsome enough. Shaven and natural heads alike were jammed against the mesh, fingers were desperately hooked into it, and I did not dare to think what might happen if someone's nerve gave way under the strain: certainly there would be no way of rescuing them. It was the most sinister form of crowd control I had ever encountered, entirely without violence but utterly brutal none the less. I was beginning to think that it might be sensible to forego this temple when one of my companions from the bus came up and, seeing my look of dismay, pointed to a notice I had missed: Special Entrance 25/-. "Included in price of our ticket," he said, grinning sympathetically. "So we can avoid all this."

We walked round the side of the temple and skirted a complex of buildings behind, all separated by little courtyards. A larger one was arranged like the toll stations on a highway and this is where the cage began; or, rather, two cages running parallel, each with a booth where officials regulated the flow from then on. Few people were about, which must have meant that this was one of the temple's quieter days. As I held up my ticket and started to walk through, the officiating priest stopped me and passed a sheet of paper across his counter for me to fill in. By signing it, I acknowledged that although I belonged to the ―― religion, I also subscribed to the view that Lord —— (whichever Hindu god I had in mind) was divine. It was my passport to the innermost secrets of the shrine. Hinduism could sometimes be very accommodating to those who were prepared to meet it halfway.

After walking a few hundred yards along a virtually empty cage I was certain that I could not have handled the claustrophobia of the common confinement. I and the other people from the bus were able to move freely almost until we reached the temple doors, but long before that we were walking beside the cage jammed with patient, submissive, herded humanity, hundreds of people who still had an hour or two to pass before they were released from their captivity. They looked at us blankly, hopelessly even, through the spaces in the thick steel mesh, hooked their fingers more firmly on to the wires as though pleading for our compassion. I could not empty my head of even more terrible images: animals penned up before slaughter, people being sent to the gas chambers.

Eventually the two cages came to an end and we were obliged to take our chances with all the other emerging pilgrims a few yards from the temple doors. There the jostling began, among people whose great natural gentleness had always been tempered by an imperative to fend vigorously for themselves or go under in time of need. Entering that temple was like trying to get out of an English football ground just after the final whistle has gone, with even greater premonitions of disaster by crushing or trampling underfoot in a narrow space. So conscious was I of the recent catastrophe at Kumbakonam that I was braced against the possibility of a lathi charge, and thinking how I might possibly escape. Just inside the entrance, in a space that no one dreamed of invading, policemen were indeed lounging watchfully without the slightest hint of piety. They kept their eyes on everyone, but most especially on those who had perhaps waited half a lifetime for this moment, and who went into spasms of elation as they reached it after those final hours of pent-up emotion in the cage. A young man elbowed me in the ribs to get there faster, kept clasping his hands above his head, almost jumped up and down in his haste to see and be seen by divinity ("I'm here, Lord, here I come at last!"). Other people smote their heads, beat their chests in their fervour. The turmoil was such that it was impossible to study the structure of the temple itself, though I was vaguely aware of the gold sheathing on the outside of the sanctuary, rising above white marble walls.

Pushing and shoving each other along, all but stumbling at steps and tripping over everybody else's feet, we came eventually into the holiest place of all, a narrow passage where the Lord Venkateswara could be descried dimly in a niche at the far end. The smoke of incense drifted about Him and with only low-wattage light bulbs and oil lamps for illumination it was impossible to make out His features; there were, also, too many other things going on which distracted my attention: the press of excited people all around, and a loud throbbing incantation of OM, which must have been coming from an amplified tape, for I could see no sign of anyone chanting. There was no time to pause and contemplate; a ceaseless pressure of bodies behind propelled me forward so that I did nothing but gesture to the Lord as I was hurried past. Immediately beyond, two priests stood half naked beside a flaring lamp, through whose flames everyone passed his hands. The first priest then spooned a liquid into the upraised palm of each pilgrim, and I bent to peer more closely at mine; whereupon he, thinking I was about to drink, hissed loudly in my ear, "The head, the head!" It was the anointing, confirmed by the second priest, who pressed a silver seal upon my moistened brow as I shuffled awkwardly along and quite failed to satisfy the hand he adroitly cupped in my direction as I went past. It was a relief to reach the open air again in the less congested courtyard, where people stood or sat and prayed with their eyes steadily on a silver arrow inset in the golden vimana above. Within the dome where the arrow pointed was a representation of Hanuman, the monkey god, friend and ally of Lord Vishnu in His seventh incarnation as Rama. Hanuman it was who rewarded such a high percentage of petitioners most favourably; and who, in consequence, stimulated a great deal of the temple's legendary income.

At that moment a strange yet familiar noise rose above the frenzied clamour of the pilgrims, a rhythmical clashing which resembled the famous smack-whoosh of spears and shields in the soundtrack of the film *Zulu*. I went in search of its source and, rounding a corner in the yard, came upon yet another cage set against the outer wall and this time provided with a door, which was padlocked on the inside. In the half-light of two feeble bulbs, men were crouched over huge piles of coin which they were systematically sieving through long trays in order to separate the different sizes for easier accountancy. Yet charity mingled engagingly with profit at the shrine of the Lord Venkateswara in Tirumala. As each pilgrim left the precincts it was necessary to pass a cubby-hole just before the exit. From this into every supplicating hand came a large wooden spoonful of sustenance, a stodgy mixture of jaggery and nuts which was intended to confer both spiritual and corporeal nourishment on the departing traveller.

That night, I heard that Sathya Sai Baba had left Puttaparthi and would be spending the next week or so at Whitefield. The news came to me from Kamala Das's son, who edited one of the Bangalore newspapers and had been keeping an ear open on my behalf for the past month or so. If I came at once, said Monoo, I would almost certainly be able to see the guru, even if I wasn't allowed a private audience. Next day I took train to the most untypical of all the Indian cities I know, a dapper centre of high-tech industry, swarming (it was said, and I could well believe it) with more motor scooters than anywhere else on the subcontinent, a sure indicator of relative prosperity. Bangalore was a very pleasant place, well named the garden city, but it was not as much to my taste as some of its less prosperous, less up-to-date, more garbage-ridden rivals. It was just a bit bland by Indian standards, and blandness was the very thing above all others that India did not represent to me: it was the strong and contrasting flavours of the subcontinent that had brought me here time and time again for a quarter of a century. Yet even Bangalore had secured for ever its place in my memory. For I was boarding a plane to India at Heathrow in 1984 when I heard that Indira Gandhi had just been assassinated; I saw the smoke rising over the rioting Old Delhi when we paused in the capital with armed police surrounding our Jumbo on the tarmac; and I grieved with friends in Bombay as we watched the funeral together on television. Later that month, in Bangalore, I was among the thousands who moved slowly through the great glasshouse in the Botanical Gardens, where some of her ashes rested in a silver casket amidst the scent of many flowers before continuing their journey around the land she had given her life for. I would not willingly have been anywhere else on earth at that time.

The word that Lord Vishnu's avatar was down from the hills had reached Bangalore's auto-rickshaw wallahs well ahead of me: they sharply identified potential fares at that season of the year, too. As I stepped out of the railway station, every hustler in sight bore down on me with a common cry of "Sathya Sai Baba?" But Monoo had sent a driver who whisked me off to the faded amenities of the Bangalore Club, where the British had once isolated themselves in bungaloid splendour from all but menial Indians, and where one could still take afternoon tea on one's own very private verandah. This came in the sort of imitation-silver teapot whose handle scorches the fingers, and was obviously a relic of catering in the time of our Raj, though I had first known its like with brews of Typhoo Tips in the Kardomah Cafés of my boyhood in northern England, which were named thus so as to infuse the working classes with a sense of wonder at the imperial exotic. I found it wryly satisfying, as I sipped the Bangalore Club's best Nilgiri, that in this modest fashion I appeared to have completed more than one circle.

Monoo appeared a little later to make sure that I was comfortable. I had met him only briefly in Trivandrum and there he had been preoccupied with a scoop about state politics. He was a plump man in his early forties, all forehead and nose above a moustache, a small mouth and a smaller chin. He had a nicely sly sense of humour, eyes amused behind his glasses when he casually mentioned that he belonged to a family of freedom fighters. That evening we were entertained to supper by one of Sai Baba's most ardent followers in the city. Balu was a considerable painter who, for more than thirty years, had increasingly been experimenting with collage; which was not, he explained, an invention of the Cubists, as I had supposed, but had originated in nineteenth-century South India.* He was a widower of about my own age, slightly built, with hair that had receded almost to the crown of his head but then fell blackly to his neck on either side. He had a studious, aquiline face, and the eyes were very soft behind large horn-rimmed spectacles. A very gentle man, he spoke of the guru and all his works in de-

---

* Cloth, baubles and other materials were commonly stitched on to paintings by Raja Ravi Varma (1848–1906).

voted terms that were almost childishly innocent. He told how
he and his wife had once met Sai Baba, "who graciously granted
us a private interview which was truly fantastic. A flood of love
shone from his eyes and face as he spoke about the young
people. His face has a special charisma, his love and compassion
give it a special halo." When Balu described Puttaparthi he called
the ashram there "a paradise of absolute peace and serenity".
When he mentioned the Super Speciality Surgical Institute he
said, "We have a hospital designed like Buckingham Palace." And
when I wondered why, he smiled sweetly and replied, "Because
the patient is God, too. So we want him to feel like God." I was
not surprised when Monoo told me later that Balu was one of
Sai Baba's most effective propagandists in India. He had painted
him several times.

My friend was a sophisticated man, one of the most practised
political journalists in the land, well accustomed to seeing through
deceptions, manipulators and the quid pro quo of patronage.

"Do you think Sai Baba is a reincarnation?" I asked him. "An
avatar of Vishnu?"

Monoo wobbled his head emphatically. "I think he is very genuine," he replied.

We set off early next day, with Monoo beside the driver of his
editorial Ambassador, Balu and me in the back. Bangalore was so
far above sea level that its breakfast times felt like spring at home:
though the day would be hot later on, there was a lovely freshness
in the air as we sped out of the city, past the National Aeronautical
Laboratory, the Air Force HQ and many civilian premises that were
also as computerised as anything in the western hemisphere. We
joined the main highway east and left the suburbs behind, to enter
an undulating landscape where cattle grazed and tractors hauled
high-sided wagons full of harvested crops. Balu answered more of
my queries about Sai Baba – "He is not materialising things so often
now. He is concentrating more on education and health" – but when
I said something to Monoo, the editor held up his hand apologetically, because he was still saying his prayers. I hadn't thought of him
as a religious man, assuming that he was probably agnostic like his
parents. I had not expected him to go with me to Whitefield, but
he had announced over supper that nothing ("Not even Cabinet

crisis!") would prevent him from accompanying me. He had long wanted to meet the holy man, and now the propitious time had come.

We had been driving for nearly an hour when we rolled down the last long slope into Whitefield, which seemed much like any other small Indian community straddling a main highway, except that one or two Westerners were shopping at its various stalls. We went straight through and over a level-crossing before we reached our destination.

"This is Brindavan," said Balu proudly; and then, anticipating me, he added, "Which was the supreme paradise of Lord Krishna, a place of untold delight."*

We stopped near a pink-washed wall with stone lotus flowers at intervals along the top and a number of slogans daubed in black upon the side. Down Down Management We Want Justice, said one; Love is God, according to another some yards away. "Students!" said Balu, beaming at everything in sight. On the other side of the wall the roofs and domes of many buildings could be seen, including a pre-stressed block with a clock tower which sprouted a huge pink lotus flower. Under the clock were the words Sri Sathya Sai Institute of Higher Learning. Many of the students were outside the wall, rummaging in stalls on both sides of the street, which sold all the things familiar from any temple bazaar, but this time especially loaded with tapes of Sai Baba, and many, many pictures of him: on badges, books, calendars, posters, as well as cheaply framed ikons. Not as many white faces were weighing up these things as brown, but there were plenty of foreigners about. They were among the figures sauntering down the road towards the ashram's entrance with prayer mats bundled under their arms. They went in beneath an arch surmounted by a disc which incorporated a Christian cross, the moonstar of Islam, the Buddhist wheel of time, a lotus flower and the Sanskrit version of OM. This was held in place by two angel figures with beating wings that might have been copied from any reredos of the later Renaissance. Through the arch I could see that all the buildings on the campus appeared to have been freshly painted

---

* Krishna is an incarnation of Vishnu, and in some of the early Sanskrit texts (e.g. *Bhagavata Purana*) the names are used interchangeably.

in what was clearly the dominant Brindavan colour scheme of pastel pink and heavenly blue.

Balu led us a long way round the sides of the wall to an entrance open only to friends of the family. When we stepped inside I realised that we had come through Sai Baba's garden gate. In front of us was an expanse of lawn, with a couple of malis sweeping the dew carefully from the grass, which was enclosed by flowerbeds. In the centre of the lawn was a building that might easily have been planned for Disneyland, a pastel-coloured, three-storeyed rotunda that was yet another attempt to reproduce the outline of an open lotus blossom. "Sai Baba's home," said Balu as we strolled towards it round the circumference of the lawn. His voice, never loud, had become quieter than ever, distinctly reverent. I was aware of my heartbeat, which I usually never notice: I was nervously excited at the prospect of meeting this commanding and hypothetically divine figure. What on earth was I going to say to him?

But we passed on along the garden path until we reached some stone slabs where we sat in the shade of trees. Behind us was an area of sand with a figure of Krishna in the middle and a large pen containing live deer at one end. I could now see that down this side of Baba's house was an aviary, with doves, cockatoos and other birds inside. There was quite a lot of coming and going around the house, by men in white shirts and slacks, wearing the blue neckerchief of official status. I was asking Balu about these when a young fellow looked at us severely and held a finger to his mouth. We took the hint and moved on until we reached an elaborate gopuram which marked the further boundary of the private compound. It, too, incorporated the disc of many faiths, but these supporting angels were not so much rococo as interdenominational, with limper and perhaps underpowered wings. OM and other words had been inscribed in Sanskrit on the ground beneath the arch, an arrangement of marigold petals glowed beside the white characters, but remained undisturbed by the monkeys who scampered over the gopuram and swung from some of its projections.

Beyond was an enormous and sandy parade ground, with the institute and other buildings I had already seen ranged along two of its sides. At the far end of the parade stood an enormous fig tree, which arose from the middle of a corrugated iron roof that was held up by dozens of struts and had been built to shelter a lot of people. As we walked on towards this, I was aware of many women sitting in regimented files on the sand to our left, under the open sky, well away from the shamiana. Men were similarly arranged on the far side of the fig tree and, with the sun having now climbed high, the day had become much too warm for either group to be comfortable. We three reached the shade and Balu indicated that we should sit halfway along a white line that had been drawn across the ground from the perimeter of the shamiana to the base of the tree; a similar line faced it a few yards away, to indicate a marked path leading from the open parade ground to some steps which had been built round the fig. At the top of these, on a yellow pedestal, was a coquettish Lakshmi, legs crossed as if about to twirl into some exuberant choreography, and heavily garlanded with ropes of marigold and other flowers.* I looked round at the emptiness of the shaded area that no one else was sharing yet, unaccustomed to having been given so obviously the best seat in the house before the doors were thrown open to the hoi polloi. Balu sensed my uneasiness and pointed to the steps below the goddess. "This is where Sai Baba gives darshan. Everyone will come here in a minute." There must have been at least a couple of hundred women now sweltering patiently, cross-legged on the sand: they reminded me of refugees, resigned, obedient, awaiting the charity of some international agency. Several had infants and these, too, endured the tedium and the heat equably. A number of Indian women, clad without exception in the sari, stood around in attitudes of authority.

Someone somewhere gave a signal. Suddenly a file of squatting women rose en masse and all semblance of order dissipated in a cloud of dust, as they raced each other across the parade ground to reach the shamiana first and secure the best positions. Now they were like schoolgirls anxious to hear the visiting luminary dish out prizes at the end of the annual sports day. But among those who secured prime positions opposite us on the other white line were a couple of Westerners with very grey hair. Another command, and a second file leapt from the sand in a headlong rush for the next

* Lakshmi was the consort of Vishnu/Krishna.

best seats, but were frustrated by marshals who arranged them in a line some distance behind the first. A fourth file was eventually awarded the space just behind the front rank and I wondered whether this was a form of discipline, to teach resignation to people who thought they had secured the most advantageous positions out in the sun. No one seemed in the least put out by the perverseness of the arrangement. The women in the front row sat in a glow of anticipation, looking pleased with life. Some fingered long-stemmed roses and one arranged neatly in front of her three transparent packets of coloured powder.

The men, too, were released and came pouring under the shamiana without let or hindrance in a disorderly mob. Also unlike the women, whose dresses were colourful, these disciples were not often clad in anything but white, and there were many more Westerners than Indians among them. Several wore a scarf or beads round their neck and one fellow had a tin full of Coffy Bites. "Just wait until Sai Baba starts distributing vibhuti," said one laid-back American voice to another. "It really is something else." There was a babble of conversation everywhere but a number of both men and women had settled into a meditation pose and sat motionless with eyes closed, contemplating hard. One girl did some prolonged neck-swivelling exercises. An old Indian behind me, one of the few poor-looking people in that congregation, was reciting to himself from a grubby Sanskrit text. The babies and other children were still exceptionally even-tempered in the heat. There may have been 500 people now.

A heavy Victorian chair with plum upholstery was manhandled on to the wide step below Lakshmi, and a matching footstool was placed in front of it. A number of young acolytes appeared and sat in the dust around the edges of the multitude. One took position directly in front of Balu, who was on my left: Monoo was on my other side. Much older functionaries, who looked as if they might have exchanged prosperous careers for this, paced the sand thoughtfully in the sun. Light had begun to glare from the parade ground. It was refreshing to let the eyes rest on the plantains, the palms and the other trees that grew behind Sai Baba's gopuram.

We had been sitting for nearly half an hour before he appeared, and the buzz of conversation instantly stopped. A woman had been rearranging her neighbour's shawl but her hands dropped to her sides at once. All heads opposite me turned sharply left, as the guru emerged from his compound, accompanied by a tall and elderly man carrying a plastic shopping bag. Sai Baba was shorter than him by several inches, he was wearing the long-sleeved robe of deep orange that was familiar from every picture, and even from a hundred yards away the famous bushy Afro hairstyle was obvious. He was taking his time to reach us, sauntering across the sand and not stepping in a straight line.

"Does he always move as slowly as this?" I whispered.

Balu wobbled almost imperceptibly. "He is clearly in thought, he is contemplating some problem, I think."

As Sai Baba wended his way towards the fig tree, a murmur of acclaim arose from the mass of worshippers and several aimed their cameras, their flashbulbs even, in his direction. "It is permitted," said Balu. "We have nothing to hide here."

A few yards from the edge of the crowd and Sai Baba began to acknowledge us, cupping his hands slightly and gesturing with them towards his chest, nodding benignly the while, accepting the homage of the faithful. I wondered if he had ever seen pictures of the Pope using exactly the same mannerisms on the balcony of St Peter's.

He reached the edge of the men's semicircle first, though the women's enclosure had been nearer to him when he emerged from his compound. People half rose from their squatting positions, moved towards him, offered him things – roses, sweets, pieces of paper that looked like petitions, letters even. A young Indian with a look of utter devotion on his face began to speak to this divine, almost certainly in supplication judging by his expression. Sai Baba took the offerings, flinging the roses across to the women with a faint grin, scattering the sweets among the men; and people scrambled for these things without any thought for adult dignity. The letters and other pieces of paper he held on to. He had strong-looking hands, but the fingers were long, not thick. As he moved slowly along our front row, collecting, nodding, gesturing, I could at last make out the features of his face, which was that of a coffee-coloured and pudgy elf with an engaging smile, all nestling within that great black halo of hair. He had thick eyebrows, a fleshy neck and double chin, lips that might not have been naturally as red as they appeared. His nose was on the beaky side with its nostrils spread wide.

I was dumbfounded by what happened next. Sai Baba moved in front of me and I raised my hands to give him namasti in the usual Indian fashion, as did everyone else in the congregation who wasn't greeting him more extravagantly. At that moment he stopped and made a circling gesture with his right hand, which was not quite closed, with the palm face down. The sleeve of his gown inevitably shook when he did this. And then, looking me straight in the eyes, he addressed me in a light baritone.

"You like vibhuti?" he said.

Involuntarily, without thinking, I held out my hand. He dropped into it a small quantity of grey-white dust from his fingertips. Then reached forward and pressed some more on my brow. There was a concerted "Ah!" from all around me, and the air was filled with flying Coffy Bites. Balu swiftly produced a piece of paper and I poured the dust or ash or whatever it was into this. My hand was suddenly seized from behind and the old Indian who had been reciting scripture rubbed his forehead in my palm, muttering words of devotion and gratitude. People near us were grinning and nodding with approval. Monoo seemed deeply impressed and kept shaking his head wordlessly. Balu looked as if all his prayers had just been answered perfectly.

Sai Baba had moved on by the time I focused on him again. He reached the dais in front of Lakshmi but, instead of taking his seat there, he continued through the ranks of the men, working his way to the back of the shamiana, which he then walked round to the rear ranks of the women, moving slowly, gesturing as before but not bestowing any more vibhuti so far as I could see; nor did he come near the front rows across the aisle from us. A groan of disappointment could be heard opposite when it was realised that he was wandering back towards his own compound, having spent no more than fifteen minutes giving darshan this day. Normally, according to Balu, we might have expected five or six times as much. There were scores of women who must have been sorely disappointed by this scant return from the man they believed to be Lord Vishnu come to earth again. I remembered Nancy, the American who turned from him because he had not paid her the attention she craved, who needed to offer her life to some saviour of the world who recognised her more demonstratively.

He was dividing his time carefully this morning. Many people followed as far as they were allowed to go, well this side of the gopuram. Through its arch Sai Baba could be seen addressing with vigorous gestures a concourse of young men who were sitting around the edge of his lawn, students from the Higher Institute; one I had noticed earlier with *Principles of Marketing* in his hand. The excluded faithful watched with longing in their eyes: a young white man stood with hands clasped in prayer as he gazed and gazed with an adoration that some lover might have hoped to see, but never would. After Sai Baba had given the students somewhat longer than he had spent in darshan, he withdrew to the steps of his pink lotus house with the institute's principal, and they stood there talking for some more minutes between two rows of potted plants. When Sai Baba stood with hands behind his back, as he did now, his shape beneath the orange cassock was not at all that of a Hindu ascetic, though it resembled the outline of many a Christian prelate. The principal knelt down and kissed the feet of his master, who then turned, went inside and was gone.

"He is in very contemplative mood today, I think," said Balu. "Needing to recharge his spiritual batteries."

I had forgotten my nervousness at the half-expectation of a private audience. A little vibhuti still adhered to the palm of my right hand and I licked it tentatively. It was quite without flavour, mostly as fine as talc, but there was something slightly gritty in it as well. I was surprised how little it mattered to me whether it was what it purported to be, or merely the result of a deft conjuring trick. I had no doubt at all that I had been singled out by careful prearrangement. Though it had not occurred to me before the materialising, I was now quite certain that the young acolyte in front of Balu had been sent there as a marker.

The three of us made our way back to the main road, where the souvenir stalls were doing brisk business and where the editorial Ambassador awaited us. We were about to drive off when an ancient beggar woman approached the vehicle. Monoo muttered something to his chauffeur, who groped in his pocket and handed some paise through the window. The old body looked at it sourly and made it plain she thought it inadequate.

"We have inflation here, too," said Monoo over his shoulder.

"Some of them are really quite rich," echoed Balu, as the car lurched on to the highway back to Bangalore.

# San Thomé

I returned to Madras next morning, and booked myself on to the first available flight home. A few hours before I was due to leave for the airport, I rose early and took an auto-rickshaw through the quietened city, past the gaunt concrete bowl of the cricket stadium, to the sands beyond. There I paid off the driver and watched the fishermen bringing in their catches from the Bay of Bengal, coming out of the sunrise across the sparkling sea, and hauling their high-stemmed craft up the steeply shelving shore, where the waters seethed and swirled and tried to suck them back again. Young men on horses cantered by, making the most of exercise while the day was relatively cool, and a few people strode along the tideline, enjoying the cleansing freshness of the hour. I walked lazily along Beach Road, taking my time over every step, relishing India while I still could, looking forward to my native hills after too many weeks away, yet reluctant to let go of the subcontinent once more.

I reached the basilica of San Thomé just as the 7.30 a.m. mass in Tamil was finishing. The church was packed and already people were waiting outside to take the places of the departing congregation before the mass in English began. I couldn't see the slightest differ-ence between one crowd of worshippers and the other, and thought that their choice of service perhaps depended on the hour rather than on the language used. Many things echoed different cultures in there, and more than one understanding of God. A lifelike Christ crucified on the high altar was dressed in full canonicals with a crown on His head, but His feet rested on a lotus flower and two peacocks averted their eyes from the flow of blood. At the west end of the church, a sort of shopkeeper's sign with interior lighting hung over the pews, much like the illuminated notices I had seen over the holiest shrines at Madurai, but this one insisted that Jesus Saves. The basilica had been rebuilt just before the turn of the century in a whitened Gothic style that looked as if it had come straight out of an English Victorian pattern book, but it stood on the site of a predecessor which the Portuguese had erected in 1522. Nestorians had been the first Christians there, though. It was they who built a chapel over the place where the Apostle Thomas was buried after his martyrdom a few miles away.

It was the First Sunday in Lent, and halfway through the mass, the priest reminded these faithful in both English and Tamil that "we are to eat abstinence every Friday, without meat, fish, prawns or eggs." Most of them looked as if their diet was rarely as ample as that, small and delicate people with skin stretched tightly over fine bones. Yet in the porch there was a notice inviting them to sign up for a pilgrimage to the Holy Land and Rome (including an audience with the Pope) at a price that would have been prohibitive to anyone in Madras but the well-to-do. The singing sounded like a blend of European Catholicism and Negro spiritual. The communion hymn was "Amazing Grace". From start to finish, the service was conducted to the background rhythm of drums and flutes, which drifted through the open windows and doors from the Kapaleeswarar Temple in the next block, where other devout believers were hailing the Lord Shiva and his sixty-three saints.

When the mass was over some people lingered and descended to the shrine. At the foot of the chancel steps a railed-in flight of stairs led down to a small crypt, where candles guttered on an altar above a stone slab. According to the authorised traditions of the Roman Catholic Church, the apostle's remains had long since been removed, first to Mesopotamia in the fourth century, eventually to the Italian Adriatic coast. But at San Thomé they were still allowed to venerate two objects associated with Didymus. One was a spearhead, which was held to be from the weapon that dealt the mortal blow in AD 72. The other was a fragment of the saint's finger bone, which every communicant in the archdiocese verily believed to be from the hand that touched Christ's wounds, as reported in John. The relics were encased in their separate vessels, the spearhead in cumbersome silver, the bone more neatly in gold, each with a little inset window so that they could be seen for what they were said to be. With the same humble certainty that had directed the old fellow who seized my sanctified hand at Brindavan, the Christians of San Thomé approached the relics and prostrated themselves in the full exhilaration of their faith.

Which I did but sceptically share. As I took my turn to kneel in the crypt I was convinced most of all that Doubting Thomas was my man. If ever I had adopted a patron saint then surely he would have been the one. It was not that I found it difficult to accept divinity, to marvel at mystery, to believe in miracles: these had never been my stumbling blocks, for I was a naturally credulous man. But every faith I had examined, most of all that into which I had been born and in which I would die, insisted on something that I could not do: and that was to surrender myself to all that it offered of goodness, to all that it demanded of self. This unwillingness touched everything that happened to me every day of my life, as Mr Anthony in Cochin might have testified, but my dilemma was essentially a spiritual one. Gentle George Herbert had also spoken for me, near sixteen hundred years after Thomas Didymus:

> Love bade me welcome: yet my soul drew back,
> Guiltie of dust and sinne.

And so, unwilling to surrender all that was required of me, my far too logical and sceptical mind became my shield and my defence. I could no more ignore religion and deny my instinct for the numinous than a child could abandon its comforter or the earth defy the natural law regulating its passage round the sun. But I had long since ceased to hope that one day, with Herbert, I might sit and eat with the true and certain believers in a kingdom of heaven. And India, above all the places I knew across the earth, had helped me to come to terms with this, had taught me no longer to strain and fret against my inadequacy; for India was, above anywhere else, the land where every distinction of faith, every equivocation, every contradiction, every doubt, every reticence was commonplace, often glorified and always accepted as if any variant at all was the natural condition of man. For that reason alone, I could have surrendered myself to the spirit of this country without any ifs or buts. There were, in fact, many reasons why such a submission was possible: for all its manifold and obvious darknesses, India had cast a spell over me, as much as any land could that was not my own. Kneeling there at the shrine I wondered when and even whether I would see the subcontinent again. Once, the prospect of my end would have alarmed and tormented me, but I had since come to accept it calmly and with curiosity, almost disinterestedly, as though it were an abstraction, something quite detached from me, stripped of its old power to hurt and terrify. I believed India had played a big part in teaching me how to accept that as well.

The candles burned brightly on the marble slab above the spot where Thomas had been, as the wax trickled down their stems and formed thickening buttresses. Shadows flickered across the petitions people had scribbled on scraps of paper and left there for the inter-cession of the saint. I said my own last prayers in India, and asked that I might be allowed to return before long. Then I went out into the blinding light of day.

# Postscript
(to pages 76–83)*

*Fortnightly report of the Madras States Residency to the Government of India in New Delhi, and the Secretary of State for India in London. Fortnight ending October 31, 1946.*

## FESTIVITIES CONNECTED WITH THE MAHARAJAH OF TRAVANCORE'S BIRTHDAY THROUGHOUT THE STATE . . .

2 Synchronising with the birthday festivities, serious disturbances broke out in and around the highly industrial areas of Alleppey and Shertallai (near the Cochin border) under communist influence and inspired by the leadership of disgruntled ex-Army and ex-INA men with the declared object of defying law and order. The disturbances were violent and fairly widespread; and armed with country bombs and explosives, crowbars, axes, areca nut spears etc, the rioters murdered a Sub-Inspector of police, a Head Constable and two Constables at the very start. Reserve Police and State Forces reinforcements were rushed to the spot, martial law was proclaimed in the affected areas, and stern and swift measures were taken under the personal supervision of the General Officer Commanding State Forces and the Inspector General of Police to suppress the disturbances. Many prominent communists have been arrested and quiet has almost completely been restored. Many of the ringleaders have surrendered to Government, though quite a number of them have escaped to outlying British Indian and Cochin

*   From India Office archives, London. L/ P & S/13/1299 File 27 (2) FR 20/46 and FR 23/46; and from L/P & S/13/1285 File 16 (2) 2274 P.

State territories. Measures to prevent any recrudescence of the trouble have been taken . . .

15 . . . There is a largely prevalent public opinion that one of the important contributory causes leading to the recent disturbances is that whereas the ordinary man has plenty of money there is very little of primary necessity – food – that he can buy therewith.

Lieut-Col C. G. N. Edwards CIE, Resident to the Madras States

*Confidential Code Telegram from Government of India in New Delhi to Secretary of State for India in London, 31 October, 1946.*

Violent disturbances started near Alleppey on October 24th. A crowd of about 500 including ex-soldiers in uniform stopped traffic and attempted to seize water works. Police opened fire, killed one man wounded one. Mob dispersed but reassembled in greater strength estimated about 2,000 in another place. They were armed with knives, spears, sticks, axes, a few firearms and followed military tactics, seeking to surround the detachment of troops sent against them. Troops opened fire. Mob dispersed but went to isolated police stations where they killed one sub-inspector, one head constable and two constables. They also broke culverts and cut communications. Travancore Government sent strong military and police reinforcements on 25th and declared martial law on 26th in two taluks Alleppey and Shertallai areas. On October 27th strong military party proceeded from Alleppey against rebel mob concentrated on sandy area near Alleppey. Troops were attacked at three points by very violent mobs armed with spears, daggers, swords, axes and country explosives. Troops opened fire at three points. Mob sustained casualties and disappeared inland. Troops took twenty prisoners with weapons and collection of many other weapons. Three sepoys were injured, one by spear, one by stone and one by gunshot wound. Situation at Alleppey/Shertallai area now under control but it cannot yet be said that rioters will not reassemble elsewhere . . . A notable point throughout whole disturbances was number of men in military style uniforms, obviously ex-soldiers who organised movements on sound strategic lines. A dangerous weapon used by mob was sharpened length of bamboo or areca nut used as throwing spear. END.

*Fortnightly report of the Madras States Residency, fortnight ending December 15, 1946.*

1 As fantastic reports of deaths due to police and military firing during the disturbances are being published by communist journals outside the state, the Travancore Government have verified all the information before

them and published a Press Note according to which the total number of deaths is about 190. Responsible persons belonging to different organisations like the State Congress, SNDP (Ezhuva) and NSS (Nair) have, after visiting the areas, accepted the correctness of the figures given in the Press Note. Government have placed no restrictions on anyone visiting those areas and have assured that they would investigate any information given by any person . . .

Lieut-Col C. G. N. Edwards CIE

*(To which was added by another hand when the report reached London)*

It seems about as difficult to get reliable figures of riot casualties in Travancore as it is in Bengal. The figure of 190 in paragraph 1 compares with estimates running up to (I think) 2,000!

# Glossary

**achkan** a long coat, buttoned at the high collar and flared a little below the knee.

**aratti** a religious ceremony employing flame, intended to ward off the evil eye from a deity or human being.

**avatar** the incarnation of a god.

**Ayurveda** literally "the knowledge of health/ vitality/ longevity". Ayurvedic practice is the traditional and naturalistic form of Hindu medicine.

**banian** a piece of cloth that covers both the upper and lower parts of the body.

**betel** a variety of palm tree (*areca catechu*) whose nut and leaf is used in the digestive concoction **pan/paan**.

**bhajan** sacred song/hymn.

**bidi** rudimentary form of cigarette, made of rolled tobacco leaf and held together with thread.

**bimah** pulpit in a synagogue.

**brahmacharyn** a religious student or pupil.

**chappals** sandals.

**chhatri** turret with a roof resembling an opened umbrella.

**choultry** simplest form of pilgrim accommodation at religious shrines; a resting place.

**darshan** literally "viewing, looking at", and the occasion of a deity making Him or Herself accessible to followers.

**devadasi** woman whose life was dedicated to the temple, held to be married to the god. She was invariably there for the pleasure of the priests.

**durbar** the court of an Indian princely state, not merely the occasion of its gathering, which is the usual interpretation in the West.

**gadi** throne, both literally and figuratively.

**godown** storage shed/room, warehouse.

**gopi** one of the shepherdesses usually associated idyllically with Krishna.

**gopuram** wedge-shaped tower found distinctively in the temples of Tamil Nadu.

**jackfruit** tree (*artocarpus heterophyllus*) whose sweet and chewy fruit tastes like a cross between mango and banana.

**jaggery** a coarse brown and unrefined sugar, from cane or various palms.

**lakh** 100,000.

**lathi** bamboo staff with iron tip; used by Indian police as truncheon.

**lingam** phallic symbol associated with Shiva.

**lunghi** distinctive South India male garment; cloth wrapped round hips to form ankle-length skirt.

**Mahabharata** one of the two great epic texts of Hinduism (**Ramayana** is the other), which runs to eighteen books in verse, of which **Bhagavad Gita** is one. It is about seven times the combined length of *Iliad* and *Odyssey*.

**mali** gardener.

**manjira** castanets, made of brass.

**namasti** most common form of Indian greeting, with hands placed together in front of face.

**neem** a variety of cedar tree (*toona ciliata*), very common in India.

**paan/pan** concoction of spices, lime, crushed areca nut, served on betel leaf, which is rolled up and chewed to aid digestion.

**paise** smallest unit of currency: 100 paise = 1 rupee.

**pakori** savoury dumpling, deep-fried and stuffed.

**peepal** (*ficus religiosa*), tree which orthodox Hindus regard as sacred.

**satyagraha** literally "truth force". Mahatma Gandhi used this expression to describe non-violent protest, employed by him first in South Africa, later against the British Raj in India.

**shalwar kameez** two-piece garment for women, traditional in northern India and Pakistan. The kameez is a shirt, the shalwar ankle-length pants.

**shamiana** an awning, or a roofless screening enclosure of canvas or calico.

**twice-born** the top three categories of male in the Hindu caste system – Brahmins, Kshatriyas and Vaishyas – regard themselves as "twice-born" when they are initiated as children into their religious duties and privileges. The ceremony includes investiture with a "sacred thread" which is thereafter worn at all times.

**vibhuti** sacred ash smeared on the body, generally in imitation of Shiva.

**vimana** tower/dome above the temple sanctuary.

# Index

Page numbers followed by *n* denote
reference to footnotes.